THE FEMALE ATHLETE'S BODY BOOK

How to Prevent and Treat Sports Injuries in Women and Girls

GLORIA BEIM, M.D.
and RUTH WINTER, M.S.

Contemporary Books

Chicago   New York   San Francisco   Lisbon   London   Madrid   Mexico City
Milan   New Delhi   San Juan   Seoul   Singapore   Sydney   Toronto

The McGraw·Hill Companies

Library of Congress Cataloging-in-Publication Data

Beim, Gloria.
    The female athlete's body book : how to prevent and treat sports injuries in
women and girls / Gloria Beim and Ruth Winter.
        p.   cm.
    Includes index.
    ISBN 0-07-141175-5
    1. Women athletes—Wounds and injuries.   2. Women athletes—Health and
hygiene.   I. Winter, Ruth, 1930–   .   II. Title.

RC1218.W65B456   2003
617.1′027′082—dc21   2002041439

1 2 3 4 5 6 7 8 9 0   AGM/AGM   2 1 0 9 8 7 6 5 4 3

ISBN 0-07-141175-5

Interior illustrations by Robert Winter
Interior design by Monica Baziuk

McGraw-Hill books are available at special quantity discounts to use as premiums and
sales promotions, or for use in corporate training programs. For more information, please
write to the Director of Special Sales, Professional Publishing, McGraw-Hill, Two Penn
Plaza, New York, NY 10121-2298. Or contact your local bookstore.

The information in this book is not intended to be a substitute for the medical advice of
physicians. The reader should consult with her doctor in all matters relating to health.
Although every effort has been made to ensure that information is presented accurately in
this book, the ultimate responsibility for proper medical treatment rests with your medical
professional. Neither the authors nor the publisher can be held responsible for errors or
for any consequences arising from the use of information contained here. The stories
included in the book are true, but identities have been changed to protect privacy.

This book is printed on acid-free paper.

To my parents, Jack and Adele Beim, who always gave me the strength and inspiration to pursue my dreams and who made me what I am today. To my beloved husband, Erik Klemme, who gave me my beautiful little girl, Skylar.
—GLORIA

To my husband, Arthur Winter, M.D., Director of the New Jersey Neurological Institute, for his support.
—RUTH

CONTENTS

Introduction 1

Part (1) **ATHLETIC ENDEAVORS**

1. Basketball: Hooping It Up 11

2. Soccer: Getting a Kick 21

3. Volleyball: Net Gain 35

4. Softball: Getting to Home Plate Safely 41

5. Tennis and Racquetball: Courting Fun 49

6. Lacrosse and Field Hockey: High-Speed Goals 65

7. Skiing and Snowboarding: Hot Sports in the Cold 71

8. Ice Skating and Ice Hockey: Ice Maidens 89

9. Swimming: Wet and Wonderful 101

10. Scuba Diving: Exploring Another World 115

11. Biking: Popular Pedal Pushing 127

12. Rock Climbing: Upscale 147

13. Walking and Running: On Your Feet 167

14. Golf: In the Swing of Things 187

15. Weight Training: Gaining Strength 199

16. Gymnastics and Cheerleading: Twist, Tumble, and Shout 205

Part ② ATHLETICS FOR LIFE

17. Girls on the Go 217

18. Pregnant Athletes: Baby on Board 225

19. Mature Athletes: Never Too Old to Play 237

20. Nutrition for the Female Athlete 251

Part ③ INJURY PREVENTION AND TREATMENT

21. Upper Body Injury and Therapy:
Neck, Shoulder, Elbow, Wrist, and Hand Injuries 271

22. Lower Body Injury and Therapy:
Hip, Knee, Leg, Ankle, and Foot Injuries 303

23. Conditioning Exercises 331

Index 355

INTRODUCTION

WHY CAN'T A WOMAN be more like a man?

This refrain echoes through the arenas, playing fields, and locker rooms of the world. The fact is we women athletes cannot and should not be more like male athletes. Our female bodies are constructed and function differently from men's, and that gives us both advantages and disadvantages. Unfortunately, many coaches, physicians, and athletes have not recognized the differences; as a result, female athletes often have inadequate training, suffer unnecessary injuries, and may not reach their full potential.

The enactment of Title IX in 1972, federal legislation that prohibited sex discrimination in sports, has spectacularly fueled female participation in athletic activity. The number of women in sports has increased 22 percent in 10 years. In fact, 40 percent of high school athletes are girls. The emphasis on fitness has encouraged females of all ages to participate in sports, most of them just for the sake of fun.

As an orthopedic specialist who has treated female patients from amateurs who play just for fun to Olympic athletes seeking gold medals, I* have seen many injuries that could have been prevented or that should have received earlier treatment. One of the most important of parts of my treatment of female

---

* This book was written by two authors who have chosen to write from a single, first-person point of view for the sake of simplicity.

1

athletes is teaching them how to continue their sport and prevent injuries. I urge them to participate in year-round or off-season conditioning. Year-round conditioning not only decreases the risk of injury but also enhances performance.

If you are an athlete who wants to excel, prevent injuries, and receive appropriate treatment, this book will help you educate yourself about both your vulnerabilities and advantages. You will learn about your body, how it works, and what that means for your chosen sport. In this introduction, I will discuss how some of the differences between male and female bodies affect women's sports; the dangers of the female triad; why your knee is one of the most vulnerable parts of your anatomy; and the influences of puberty, menstruation, menopause, and pregnancy.

SEX MAKES A DIFFERENCE: FEMALE ATHLETES ARE UNIQUE

There are a lot of myths about women athletes, but here are a few things that are true—things that aspiring and practicing athletes should bear in mind.

The Vulnerable Female Knee

Historically, for example, it was believed that women's wider pelvis and shorter stature gave them a lower center of gravity and thus a better sense of balance. The truth is that men and women have only small differences in their centers of gravity, which are determined by height and body type rather than sex. A wider female pelvis, however, is important in other ways. For many women, a wide pelvis can produce an increased angle at the knee (Q angle), which can make the knee more vulnerable to injury than a man's knees. (See Figure 1.)

Men and women also are different when it comes to flexing their knees. When women bend their knees, their thighbones (femurs) give less support to their kneecaps (patellae). This is why female athletes frequently suffer from the patellofemoral syndrome, which includes many types of knee pain and injury. Those who play sports such as volleyball, basketball, and soccer expose themselves to increased risk for knee problems because in these pivoting sports, they often have less muscle protection at the knee than do their male counterparts.

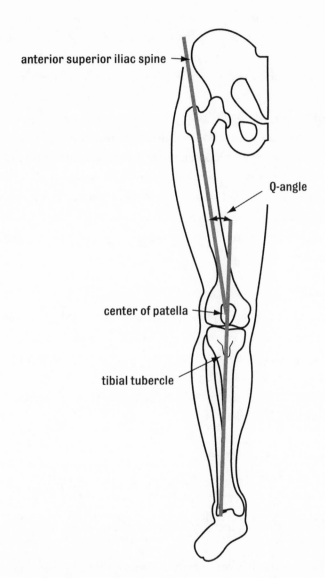

anterior superior iliac spine

Q-angle

center of patella

tibial tubercle

Figure 1

Churning and Burning

Men metabolize energy differently than women. Metabolism is the way you process food into tissue elements and into energy for use in the growth, repair, and general function of your body. A woman's resting metabolic rate (RMR) is 5 percent to 10 percent lower than a man's. If you have developed your muscles through sports, however, your RMR will burn increased calories while you are at rest. If you don't exercise and are on a weight-loss diet, you will deprive your muscles of protein and conditioning, decrease the size of your muscles, and lessen your RMR. So commit yourself to regular exercise. It will increase your metabolism and assist you in maintaining a healthy weight.

How Much Oxygen Can You Carry?

The fellows around you may have still another advantage. Men have approximately 6 percent more red blood cells; therefore, their blood may be able to carry oxygen to body tissues more efficiently than yours can. You also have a lower amount of iron stored in your body. In addition, if you menstruate, you lose iron during your periods and you probably have a lower dietary intake of iron than men do. This combination of factors often results in iron deficiency anemia, so check Chapter 20 on nutrition.

Throwing a Ball

In general, females have shorter limbs relative to body length than males do, especially in the arms (upper extremities). This relative shortness, combined with a female's generally narrower shoulder girdle, may cause you to have a shorter lever arm, which can affect throwing mechanics in many ball-and-racquet sports. In turn, you may also be more prone to specific injuries, which will be addressed in later chapters.

Bones, Hormones, and Athletic Performance

You've probably heard about osteoporosis, the thinning of the bones that can occur in nutritionally deprived girls and in many women after menopause. If you are a young female on a starvation (anorexic) diet or if you are postmenopausal, you may develop decreased bone density, which can increase your risk of broken bones during athletics. If you have been through menopause and you want to pursue a sport, you would be wise to have your doctor do a bone density scan. Your doctor can tell you whether you are at risk and what you can do about it.

Amenorrhea and Osteoporosis

Surprisingly, anorexic young females and postmenopausal women are not the only ones at risk for low bone density. High endurance athletes such as marathon runners or triathletes may be vulnerable even in their 20s because the continuous exertion required by their sports can lower their estrogen levels causing them to stop menstruating. This may weaken their bones. Cessation or irregularity of menstruation can be a problem in female athletes. Athletes who develop abnormal periods (oligomenorrhea) also have reduced bone mineral density, as much as 20 percent lower than that of women athletes who have normal periods. Oligomenorrhea is most prevalent in endurance athletes. Twenty-eight percent of female college varsity athletes, 13 percent of female basketball players, and 57 percent of female cross-country runners reportedly have menstrual irregularities. Ballet dancers and cyclists also have shown a higher incidence of amenorrhea (absence of menstruation).

Studies show that most menstrual problems that occur in women who exercise are due to inadequate food intake rather than to the exercise itself. Bone mineral density has been shown to be inversely related to age of menarche (a woman's first menstrual period); athletes with delayed menarche appear to enter adulthood with irreversible bone loss. Some believe it is caused by exercise-induced raising of the male hormone testosterone and the lowering of the female hormone estrogen in women athletes. Whatever the cause, failure to reach peak bone mass, premature bone loss, and poor mineralization of bone (because of stress) all make the athlete who does not have periods (amenorrheic) more susceptible to stress fractures.

Infertility is another important consequence of athletic amenorrhea. Exercise-associated infertility is usually considered reversible with reduction in training.

If you are suffering from menstrual irregularities or an absence of menses, your doctor may recommend calcium supplements, nutritional counseling, decreased training, and medications to increase bone density.

THE FEMALE ATHLETE TRIAD

A serious and potentially fatal nutritional aberration is known as the female athlete triad—eating disorders, stress fractures, and amenorrhea. It involves a female athlete who focuses on being thin or lightweight, eats too little, and/or exercises too much. The prevalence among female athletes has been reported to range from 15 percent to 62 percent depending on the activity, according to WomenSport International. Athletes in any sport can develop one or more parts of the triad. At greatest risk are women who are involved in sports that reward thinness because of appearance (i.e., figure skating, gymnastics) or improved performance (i.e., distance running, rowing). Some female athletes suffer low self-esteem or depression, and may focus on weight loss because they think they are heavier than they actually are. Others feel pressure to lose weight from athletic coaches or parents.

Recognizing the female athlete triad is the first step in treating it. See your doctor right away if you think you might have an eating disorder, miss several menstrual periods, or suffer a sports-related stress fracture. Give the doctor your complete medical history, including prior fractures, prior surgeries, calcium or vitamin supplements, medications (including birth control pills), alcohol consumption, and family history of osteoporosis or other bone disorders.

The doctor will give you complete physical and pelvic examinations and may use laboratory tests to check for pregnancy, thyroid disease, and other medical conditions. In some cases you may also get a bone density test. Treatment for the female athletic triad often requires help from a team of medical professionals including a doctor, a nutritionist, and a psychological counselor.

BREAST PROTECTION

More annoying than life-threatening concerns include breast discomfort, a common complaint of women who exercise, especially among those who have large breasts. During the menstrual phase, fluid retention can make even women with small breasts uncomfortable. Tight-fitting garments and activities such as jogging or swimming and exercise in cold weather may also cause nipple trauma. A properly fitted sports bra will usually counteract breast discomfort. A note of caution: breast trauma in contact sports has been shown to increase the risk of breast cancer; consequently, chest guards are very important for athletes such as soccer goalies and softball catchers.

CARING FOR YOUR UNIQUE ATHLETIC FEMALE BODY

Your anatomy and physiology are significantly different from those of a male athlete. You must be aware of your body's needs to avoid injury and undergo the best training techniques available. Overall, female athletes have the same number of serious injuries as male athletes do, yet in some sports women are more susceptible to certain types of injuries, such as noncontact injuries to the anterior cruciate ligament (ACL), a major stabilizing structure in the knee.

By reading this book you will gain the knowledge necessary to reduce the chance of injuring yourself while pursuing your sport. Should you experience an injury, the descriptions of the most current treatments available will help you recover. We hope this book helps you perform at your best and get the most from your sport.

ATHLETIC ENDEAVORS

1

BASKETBALL

Hooping It Up

REBECCA LOBO, one of the first women's basketball superstars, knows well the vulnerability of the female basketball player's knee.

She was the youngest member of the 1996 USA Women's Olympic Team that won the gold medal at the Atlanta Games. She was signed by the Women's National Basketball Association (WNBA) and assigned to the New York Liberty in January 1997. She suffered a torn anterior cruciate ligament (ACL) in her left knee during the first minute of play against the Cleveland Rockers in the season opener on June 10, 1999. The ACL is the ligament behind the kneecap that connects the thighbone to the shinbone and is responsible for knee stability. Surgery was done and she tore the same ACL again on December 12, 1999, while playing in a controlled rehabilitation session. She refused to be sidelined and worked hard at rehabilitation. She scored her first basket two years later when her team played Cleveland.

Now a Houston Comet, Lobo is a wonderful role model for young athletes. A political science graduate of the University of Connecticut, at 21 she coauthored the mother-daughter autobiography *The Home Team* (Kodansha International). Rebecca is very active in breast cancer research organizations because of her mother's battle with the disease. Her mom, Ruthann Lobo, a former middle school cross-country coach, is currently the Title IX compliance coordinator for a school district.

Rebecca Lobo is six foot four, but you don't have to be tall to play basketball. It is the number one sport in which females participate at the high school and collegiate levels. It is also the most popular women's spectator sport.

Dr. James Naismith, a minister, doctor, and educator at the University of Kansas, invented the game in 1891 as a sport to be played indoors in the winter. The game had 13 basic rules and was played with a soccer ball, peach baskets, and nine players to a side.

Women were into basketball early. Less than a year after Naismith's first game was played, gymnastics instructor Senda Berenson Abbott adapted basketball for students at an all-women institution, Smith College in Massachusetts. Women were not permitted to self-govern their competitions, however, until 1924. Organizing and gaining recognition for female basketball players has been a bit less difficult since 1996 when the U.S. women's basketball team won the Olympic gold medal. The game since then has been increasingly popular among elementary school, high school, and college females.

The sport is not without its physical hazards. Women's basketball is supposedly a noncontact sport but players do crash into one another. In fact, more female players are hurt during their games than males during theirs. The following are common female basketball injuries, many of which can be prevented with good conditioning, a safe environment, and proper equipment. For more detailed information on each body part's injury and therapy, refer to Chapters 21 through 23. Chapter 21 has detailed information on upper body injuries and therapy, Chapter 22 explains lower body injuries and therapy, and Chapter 23 contains conditioning exercises to strengthen your body and improve your flexibility.

BASKETBALL KNEES

You do have to protect your knees—female college basketball players are three to five times more likely than males to tear their ACL. The ACL is a major stabilizing structure in the knee. In women's basketball—as in volleyball, soccer, and other sports where our knees are subjected to turning, twisting, and jerking—ACL injuries are common because most women don't have muscles as strong, quick-acting, and balanced as those of males supporting our knees.

For example, at the U.S. Olympic basketball trials for men and women in 1988, coaches picked the elite male and female players in the country. Of the 64 female basketball players at the Olympic trials, 20 had to undergo knee surgery after playing while only 6 of the 80 male participants needed surgical knee repair.

So you should work to strengthen the muscles that support your knees but there is a caution. It has been discovered women who strengthen the quadriceps in the front of their thighs more than the hamstrings in the back of their thighs actually *increase* their risk of ACL injuries. Your muscles must be in balance to protect your knees.

In addition to the disparity in muscle protection of the knees, studies have found differences between female and male basketball players' body mechanics while performing jump shots, rebounds, and pivots. Females maneuver the court with less knee flexion than males. Therefore, you can see that it is vital that you not only strengthen muscles around your knees, but also work on your flexibility.

BASKETBALL SHOULDER

The most common upper body injury in basketball is a partial dislocation (subluxation) of the shoulder joint. This injury typically occurs when you block a shot with your arm up, out to the side, elbow bent, and hand back as if cocking your arm to throw a ball. If you go for a shot or a rebound with your arm stretched over your head in that manner, and an opponent knocks your arm backward, you may end up with a partial or even a complete shoulder dislocation.

If you feel that your shoulder may have come partly out of joint, you will probably feel some kind of pop or shift inside your shoulder and it will be quite sore. By the next day it may really hurt, and you may have trouble raising or rotating your arm. Rest may ease the pain, but your shoulder muscles will still be weak. Without therapy, the shoulder will likely go out on you again.

If your shoulder comes completely out of the socket, you will have severe pain and be unable to move your arm away from your side. You may even have difficulty breathing deeply because of the pain. It is a terribly uncomfortable situation, one that requires immediate care by a physician for both diagnosis and treatment (getting the shoulder back into place). I can speak firsthand about the pain because in the past I have dislocated both my shoulders and it was very memorable. As soon as the shoulders were put back into place the pain was minimal.

Once a doctor puts your shoulder back into place, your arm will be in a sling or an immobilizer for one to two weeks. Then physical therapy will start.

In some cases, surgery may be necessary. When I see a first-time dislocator, I make every attempt to treat her without surgery. It is important for me to determine whether my patient injured a ligament or tendon. For subluxators, where the shoulder only comes out part of the way, surgery is less likely to be necessary unless partial dislocation happens repeatedly. I see many college basketball players who come to the clinic complaining of shoulder pain but are unaware that they have shoulder instability. When I examine them, it is clear to me that their shoulders have some looseness or instability.

BASKETBALL HEAD BANGERS

Crashing heads with another player, falling down and hitting your head, or being smacked hard with a basketball can cause a concussion. According to surveys by the National Collegiate Athletic Association (NCAA), concussions occurred in 4.9 percent of all women's basketball game injuries between 1989 and 1998. A concussion can be serious, and you could be unconscious for a brief period of time. Or it can be relatively mild leaving you with a headache or nausea for a few hours. No matter how much you wish to play in a game, if your head is "ringing" or you have lost consciousness even for a moment, you should be out of the game and examined by a physician. If you suffer multiple mild concussions in one season, they can be cumulative and cause severe irreversible injury to your brain. Therefore, any concussion, however mild, should be evaluated by a trained professional.

BASKETBALL NECK

Women basketball players suffer more neck injuries than men, again because their neck muscles are not as strong. Looking up to throw into the basket or falling down and getting a whiplash can cause ligament stretching and muscle spasms in your neck.

BASKETBALL BACK

If you come down from a rebound off balance, you may strain your back. Jumping and twisting put great strain on your back muscles, and you may not be able to absorb all the shock. If you are tall—and most basketball players *are*—one of your legs may be slightly shorter than the other. This discrepancy can lead to lower back pain. You may also have a long back and need to strengthen your muscles to stabilize your spine. Therefore, you have to strengthen those back and abdominal muscles. A lumbar corset or brace may be recommended for a patient with chronic lower back problems, but this is unusual in this sport. A neoprene back brace is a little more common; it doesn't replace the need for muscular strengthening but can relieve some of the symptoms.

BASKETBALL WRIST

Sprained and even broken wrists commonly result from players falling to the floor. You instinctively put out your hands to stop your momentum, and your wrist then absorbs the shock. When falling onto an outstretched hand, a small bone in your wrist—the scaphoid or navicular bone just behind the base of the thumb—is at great risk of being broken. If you break your scaphoid bone, your wrist will still move and function, but there will be pain and possibly swelling. So just because you can move your wrist and fingers doesn't mean that it isn't broken. It is very important that your injury be evaluated by an orthopedist or sports specialist because this bone is at risk for major problems if the injury is not diagnosed correctly.

BASKETBALL FINGER

Broken or dislocated fingers are common in basketball. A broken finger usually occurs when you try to deflect a pass and it hits the end of your finger. In that case, a tendon may rupture and a piece of bone can break off with it.

If it doesn't respond to an ice pack you should have your finger x-rayed to determine if it is broken. If there is any deformity of the finger or a lot of swelling, I recommend an x-ray to rule out a fracture—especially at one of the finger joints. If you do have a fracture (even a small one) at the joint and it is not treated early, you can suffer from stiffness or joint pain, which may not be correctable.

You can dislocate your finger if the ball hits it sideways. In my experience, it usually occurs in the middle joint between the joint closest to your fingernail and the knuckle joint. Your finger will appear terribly deformed. Immediately pulling on your finger usually puts it back in place and relieves the terrific pain. However, you should have the finger x-rayed because it may also be broken. If you allow a broken finger to go untreated, eventually it may lose its mobility.

BASKETBALL HAMS

The hamstring muscles in the back of the thigh are called into action in all running sports. Hamstring pulls are common among basketball players because of their sudden acceleration, for example, as they drive to the basket. Hamstring strains are nearly twice as common in females as in males during practices, but during games the incidence is about the same. The treatment is rest and ice, followed by a stretching program. Many players now wear rubber thigh sleeves under their shorts to keep their thighs warm and give their hamstrings some support. Prevention is the best treatment so be sure that you warm up and stretch before play and cool down after play.

BASKETBALL ANKLE SPRAIN

Reports from high school basketball coaches reveal 31 percent of the girls playing the game injure their ankles. Among college female basketball players, the ankle has been the most commonly reported injury. An ankle sprain usually results from a player stepping on another player's foot while coming down from a jump or while running up the court. If you turn or twist your ankle, you must get off the court and let your trainer or team doctor (if available on the sidelines) take a look at it. If you are having trouble walking off the court, you are probably done for the day.

Swelling and pain should give you cause to see a doctor and get an x-ray. It is often difficult to distinguish between a sprain (which is much more common) and a fracture. (See Figures 22.3 and 22.4 in Chapter 22.)

ACHILLES TENDONITIS

The Achilles tendon, extending upward about six inches from the back of the heel, is the thickest, strongest tendon in the body. It binds the muscles of your calf in your leg to your heel bone. Basketball players can suffer acute injuries to the Achilles causing inflammation of the tendon (tendonitis) from turning the foot over while running or straining through overuse or while jumping.

As always, overuse injuries can often be prevented with an intensive stretching and warm-up program. Treatment consists of physical therapy, cross training, and anti-inflammatory medications (as tolerated). If you do not treat inflamed tendons, the pain can progress and the problem can become much more serious. Repeated tendonitis can weaken the Achilles tendon and cause scar tissue to form. You may go up for a jump shot one day and all of a sudden rupture your tendon.

Each year I see about a half-dozen basketball players with Achilles ruptures. This is one of the most severe injuries in sports. Because of the generally younger age groups in basketball, I have not seen many Achilles ruptures in high school or college players. Achilles ruptures are much more common once you hit 40, but they also occur in younger people and when they do they need prompt attention.

Most of my patients describe an Achilles rupture as similar to being shot in the back of the leg. Sheila, for example, had an acute sharp pain when she took off quickly to run to the other end of the court. She fell down and was unable to walk. Swelling occurred within an hour of the injury, which happens quickly because Achilles tendons generally bleed a lot when they are torn. Sheila came to my office with an obvious rupture of the Achilles. Because she was an avid athlete, I recommended surgical repair of the tendon. You can treat these with a cast but if you repair them surgically the tendon will be stronger, will have more endurance, and will have a lower rate of rerupture. After surgery, Sheila wore a cast boot and entered physiotherapy. Within four months, she was healed and ready to return to basketball.

FOOT AND STRESS FRACTURES

Stress fractures are more common in female basketball players than in male players—twice as common during practices and more than *four times* as common during games. Specific reasons for the increased rate of stress fractures in females include hormonal imbalance, disordered eating, improperly fitting shoes, and reduced strength.

If you experience a sudden pain on the outside of your foot while running, it may be a stress fracture. If both the top and bottom of the foot hurt and the foot swells up, have it x-rayed to see whether any bones have cracked. The most common stress fracture among basketball players occurs in the bone behind the little toe. A Penn State study revealed that NBA players come down on their feet with as much as 14 times their own body weight after a layup. The NBA is now studying the connection between such high-impact landings and stress fractures.

In the past, basketball shoes for female players were simply smaller versions of the shoes male players wore. There has been progress in the development of athletic shoes contoured to the female athlete, with the true shape of women's feet and reduced heel width. Don't compromise quality in the interest of economy. I also recommend cotton socks that absorb perspiration and give added support to your foot.

PLAYING WELL

Recognizing the differences between female and male basketball players has led to better training and conditioning for women. If you are going to play basketball, which requires jumping, turning, and twisting, you should be prepared to protect your knee against rotational forces, your shoulders against dislocation, and your feet against stress fractures. The necessary ingredients, of course, are good coaching, regular practicing, and conditioning.

Like other running sports, basketball requires superb conditioning. You must be able to exert a burst of speed to get by the person guarding you and have the endurance to run the court for an entire game. You can perform running drills that combine these aspects. Endurance running drills are just long, slow runs, from three to five miles a day, that get your heart into the training range. This gives you the strong base of aerobic conditioning necessary for stamina. Once you have built up your base level, start interval training. Repeated sprints of varying distances with short rests in between will give you the speed and quick recovery you need for basketball. You also should develop good first step and side-to-side agility (see Figure 23.34 in Chapter 23). Running in a figure-eight pattern will accomplish the same thing.

Although many injuries that result from the physical nature of basketball cannot be anticipated, you can take preventive measures. Increasing your muscle strength and your cardiovascular endurance will allow you to compete well in the game and will also protect you from injuring yourself.

The American Academy of Orthopaedic Surgeons (aaos.com) offers the following tips to prevent basketball injuries (reprinted with permission from the American Academy of Orthopaedic Surgeons):

- Play only your position and know where other players are on the court to reduce the chance of collisions. Don't hold, block, push, charge, or trip opponents. Use proper techniques for passing and scoring.
- Use protective knee and elbow pads to protect yourself from bruises and abrasions.
- Use a mouth guard to protect your teeth and mouth.
- If you wear glasses, use safety glasses or glass guards to protect your eyes. Polycarbonate lenses should be used during athletic activities, particularly in sports such as basketball where there is significant risk of eye injury.
- Do not wear jewelry or chew gum during practice or games.
- Avoid outside courts that are not properly lighted in the evening.
- Do not play in extreme weather conditions.

For more information, check out these resources:

Rebecca Lobo's "The World According to Me" at her website, rebeccalobo.com. She is also the spokesperson for Body1.com and for a website on knee treatments and injuries, knee1.com.

Women's National Basketball Association (WNBA), wnba.com. This site offers information about national basketball teams and other opportunities in the sport for women.

The National Collegiate Athletic Association (NCAA) basketball program, ncaabasketball.net. It sponsors and promotes events throughout the college basketball season for girls as well as for college-age players.

2

SOCCER

Getting a Kick

WOMEN'S SOCCER IS ONE of today's most popular sports, yet not so long ago, females were forbidden to play it. In fact, until fairly recently, it was still a male-dominated game.

Versions of soccer were played as far back as ancient Rome. The modern sport, however, was established in 1863 in London by the Football Association and was declared a game for males only.

U.S. women sometimes played soccer in gym classes, intramural college competitions, or during pickup games. Soccer was considered a male sport. Then came Title IX of the Education Act of 1972, and colleges began to create women's soccer teams. By 1981, the NCAA had established about 100 varsity programs, and many soccer clubs sprang up. Of the players in the United States today, 43 percent are girls and women; 22 percent of worldwide players are female.

The benefits of soccer for the female athlete's body are many. To play any position, except goalkeeper, is to have a complete lower body and cardiovascular workout. The sport involves all muscles of the lower body and promotes good eye-foot coordination. It requires endurance training. The female athlete runs and sprints more than 100 times in the average game. Therefore, soccer promotes aerobic fitness. Another advantage to the game is that nearly anyone can play. Size is of much less importance than it is in basketball. With an array of specialized positions, soccer encourages teamwork and participation by people of varying abilities. It's a fun way to become physically fit, and it improves self-esteem and body image.

The bad news is that soccer is one of the female sports with a significant rate of injuries. The game demands the ability to turn quickly, pivot, jump in the air, run forward and backward, and use the head to hit the ball. It also involves physical contact with other players (and often the ground), resulting in minor bumps, scrapes, and bruises—especially to the shins, which is all part of the game.

Studies comparing indoor with outdoor soccer injury rates reveal that indoor soccer players encountered 6.1 times the injuries that outdoor soccer players do. Higher injury rates in indoor soccer happen because of a number of factors, including the hard playing surface and collisions between players and the walls bordering the field of play. It was also found that more injuries occur in games played on artificial turf than on natural grass outdoors.

What about injury rates and positions played? The goalkeeper's number-one priority is to stop the ball from getting into the goal. This is expected of her regardless of what might happen after the save has been made. Goalkeepers, as a result, often hurt their hands, elbows, hips, and head. These areas are at risk because of the stresses placed on her body to stop a ball that may be traveling at more than 70 miles per hour. When diving to stop shots, a goalie often lands on her hip and suffers cuts, scrapes, and bruises. In some cases, blood collects around the top of the thigh bone at the point of the hip. A goalie may also dislocate and break fingers because of the high-speed impact of the ball coming at her. Despite wearing pads, she can also fall on and injure her elbow. An example of this is an upper V shot where the goalie dives for the save and lands hard on her hip or elbow. There have been, and continue to be, equipment advancements to reduce goalkeeping injuries. In the last couple of decades goalkeepers have been using gear with increased padding, including padded gloves, pants, shorts, and jerseys.

A common problem in women's soccer is overuse injuries, which occur when repetitive pounding or stress on your body causes a progressive failure of muscle, tendon, and/or bone. Stress fractures, cracks in the bones, are more common in females than males. Factors that predispose female soccer players to develop these bone cracks include training and equipment errors as well as biomechanical abnormalities. Training and equipment errors identified in some studies include a sudden change in playing surface; an abrupt alteration in training schedule, including increased distance, intensity, or speed of activity; or insufficient recovery time between sessions. Inappropriate shoes may contribute to a stress fracture, particularly in soccer players whose cleats are worn out and in poor condition and therefore do not properly control rear foot and front foot motion.

The goalie isn't the only one at risk during a game of soccer. Every member of a soccer team can and often does suffer injuries, the majority of which are minor but some of which can be serious. The following are common female soccer players' injuries. Many of them can be avoided with good conditioning, a safe environment, and proper equipment. For more detailed information on each body part's injury and therapy, refer to Chapters 21 through 23. Chapter 21 has detailed information on upper body injuries and therapy. Chapter 22 explains lower body injuries and therapy, and Chapter 23 contains conditioning exercises to strengthen your body and improve your flexibility.

SOCCER LEGS, KNEES, AND FEET

During practices and games, female soccer players are most likely to injure the upper leg, knee, and ankle.

The Ankle Sprain

This is probably the most common overall soccer injury. You usually get it by stepping in a hole or divot or on another player's foot. A sprained ankle involves tearing of ligaments, the tough, flexible, fibrous bands that connect bones. If your ankle is injured and you are able to stand on your own, you probably can walk off the field by yourself. If you are able to do so and then perform a deep knee bend and jump on the affected leg relatively comfortably, you may be allowed to return to the game. If you are unable to do these things, use the RICE protocol. (See Chapter 22, Figure 22.4.)

The Muscle Strain or Pulled Leg Muscle

Soccer demands sudden acceleration and direction changes, which can cause muscle pulls. In a typical muscle pull, the affected muscle is abnormally stretched causing a tear, which then produces bleeding, swelling, and pain. Tearing of the muscle tissue may be seen only microscopically. However, if the tear is very large, you may be able to feel or see a defect in the muscle. It is important to start treatment within the first 24 hours with the usual RICE regimen. (See Chapter 22.) The treatment involves wrapping and icing the muscle and then gently stretching it. Once you regain a significant amount of flexibility, you should begin a strengthening program. When your muscle is no longer tender, has full motion, and has strength equal to the same muscle on the opposite side of your body, you may be allowed to return to soccer.

A contusion, or charley horse, is caused by direct trauma to soft tissue, usually a muscle in the body (e.g., the thigh). If severe enough, this can be a devastating injury. I treated a 17-year-old soccer player, Cindy, who was kicked forcefully in her thigh by an opponent. She had some initial pain but felt OK to finish the game. She did not seek any treatment until the next evening when she could not even bear weight on the leg. She was treated in the emergency room and given crutches and instructions to use ice. Six weeks later, she still had severe pain in her thigh and was unable to return to soccer. Cindy ultimately recovered after four months of rehabilitation. If you suffer a muscle contusion that does not resolve within several weeks, you should seek advice from an orthopedist.

Muscle Cramps

These involuntary muscle contractions can be extremely painful when they occur during a soccer match. If you have a muscle cramp in your lower body you may not be able to walk and will probably have to lie down on the field.

So why does this happen? It can be due to several factors, but most likely you're lacking sodium, calcium, potassium, magnesium, or some other mineral in your muscles.

How to Avoid Muscle Cramps
1. Maintain a well-balanced diet.
2. Take a multivitamin every day.

3. Develop and maintain a lower body stretching program.
4. Drink 16 ounces of water 30 minutes prior to your match.
5. Drink 10 ounces of water 10 minutes prior to your match.
6. Drink every chance you get during the match.
7. Loosen your socks or shin guards during halftime.

How to Treat Muscle Cramps
1. Stretch the cramped muscle.
2. Massage the cramped muscle.
3. Drink fluids.

Once your cramps have subsided you may be able to keep playing. However, take every opportunity to stretch the muscles that are giving you problems. You can do this during substitutions, goals, or other ball-stop situations.

SOCCER KNEE

Your knee is particularly vulnerable in soccer because of the kicking involved and because of the inherent female vulnerability of your anterior cruciate ligament (ACL), a major stabilizer in your knee. The percentage of ACL tears in women as compared to men is higher in all sports tracked by the NCAA, although the difference in soccer is dramatic. Extrinsic factors that contribute to the incidence of ACL injuries include the field, cleats, and rules of the game. The mechanism for noncontact ACL injuries is associated with landing from a jump while cutting or with sudden deceleration. Pivoting is also a major factor in ACL tears. Researchers have found that if basketball and soccer players are coached to land with bent knees and to make pivots with a three-step stop with a flexed knee instead of a sharp turn, it results in an 89 percent reduction in ACL injuries.

Soccer players suffer the same kinds of knee injuries as football players do. If you take a blow to the knee from the side with your cleats dug into the ground, you can damage ligaments or cartilage. If you feel a pain on the side of the knee (usually the outside) that took a blow from the ball or another player, the injury may just be a bruise. If, however, you feel the pain on the opposite side of the knee, you may have sprained the ligaments and possibly torn one of the cartilages of the knee. Signs of a cartilage tear include catching, locking, swelling, and pain.

A sudden rotation of the knee with your foot fixed to the ground, such as when you plant your foot to go upfield, can cause a devastating knee injury. The torque on the knee can tear the medial collateral ligament (MCL), the anterior cruciate ligament (ACL), and the medial cartilage (meniscus) in the knee (see Figure 22.1). This injury, known as the Terrible Triad of O'Donohue, can leave you with an unstable knee.

Any injury to a knee ligament must be considered serious. A sign of a torn ligament is buckling of the knee when you turn on it, even when walking. If the knee does not improve within a day or two, see a doctor. If the swelling or pain is severe, see your physician immediately. The collateral knee ligaments may heal with a rehabilitation program without surgery, but you cannot fully recover from these injuries without supervision. Bracing and rehabilitation are essential for the best possible result. Other knee ligaments, such as the ACL, cannot heal and may require surgery.

Knee fractures are rare in young women, but they do occur occasionally. In some cases, surgery is necessary for these fractures but it's more common for cartilage tears. No matter what the treatment, rehabilitation is essential for a good outcome and the ability to return to a preexisting level of play. Prevention is always the best medicine, therefore, the importance of proper techniques—keeping body weight over the ball of the foot and strengthening the lower leg—are extremely important.

SOCCER SHIN

The shin is the front part of the leg from the knee to the ankle. A shin contusion is a bruise to either the bone or the muscle beside the shinbone. When you get kicked in the shins, it is really painful because, unlike other areas of your body, your shin has very little natural padding. You may feel like your leg has been hit by lightning. The natural response to this type of injury is massive bleeding under the skin. This may put pressure on nerves, which will result in tremendous discomfort. If not appropriately treated, the nerves may have so much pressure on them that they stop doing their job. The result may be an inability to pull your foot upward—a condition called a drop foot—or an area of the leg or foot may feel numb or tingly.

When you return to soccer, be sure to wear a proper shin guard and place some foam in the shape of a doughnut in between the injured area of your leg and the shin guard. Ice your leg again after each practice or game.

BROKEN LEG

One of the most serious soccer injuries is a fracture of both bones in the lower leg (tibia and fibula). The tibia is the larger of the two, located just underneath the skin where there is no muscle. In soccer, this injury occurs when two players going for the ball at the same time collide. If your opponent misses the ball and kicks you with enough force, it can break one or both of the bones. You will need to have the leg splinted before you can be transported to a hospital. Then you will need a cast or possibly surgical insertion of a metal rod or a metal plate with screws to hold the bone fragments together. These bones may take months to heal.

If you are kicked on the outside of the leg, you will usually fracture only the fibula. This is not as serious because most of the fibula does not bear weight. The treatment is a cast or, if the fracture is in good position and not in many pieces, just keeping weight off it by means of crutches. In four to six weeks you may be able to return to play with a hard shin guard. However, if your fibula is fractured close to the ankle joint, this can be serious. Surgery may even be necessary because at this level the fibula is a weight-bearing bone.

Tibia fractures are generally more serious than fibula fractures. If there is a crack in the bone (some people call this a hairline fracture), a cast may be applied and weight bearing initiated at your physician's discretion. If you have a hairline fracture, you must stop running and jumping. Crutches may be necessary in the early phases of healing and cross training may be allowed at the discretion of your physician. Swimming may be recommended as well as limited weight training (not including weight-bearing exercises on your leg). These fractures generally take 6 to 12 weeks to heal, a process that can be monitored by x-ray evaluation.

If the fracture is more severe or if there is displacement (the bones are misaligned), surgery may be necessary. I have treated many of these fractures by inserting a long stainless steel or titanium rod. The rod enters the bone near the knee and travels down the hollow canal of the tibia toward the ankle. This surgery allows you to get out of bed bearing minimal weight on your leg the next day. It also permits full range of motion of your knee and ankle right away. Within a few weeks you can begin rehabilitation in the pool and on an exercise bike. This is a great advantage over wearing a cast for 6 to 12 weeks, which may lead to muscle shrinkage and joint stiffness.

BRUISED LEG

Since soccer is a kicking sport, you're bound to get kicked in the lower leg, usually in the shin. Cuts and bruises on the shin can be painful, and they heal slowly because of poor blood supply to that area. If your opponent's cleat was dirty, which is likely, you must clean any cuts carefully and watch for signs of infection, which include redness, swelling, and heat around the cut.

Getting kicked in the calf can also cause bleeding and bruising in the muscle. First stop the bleeding by compressing the muscle with an elastic bandage. Second, ice and elevate the calf. Continue icing intermittently for several days and then begin to stretch the muscle. When you bruise a muscle it goes into spasm and shortens, so you need to relengthen it as it heals.

SOCCER FOOT

Without good feet you are automatically defeated in soccer. Wear shoes with molded cleats or ribbed soles. Shoes with screw-in cleats present a higher risk of injury. However, you should wear shoes with screw-in cleats when more traction is needed, such as on a wet field with high grass.

It is important to have properly fitting shoes to help avoid calluses, which occur in the feet over areas of prolonged pressure and friction over a bony prominence. Treatment of calluses includes shoe inserts to help distribute the body weight on the feet, felt doughnuts to avoid further pressure on the area of involvement, or sanding of the calluses (which should be performed by a medical professional).

Improperly fitted soccer shoes and an accumulation of injuries to the feet may eventually lead to a very serious injury—rupture of the Achilles. (For a detailed description of Achilles rupture, symptoms, physical exam, treatment, and rehabilitation, see Chapter 22.)

Running in soccer can cause stress fractures of the foot, heel pain, and shin splints, as well as lower back pain and knee problems. Most of these problems can be avoided by raising the arch of your foot so that it strikes the ground properly. The current design of many soccer shoes today tends to worsen running injuries. They are too soft to protect against excessive foot roll. In many young soccer players, heel pain is attributed to growing pains or a fracture. The pain is actually due to stress on the heel bone from flat feet. Soccer shoes have no built-in arches as running shoes do. The placement of low cleats in the soccer shoe may also cause instability. The cleats are much closer together than those in a football shoe, which means you are running on a narrow base. Also, the soccer shoe doesn't help much to keep your foot from turning over. I often recommend orthotics to help prevent and treat stress fractures, shin splints, foot pain, and back pain.

SOCCER SHOULDER

When you try to head a ball, the ball may hit your shoulder or you may trip and fall on your shoulder. This can cause your shoulder to separate (AC joint separation) or you can even fracture your collarbone (clavicle) if you land on your shoulder after falling to the ground. You may also tear your shoulder ligaments, injure your AC joint, and suffer fractures or bruises to the rotator cuff. (See Chapter 21.)

SOCCER IN YOUR FACE

Being hit by a ball or another player's body can cause an eye injury so you should wear protective sports eye equipment using polycarbonate lenses during soccer practice and competition.

Soccer is the second leading cause of face and dental trauma in sports, preceded only by basketball. Potentially, getting hit in the teeth with a ball or another player's body may destroy the nerve and require root canal therapy. Braces on your teeth can increase or decrease the problem depending on how you're hit. The braces may prevent your teeth from being knocked loose or out. On the other hand, they may cause lacerations within your mouth. There are few rules for protection from mouth and face injuries and no mention of braces or other oral devices in texts for coaches and athletes. Use of protective mouth guards has been advocated to reduce injuries. During clashes in the air over the ball soccer players can also break their noses, cheekbones, or jaws. These fractures are all serious injuries that call for x-rays and treatment by a doctor.

A HIT IN THE HEAD

When players bang heads or hit the ground concussion can occur. Hitting the ball with one's head, or heading, is an important part of the game. Reporting agencies have pinpointed concussion as representing between 10 and 20 percent of soccer injuries during games. The cognitive consequences of heading the ball have come under closer scrutiny by researchers, especially after a Norwegian study reported mild to severe deficits in attention and memory in 81 percent of soccer players who had suffered concussion in a youth league. Players who headed the ball more frequently during competition had higher rates of cognitive loss than players who used the technique less often. Other researchers have expressed concern about cognitive deficits appearing in youth soccer participants after even infrequent and minor incidents of heading.

Researchers at the University of North Carolina (UNC) at Chapel Hill recently reported on a study they conducted to determine if there are cognitive deficits in college soccer players who head the ball. The UNC investigators found no impaired brain function among the players tested.

Heading is a unique aspect of the game. Despite the reassuring study by UNC researchers, a concussion is a worrisome injury. The answer is not yet definitive as to whether or not repeated heading damages a player's brain in the same way receiving multiple blows to the head can damage a boxer's brain.

Since hitting the ball with your head is an accepted and important part of the game, you should learn the proper technique: Keep your back straight and your shoulders as square as possible, and use the middle of your forehead to contact the ball. Heading the ball with your face or the top or sides of your head, besides being ineffective, can be painful and potentially dangerous to your neck.

Parents and coaches should be especially cautious about letting children play after a head injury. If a child loses consciousness, experiences temporary memory loss, complains of head or neck pain, or has numbness or weakness in the arms or legs, she should be evaluated by a physician. If there is any chance of a spinal injury, do not move her. Instead, call for emergency medical assistance at the site.

FATAL INJURIES

Although fortunately rare in soccer, deaths do occur. They are associated almost exclusively with traumatic contact with goalposts. This situation has prompted specific recommendations from equipment manufacturers and from the U.S. Consumer Product Safety Commission to ensure that soccer goalposts are adequately secured during play and when not in use.

PREVENTING INJURIES

Soccer players, like any athletes today, are expected to train harder and longer, and to start at an earlier age, if they want to succeed at the elite level. It is therefore not surprising that soccer players are experiencing an increasing number of overuse injuries. An overuse injury results from an accumulation of stresses to the involved tissues—bone, ligaments, or tendons—and can also result from the body's attempt to compensate for a previous injury by increasing the stress on another part of the body, a situation that eventually leads to tissue breakdown and overt injury at the vulnerable site.

The key to avoiding injury is getting in shape and staying in shape during the soccer season. Getting in shape or conditioning should be progressive over a four- to six-week period. The "no pain, no gain" philosophy does not apply here. One of the largest training problems is actually overtraining, which leads to overuse injuries.

Soccer players can't prevent every injury, but a good conditioning program can minimize the risk. As in most sports, you have to warm up, cool down, and work on strengthening and flexibility. However, in soccer, evidence suggests that a preseason balance-training program can lower the risk of ankle sprains. Examples of balance training include standing on one leg and having a friend toss you a ball or dribbling a basketball in a 180-degree arc while standing on one leg. Soccer demands a crucial set of skills such as passing, dribbling, trapping, and heading the ball. Nothing can substitute for repetition of these fundamentals to perfect technique and gain confidence. Start drills at a slow pace, then gradually increase the speed and intensity.

Remember, use synthetic, nonabsorbent balls on wet playing fields. Leather balls can become waterlogged and very heavy when wet, putting players at increased risk for injury. A sodden ball makes it very risky for a player to use her head to hit it. Wear shoes with molded cleats or ribbed soles. Shoes with screw-in cleats are often associated with a higher risk of injury. However, shoes with screw-in cleats are the best option when more traction is needed, especially on a wet field with high grass.

If you are physically fit and have proper equipment and good coaching, the benefits of soccer far outweigh the relatively low risk of serious injury. So get out and enjoy the world's most popular sport.

For more information, visit these websites:

WOMEN'S UNITED SOCCER ASSOCIATION at wusa.com. WUSA is the world's premier women's professional soccer league. In its inaugural season, the eight-team league featured the best players from the U.S. World Cup Championship Team and top-flight international players.

U.S. YOUTH SOCCER at usysa.org. This organization provides information about Olympic training teams as well as teams for handicapped youngsters 8 to 19 years old.

NATIONAL SOCCER COACHES ASSOCIATION OF AMERICA at nscaa.com. This association provides programs, access to insurance benefits, and many helpful publications.

UNITED STATES SOCCER FEDERATION at ussoccer.com. The Webbed Foot, the official information source for this club, features a photo gallery, updated news, and a section for ordering merchandise.

UNITED STATES AMATEUR SOCCER ASSOCIATION at usasa.com. The USASA is a member of the adult council of the United Soccer Federation, the national governing body for soccer in the United States, as recognized by the U.S. Olympic Committee.

3

VOLLEYBALL

Net Gain

VOLLEYBALL IS ONE of the female sports with the fewest injuries, but you can still get hurt. Some maneuvers are unique to volleyball, and each poses a risk of injury.

When acute injuries do occur, they usually involve blocking followed by spiking—both of which require a jump. More than half of all volleyball injuries are related to jumping. Not surprisingly, most injuries are directly related to the court surface. For example, jumper's knee (see the following section) is more common among volleyball players who play on concrete or linoleum than in those who play on softer wood courts, grass, or sand. Elite collegiate players reported five times as many injuries per hour when they played on indoor hard courts as when they played on sand courts. The following are common female volleyball player injuries, many of which can be prevented with good conditioning, a safe environment, and proper equipment. For more detailed information on each body part's injury and therapy, and refer to Chapters 21 through 23.

JUMPER'S KNEE (PATELLAR TENDONITIS)

If you have jumper's knee, you will most likely feel pain at the lower end of your kneecap and experience an inflammation of the bone-tendon junctions there. This is by far the most frequently reported overuse injury in volleyball because jumping is such a major part of the sport. Furthermore, elite volleyball players spend much of their practice time doing jump training. You are at risk for jumper's knee if you fit into one or more of the following categories:

- You play more than four times weekly.
- You are between 20 to 25 years old.
- You have played three to five years.
- You generate great power during jumping and have the highest vertical jumps.

You are also vulnerable if you experience any of the following:

- Your knees turn outward (increased external tibial torsion).
- You have lower body imbalances, especially tight hamstrings.
- You have a very deep knee bend at takeoff.

Jumper's knee usually can be managed with one to two months of conservative treatment that includes ice, anti-inflammatory medication, and alterations in training. Stretching the hamstrings and quadriceps is essential as well as balancing the kneecap mechanism by improving hip and thigh muscle strength. Good coaching for proper jumping technique can help to reduce the likelihood of this injury.

While acute knee injuries in volleyball are less common than overuse injuries, severe ligament tears do occur in more female volleyball players than in male players. I am a team physician for a college and I see at least one woman volleyball player suffering with an acute ACL tear every season. ACL tears require surgery if a player wants to continue in volleyball or any other pivoting sport. (See Chapter 22.)

LEG INJURIES

Studies of female collegiate athletes who play volleyball have found that the lead leg (left leg) takes the brunt of the force when landing during a block rather than the lag leg (right leg). Thus, when you perform blocking movements, you may experience uneven weight loading during your landing. Over a season, because of such uneven forces during jumping, cumulative stresses may affect one leg more than the other. It is important to identify which leg is overstressed so you can use conditioning and training to prevent an injury to it. This would include warm-ups with lunges in multiple directions and step downs. It should go without saying that you must also do stretches.

ANKLE SPRAINS

Ankle sprains account for a large percentage of acute injuries in volleyball. Most players hurt their ankles when they land after blocking or spiking in the front of the court. The ankle twists with the foot turned inward. This usually occurs when the blocking player's foot lands on an opposing spiker's foot that has come underneath the net and is in the "conflict zone."

You can greatly reduce your risk of an ankle sprain through a training program that teaches you how to avoid the centerline during practice and that identifies problem attackers—players who jump forward when spiking the ball.

VOLLEYBALL SHOULDER

Volleyball shoulder is the game's second most common overuse injury. It usually involves inflammation of the rotator cuff muscles and/or biceps tendons. While discrepancies exist within the teaching of proper arm swing during the volleyball attack, a scientific perspective favors a technique to reduce potentially harmful forces on the shoulder joint itself while maximizing the power generated to move the ball. If you are a hitter who is about to kill the ball to maximize the power in your volleyball attack, it is best to have your shoulders and upper arm aligned. If you line up your nonhitting shoulder with your hitting shoulder and continue that line through your upper arm, you will be in a better biomechanical position to transfer more of the strength from your shoulder and chest muscles through your arm and to the ball. You want your body and arm in a slightly more forward position to maximize this strength as well.

Volleyball shoulder can involve more than one factor. It is a complicated joint. Jennifer, for instance, was one of the stars of the volleyball team at her college. She was plagued with shoulder pain and could hardly finish the season. She would take way too much over-the-counter painkiller just to get through her practices and games. She finally came to my office because she was afraid that she could not finish the season. Jennifer denied any specific injury, but her pain had been progressively worsening. She was even having difficulty sleeping because of her shoulder discomfort.

I found she had significant pain in the shoulder when she raised her arm over her head, a sign that she had a pinched tendon (impingement). She also had tenderness in the front of her shoulder and weakness in her rotator cuff muscles. One of Jennifer's biceps tendons was weak, and the motion of one shoulder blade was not in balance with the other shoulder blade because she was compensating for the impingement. She also had evidence of mild instability, which was probably caused by slowly stretching out the capsule over time and allowing her shoulder to move slightly in and out of the socket. This can cause irritation and pain in the rotator cuff and biceps tendon. I recommended that Jennifer rest, apply ice during the day, take anti-inflammatory medication, and participate in a shoulder rehabilitation program. (See Chapter 21.)

VOLLEYBALL NERVE INJURIES

Another common injury is compression of a specific nerve in the shoulder region. Approximately 32 percent of elite volleyball players experience this type of injury at some point. The suprascapular nerve pokes through a small channel in the shoulder blade that makes its way to one of the rotator cuff muscles and gives it strength. This particular muscle is in charge of rotating the shoulder outward (external rotation) and is very important in overall shoulder function.

The injury may be the result of the floater serve commonly used in indoor volleyball to impart as little spin as possible to the ball, thereby making it difficult to pass. This serve requires the player to stop the overhand follow-through immediately after striking the ball. The result is a forceful contraction of the muscle while the muscle is being lengthened. The nerve to this muscle may, as a consequence, be stretched and injured. Most athletes who have nerve injuries of this type don't even know it. Their strength is certainly affected, and the entire function of their shoulders can be thrown off as a result by the other muscles trying to compensate. I routinely test all of the rotator cuff muscles during examinations. If I identify a significant muscle weakness, I generally recommend that a neurologist step in and do a special test, an electromyogram (EMG) to test the nerves to determine if they are working partially or at all. If the nerve is injured but still shows some activity on the EMG, the nerve injury will generally get better with time. It is important to rehabilitate the shoulder to strengthen the muscle when the nerve does work again and to address any shoulder imbalances that may have occurred.

If there is pain and the nerve is not responding to conservative treatment, surgery may be necessary. With proper treatment and rehabilitation, chances are good that you can resume playing volleyball.

VOLLEYBALL FINGERS

A thumb sprain is the most frequent volleyball-related hand injury. It often occurs in blocking. Splinting or taping can manage most finger sprains and closed fractures. Taping two fingers together (buddy taping) is the recommended treatment for ligament injuries and is particularly effective in protecting an injured finger by creating a functional mobile splint with the healthy adjoining finger. Unfortunately, the thumb does not lend itself well to buddy taping. This is because the thumb is opposable and must be independent from the other fingers. Taping or bracing the thumb to the hand can protect the thumb joints from further stresses while the ligaments are healing. Volleyball finger injuries generally heal without surgery and without interruption of the player's volleyball season—provided she receives proper taping.

VOLLEYBALL BACK

Lower back injuries are common but do not often stop players from playing. Again, jumping may be related to lower back problems because landing increases the forces on the spine. Fortunately, slipped disks (herniations) in the spine in the lower back are rare in volleyball players. If a disk should cause a problem, an appropriate treatment regimen may include decreased jumping activity, playing on softer surfaces such as sand, and a functional lower back exercise program that includes flexion and extension exercises.

As you have read, certain maneuvers and movements of volleyball make areas of your body vulnerable to acute and overuse injuries. If injury does occur, prompt diagnosis, treatment, and rehabilitation will almost always allow you to continue playing volleyball.

For more information on collegiate and university volleyball, visit these websites:

USA VOLLEYBALL at usavolleyball.org. USA Volleyball is the national governing body for the sport of volleyball in the United States and is recognized by the Federation International de Volleyball (FIVB) and the United States Olympic Committee (USOC). Its national office is located in Colorado Springs.

VOLLEYBALL WORLD WIDE at volleyball.org. This site offers information on all aspects of the sport, from beginner to professional and from high school to college to the Olympics.

AMERICAN VOLLEYBALL COACHES ASSOCIATION at avca.org. This site includes information on marketing your team.

NATIONAL GAY VOLLEYBALL ASSOCIATION at nagva.org. This organization promotes competitive volleyball in the gay, lesbian, bisexual, and transgendered community. It is dedicated to a policy of nondiscrimination, inclusion, sportsmanship, and tolerance of all viewpoints.

4

SOFTBALL

Getting to Home Plate Safely

IN A SOFTBALL GAME, when the umpire yells "Safe!" you want to be safe in more ways than one.

I joined a local softball league in my mid 30s but found little time to warm up because of my work schedule. I learned very quickly that I should practice what I preach. I got off work late one night and was behind schedule for the game. I had no time to warm up or even stretch. It was my turn to bat and I just stepped right up. I slammed one into left field and took off in a sprint for first base. By the time I got there I realized that I pulled a quadriceps muscle in the front of my right thigh. I didn't know if I could even limp to second base. I didn't want to hurt my team's position so I gritted my teeth and ran on to second and then third base. By the next day, I could hardly walk. I had significant pain and swelling in the thigh and it took me an entire week to get relief. Stretching, ice, and ibuprofen finally did the trick for me.

I see a lot of patients with this type of injury. I have always told them to stretch and warm up before practice and play. You can be assured that I now listen conscientiously to my own advice.

Softball is easy to learn and is both aerobic and anaerobic. Amateur female softball has been extremely popular for a long time. The Amateur Softball Association (ASA) annually registers more than 83,000 girls' fast-pitch softball teams—that equals out to more than 1.2 million players nationwide.

The newly formed Women's Pro Softball League (WPSL) is expected to have a full schedule of nationwide league play in six to ten markets in 2003. Teams will feature a roster of 14 female athletes who will play a 56-game schedule between Memorial Day and Labor Day. Efforts to make a success of professional women's softball have been started and halted through the years, but this time, with the success of women's professional basketball and the pool of female athletes since the inception of Title IX, things look very promising.

The majority of injuries in softball are minor, consisting mostly of abrasions, sprains, strains, and fractures. Catastrophic traumas are rare and occur when players are struck in the head or chest with a ball or bat. The following are common female softball players' injuries, many of which can be prevented with good conditioning, a safe environment, and proper equipment. For more detailed information on each body part's injury and therapy, and refer to Chapters 21 through 23.

Sliding into bases turns out to be the most common cause of recreational softball injuries, according to the U.S. Centers for Disease Control and Prevention (CDC). When you run to a base and rapidly decelerate as you slide into it, your body's full weight falls on your awkwardly positioned limb—typically your lead leg or arm—causing trauma.

Every softball season I treat several acute ACL tears. Sliding into a base seems to be the most common cause of injury. Doctors and coaches maintain 96 to 98 percent of the injuries that occur in softball could be prevented with a change in bases to make them break away.

The on-deck circle, the area near the dugout where the next batter warms up, poses another problem. In addition to using bases that break away upon impact, the CDC emphasizes that eliminating the on-deck circle and adding screens or fencing to the dugout would protect players from wild pitches, foul balls, and flying bats.

Helmets and safety equipment for catchers have already brought about reductions in injuries. If you are a catcher or are supervising a game, be sure to wear a helmet and padding.

PITCHING FOR TROUBLE

In addition to the acute major and minor traumas just described, softball can lead to overuse injuries. Pitchers commonly suffer overuse injuries in their elbows and/or shoulders. All softball players may suffer problems from throwing the ball, but these injuries usually evolve gradually. You should not abuse your throwing arm by overusing it. Relief pitchers should be available on your team, and you shouldn't pitch more than two to three consecutive innings, especially if you are not conditioned to do so. If you develop pain during a game or if you feel pain after the game every time you pitch several innings in a row, you should back off on the number of pitches the next time you play. Sometimes you may even have to stop pitching for a week or more to rehab and recover. When you do return to pitching, be sure to start with a very small number of pitches and increase the number gradually.

You have got to warm up and cool down your throwing arm to reduce your risk of injuries. As I mentioned previously, my own failure to do so once got me in trouble.

Condition all shoulder muscles emphasizing those in the back of the shoulder that are required to stop the pitching motion. Muscles in the front of the arm are naturally stronger—shoulder injuries can result from weaker ones in the back.

In softball, the underhand pitch usually does not cause shoulder problems. But a windmill pitch may cause trouble. The bulk of the throwing injuries involve the rotator cuff muscles—usually when a player stops the arm after releasing the ball. This happens particularly in windmill pitching in which the pitcher whirls her arm over her head and then has to stop her arm after she lets the ball go. The rotator cuff can also be injured or torn during play on the field. Rotator cuff injures may require surgical repair unless the tear is minor. In these cases, or in cases of severe inflammation of the tendon, I recommend physical therapy. If this fails after six months or so, surgery may be necessary. Rotator cuff tears are rare in young weekend warriors, but in the more elite athletes (especially pitchers) tears can occur because of overuse.

In some cases, a professional player or one who has pitched for many years may develop a bone spur extending from the bony arch (acromion bone) in the shoulder. When this happens, the muscles under the arch become inflamed and get pinched by the arch or the bone spur. Hypertrophied or overdeveloped muscles are not a cause of impingement. To the contrary, impingement is treated by strengthening these muscles. A lot of athletes have night pain with this syndrome. If conservative therapy fails, surgery may be necessary to remove the bone spur and any inflamed bursal tissue (the soft liquid sac that minimizes friction between body tissues) to provide more room for the inflamed rotator cuff muscles.

SOFTBALL ANKLE

Among the most common softball injuries are ankle sprains, ankle fractures, or ankle dislocations. Most of the ankle problems happen when a player slides into base. The foot gets caught under the bag; the player may then suffer a severe ankle sprain by stretching the ligaments on the outside or inside of the ankle. If the base does not give way, she may even fracture the bones at the ankle joint. Players can also strain, sprain, or break an ankle in the field while running or trying to catch a fly ball.

Another mechanism of injury is accidentally stepping on an opponent's foot and twisting your ankle. If you do hurt your ankle, you should have it x-rayed by a physician to find out the degree of damage. If it is merely a mild ligament sprain, your physician may recommend RICE therapy (see Chapter 22) and crutches until you can walk without limping. If it is a more significant ligament sprain, strain, or a fracture, you may need a cast and crutches and rehabilitation. If there is a fracture that is misaligned, you may need surgery. Nerve or vascular injury can also occur in the ankle in which the joint is dislocated. In that case, there is no time to waste; get early and aggressive treatment. Don't try to have your friend or coach put the ankle back into place—see a professional. Surgery is not always the rule for an ankle dislocation, but it can be necessary depending on the severity of the injury.

SOFTBALL ELBOW

Softball elbow is not unlike golfer's elbow (see Chapter 14). The muscles of the wrist (flexors) help pull your wrist forward and turn your hand over as you release the ball. These muscles are attached to the inner side of your elbow, which can become inflamed and painful from overuse. It was once believed that baseball elbow was caused by pitching too many curve balls, but it is now generally attributed to stress on the wrist.

Treatment is conservative including physical therapy and anti-inflammatory modalities such as medications, icing, and sometimes ultrasound.

Softball players can also suffer from Popeye elbow, an inflammation of a small fluid-filled sac (bursa) over the tip of the elbow. The medical term is olecranon bursitis. This swelling can sometimes be painless but often it is irritating or painful. The treatment usually involves RICE and anti-inflammatory medications. Sometimes a cortisone injection is necessary to reduce the swelling.

I had one patient, however, who actually required emergency surgery. Tina, who had preexisting bursitis, slid into a base and scraped up her elbow. She washed out the bleeding wound and continued to play. Two days later, her elbow ballooned. It became red and hot and she even had a fever of 101.7°F. I diagnosed Tina with infected olecranon bursitis. I had to take her to the operating room right away to wash out the infection before the infection spread into the elbow joint. Joint infections can be extremely dangerous because they can irreversibly damage the articular cartilage and therefore the joint. Tina was on antibiotics for 10 days after surgery and did very well. She returned to play in six weeks.

SOFTBALL WRIST

Repeated bending of the wrist such as that involved in throwing a softball can bring on carpal tunnel syndrome (see Chapter 21). Pressure on the median nerve where it enters the wrist through the carpal tunnel—the narrow, tunnel-like enclosure through which the finger tendons also pass—is a common cause of discomfort in the hand, especially in computer users, women over 40, and softball players (who may be all three). The RICE procedure may provide relief. (See Chapter 22.)

SOFTBALL FINGERS

Even though it's called a softball, when one hits your finger, it can tear an extensor tendon in your finger or detach it from the bone. This tendon straightens the tip of your finger. If it is injured, you won't be able to point with it. This is called a mallet finger. You must visit a physician to determine if your finger is broken. If it is, or if you have torn a tendon and fail to get proper treatment, you may be stuck for the rest of your life with a deformed digit. If the diagnosis is made early, you can often avoid surgery and just wear a splint for about six weeks. However, if the fracture is large and involves a significant portion of the joint surface or if the diagnosis is made late, surgery may be indicated. It is much better to avoid surgery because it is difficult to get full motion of your joint back after an operation, although it can be done with time, patience, and a lot of physical therapy.

SOFTBALL KNEE

Knee injuries in softball range from skin scrapes to major ligament injuries and fractures. They are often a result of sliding into bases feet first; rounding bases too fast and sharp; and/or tripping on either the ground or an opponent's foot.

I treated 42-year-old Barbara, a member of a local softball team, for a break in the top of her leg bone (tibia) at the level of the knee. I often see this type of injury in skiers, but it can occur in any sport where the leg is twisted with a lot of force behind it, such as sliding into a base. Barbara did require surgery to put in a large metal plate and screws to fix the fracture, and it took her a full year to rehabilitate back to where she could return to softball.

Unfortunately, with this type of injury, the rate of developing posttraumatic osteoarthritis is very high, and I recommended that Barbara modify her sporting activities to increase the life expectancy of her knee. For instance, I recommended that she limit her running and jumping activities and avoid certain high-compression sports such as mogul skiing.

As I mentioned earlier, ligament sprains and tears do occur in softball. They are not nearly as common as in other pivoting sports such as basketball, soccer, or skiing, but they do happen. If you slide into a base or into another player or if you just trip and twist your knee on the way down to the ground and you have pain, swelling, clicking, catching—and especially if your knee feels locked to the point where you can't extend it fully—you need to see a physician. Don't put it off. Not only will a delay in diagnosis potentially hurt your prognosis for recovery, limping around town can cause other problems in your body such as low back pain, hip pain, or pain in your other knee from overcompensating for your injured knee.

SOFTBALL HEEL

Heel pain is usually due to a flat foot, which means your foot is turned in (pronated) or has little or no arch. When you begin running with cleats, which are less stable than flat sneakers, your heels may roll to the inside quickly causing heel pain. The medical term is plantar fasciitis. This is an inflammation of the tissue that fans out across the bottom of the foot starting at the bottom of the heel.

There are other causes of heel pain besides plantar fasciitis, such as a stress fracture. It is important to have a physician rule out other potentially more severe diagnoses.

SOFTBALL TOES

Hallux valgus, also known as a bunion deformity, is a prominent bump that affects the inside of the big toe. Take the case of Cassie, a 25-year-old woman who was an active softball player. She had suffered pain in both feet for a year. Her left foot was worse than her right. Her bunions sometimes became swollen and red. She had tried over-the-counter pads to no avail. She underwent surgery to remove the bunions and to correct the hallux valgus in her big toe. Just cutting the bunion off was not enough. As is typical in this type of case, the surgeon had to cut into a bone (an osteotomy) to correct the abnormal angle of her toe so that there would be no recurrence. Cassie was able to continue playing softball. Why she had developed the bunions was unclear. Sometimes bunions are hereditary; sometimes they are the result of poorly fitting shoes (especially pointy-toed high-heeled shoes); and sometimes they are a result of stressing the joint constantly while playing softball.

Turf toe, so named because it's often the result of playing on the fake grass known as Astroturf, can cause a sprain of the big toe's joint connecting it to the foot. Treatment entails taping and ice.

PLAYING WELL

A key fundamental for a successful catcher is her setup and stance. If you are the catcher, you must be in a position to move quickly to throw or block the ball and at the same time, allow the umpire to see the pitches. In addition, good catchers have the responsibility to make questionable pitches look like strikes.

If you are going to play softball, you have to work on your arms, shoulders, and legs. See the exercises for arms, shoulders, and legs in Chapter 23. Softball is popular because it's a very social game that is easy to learn and a lot of fun to play. It is also a great form of aerobic and anaerobic exercise.

For more information about the game, write to

Amateur Softball Association of America, 2801 Northeast 50th Street, Oklahoma City, OK 73111. You can reach the organization by phone at (405) 424-5266, or visit the website at softball.org.

5

TENNIS AND RACQUETBALL

Courting Fun

You DON'T HAVE TO BE a champion to play tennis. In fact, almost all racquet sports players do it for recreation and fitness. Take Sandra E. Lamb of Denver, Colorado, for example. According to this public speaker and author of *Personal Notes: How to Write from Your Heart* (St. Martin's Press): "Tennis is the sport for me. It offers aerobic and fitness benefits, as well as camaraderie, challenge, and an emotional uplift. I find it so challenging that I will spend time routinely and consistently (three times a week) doing conditioning exercises to keep fit for it. This includes a combination of weightlifting and aerobics."

Sandra plays in a club, but tennis can be played on indoor or outdoor courts, which may be grass, clay, or synthetic. As she points out, tennis is available to many people because there are public courts in city parks. Through watching it on TV, it's easy to learn how the professionals play.

In tennis, of course, a small felt-covered rubber ball is hit back and forth over a net with a racquet fitted with strings usually made from synthetic materials. The size, weight, and strings of the racquet all may affect your ability to hit and your vulnerability to injury.

Racquetball, on the other hand, has been described as "hitting a hardball with a flyswatter against four walls until exhausted." A fast-moving game played on an enclosed indoor court, it is the newest of the racquet sports. It was developed in the 1920s by Joe Sobek, a tennis pro from Greenwich, Connecticut. He wanted an indoor alternative to tennis so he combined the rules of squash and handball to create a new game, paddle racquets, which later became racquetball. The simple wooden racquet he used has given way to a state-of-the-art frame. Surging in popularity, the game is now played by 9.3 million men and women in 87 countries.

The high level of energy expended during a game of racquetball makes it one of the most thorough cardiovascular workouts available because it involves both the anaerobic and aerobic system. If you want to lose weight, consider that in one game you can burn up to 700 calories. Despite the physical exertion, age is not a deterrent to playing racquetball. Girls as young as five participate. The National Masters Racquetball Association (NMRA) is a nonprofit organization of men and women racquetball players who are 45 and older—including some players in the over-85 category.

RACQUET SPORTS INJURIES

Injuries in all of the racquet sports are relatively common. Racquetball, squash, badminton, and paddleball players suffer basically the same injuries as tennis players but one type of injury that is specific to racquetball and squash players is the result of running into the wall or diving onto the ground for a ball. This usually involves a blow to the shoulder, but the head, hip, or knee may also be hurt. I have injured my shoulder many times doing this; have suffered a number of hip pointers (contusions of the prominent point of the iliac crest of the pelvis); and scraped my knees so often I started using kneepads.

Sandra Lamb has suffered foot problems, which she attributes to tennis—and life. "I do have some arthritis, and do try to work on preventive and precautionary medical advice to prevent further injuries," she says.

The most frequent complaints I hear from female tennis players, however, have to do with their shoulders. Laurie, 32, came to my clinic complaining of shoulder pain after she returned from a trip during which she played tennis on eight consecutive days. She had such severe discomfort by the time she got home that she could hardly sleep and was unable to raise her hand behind her head to wash her hair. She was worried that she had torn something and would need surgery. To her relief, I diagnosed her with simple bursitis, an inflammatory condition in which a sac (bursa) in the shoulder fills with fluid and causes pain (see Chapter 21). Rest, medication, and physical therapy led Laurie to a quick recovery. She was back playing tennis two weeks later, but I warned her to begin slowly and progress gradually. She had a typical overuse injury—rest is an important component to a successful outcome.

Elizabeth was another patient with a shoulder injury. At 58, she was an incredible tennis player who ignored her shoulder discomfort for two years. The pain became so severe that she could not even get a good night's sleep. When she came to my clinic, I diagnosed her with a torn rotator cuff in her shoulder. Unfortunately this overuse injury, which easily could have been treated with physical therapy and subtle changes in her tennis game, became a problem requiring surgery. Elizabeth eventually was able to return to her sport, but some players are not so lucky if the damage goes beyond a certain point. Early detection and treatment of a racquet sport injury is the best prevention against surgery and long-term problems.

Inflexibility combined with an imbalance of muscle strength can predispose female athletes to injury because racquet sports involve running, hitting, or serving a ball. For example, if your thigh muscles are weak and your hamstrings are tight, your kneecap may track off the center from your thighbone and cause significant overuse syndromes of your knee. This is a frequent cause of knee pain in the female athlete and is very common in racquet sports because of the amount of running and pivoting involved as well as the quick starts and stops. Nancy, a 28-year-old who was having severe pain in the front of her knee, is a prime example. She had very tight hamstrings and admitted that she rarely stretched before or after playing tennis. She also had a lot of muscle weakness in her quadriceps and hip abductors, which are very important for knee balance. An advertising executive and weekend warrior, Nancy was placed on a dynamic rehab program to balance these muscles. I recommended cross-training exercise (avoiding any painful activities such as tennis) to maintain fitness and increase strength. Her pain disappeared after a few weeks.

Generally, girls and women are considered more flexible than their male counterparts. However, in certain sports, some of these flexible joints become less flexible as they are increasingly exposed to an athletic activity. For instance, women are generally more flexible in their shoulders than men. However, when both sexes train for tennis, one range of motion of the shoulder (internal rotation) in the arm with which they hold the racquet becomes tighter and less flexible. To check if your shoulder's internal rotation is less on one side compared to the other, reach behind your lower back and try to touch the highest level of your spine that you can. If you are not able to reach as high with one hand as you can with the other, then there is an imbalance in your internal rotation. Once flexibility is reduced, your shoulder is at greater risk of injury, especially with overuse as you continue to play in pain (which many of us foolishly do). Other areas of your body where you may lose flexibility if you aren't careful include your lower back, quadriceps, and hamstrings, as Nancy found out the hard way. Hamstring tightness is one of the most common causes of pain in the front of the knee. Tight hamstrings are also a common cause of low back pain with or without tightness in the lower back.

TENNIS ELBOW

Though known as tennis elbow, this type of injury is common to all racquet sports. Many racquet sport injuries happen because the muscles and tendons in the forearm are not strong enough to withstand the impact of the ball against the racquet. About half of all tennis players suffer from tennis elbow at some time. Those players who are 35 to 50 are the most likely to complain of elbow pain.

Similar to male players, female tennis players get symptoms on both the outer and inner sides of the elbow. However, pain on the inside of the elbow is less common in female players than in male players—probably because males serve the ball harder and generate higher forces in their forehands.

Tennis elbow (lateral epicondylitis) is an inflammatory problem at the outside of the elbow where several tendons emanate (see Chapter 21). Tennis elbow is generally an overuse injury and comes from repetitive motions of your wrist and hand. It can also result from insufficient stretching or a poorly fitted grip on a racquet.

Outer-side elbow injuries are relatively uncommon in elite female players because these players usually use a two-handed backhand. Such injuries are very frequent, however, among recreational one-handed backhand players as a result of faulty technique, shoulder muscle weakness, and lack of flexibility in the forearm muscles, which decreases the rapid movement of the elbow through the hitting zone. The shots that are most affected are the backhand groundstroke, the backhand volley, and, occasionally, the overhead service. Tennis elbow often results when you play against a more skilled player than usual and you suddenly find the ball is coming at you harder. Your elbow ends up absorbing most of the shock. Also, you may be a little late hitting the ball because of its speed.

A second type of elbow injury, which involves pain on the inner portion of the elbow, is called medial epicondylitis or golfer's elbow (see Chapter 21). The pain is usually the result of turning the hand over the top of the racquet while hitting topspin shots on the forehand side.

Paddleball players suffer injuries similar to those of tennis players, and they are much more apt to suffer from tennis elbow. Unlike the strings of a tennis or racquetball racquet, the heavy paddle doesn't give, and this, along with the harder ball, increases the stress on the elbow.

I had tennis elbow when I was playing aggressive racquetball as a teenager. No one ever told me that I needed to stretch my forearms before playing racquetball so I never did. The discomfort in my right elbow (the side on which I held my racquet) became progressively more painful. I tried to play my regular two to three hours but could not. The pain was so bad that I was unable to even push the button on the water fountain while taking a break between games. I had pain at night. I finally saw a doctor and he diagnosed me with tennis elbow. I got better with rest (no racquetball for two weeks, which just about killed me) and stretching. When I did get back to racquetball I wore a band around my forearm.

My recommendation to patients is to stretch regularly—*before* you get tennis elbow. The stretching is easy and you can do it just about anywhere and anytime. Simply stretch your arm with your elbow straight behind you and flex your wrist upward as if you're holding an apple in your hand trying to feed a horse behind you. Hold the stretch for about 10 seconds, then repeat. Doing this stretch before you develop any pain can help prevent tennis elbow altogether.

If your elbow bothers you, you should use a composite or graphite racquet because it will minimalize the shock to your elbow. (Wooden racquets are the best for absorbing shock, but they are usually available only second-hand.) Your racquet should be strung loosely and should be no larger than midsize. An oversize racquet has a bigger sweet spot in the center, but it also has a much larger elbow-shocking hitting area around the rim. Also, a ball hit out on the rim of an oversize racquet is a shot you probably would have missed with a smaller racquet, which would have spared your elbow.

Manufacturers now produce lighter, stronger tennis racquets with increased padding to enhance shock absorption. You may want to try one of the racquets with a different style of stringing, such as one strung in a diagonal direction; they are designed to reduce shock to the arm.

An exercise program with light weights to strengthen forearm muscles and tendons will go far to prevent and to treat elbow injuries.

Wearing an elastic elbow band, either a single band or a double band with a bar, is definitely beneficial for tennis elbow. These bands compress the muscles and reduce the shock to the tendon. I usually tell patients to apply ice to their elbows as soon as they get home. Fill a paper cup with water and freeze it. Peel off the top of the cup and turn it over, massaging the elbow in small circles with the ice for 20 minutes. (You don't want to cause thermal injury by leaving the tissues too cold for too long.)

Once your tennis elbow is relieved, you may also wish to take a backhand lesson to review proper swing technique. Be sure your coach or instructor takes a look at your racquet: size, grip, string tension, etc. A poor-fitting racquet or grip can be the main culprit in developing tennis elbow.

YOUR NOT-SO-FUNNY FUNNY BONE

Another problem involves the ulnar nerve, which supplies motor function to many of the muscles of the hand, as well as the sensation of the two smaller fingers of the hand. When you hit your elbow, it's not the bone but the nerve that hurts. (See Chapter 21.) You may feel numbness or tingling in the small and ring fingers of your hand. If you have ulnar neuritis—inflammation of the nerve—the same fingers may be painful at night.

RACQUET WRIST AND HAND PAIN

On one side of the wrist there is a complex of ligaments and cartilage called the triangular fibrocartilage complex (TFCC). It is on the same side of the wrist as the pinky finger and injuries to this region can be quite painful. Injuries to the TFCC and a nearby tendon, the extensor carpi ulnaris (ECU), are common in female tennis players, especially with the recent trends in tennis: racquets are larger and there is more topspin applied to the ball. Some people use more wrist action than they did before, and this is a major factor in wrist injuries. (See Chapter 21.)

I treated a tennis player, Judy, who was complaining of severe wrist pain for several months. Rather than resting or doing another sport, Judy continued to play in pain. She didn't come to seek my advice until her wrist was actually getting locked up in certain positions. The TFCC was so chronically inflamed that the tissue had actually torn and was folding over in the joint and locking it. I treated Judy conservatively first with bracing, rest, physical therapy, and medication, but it was too late. She did require a surgical procedure. I performed an arthroscopy using a tiny fiber optic camera and small instruments to clean out tissue. She responded very well. She also learned a valuable lesson: do not ignore pain in sport! Consult your doctor sooner rather than later.

The cocking phase of the tennis swing causes the wrist to turn in the direction of the little finger (ulnar deviation). If your racquet is heavy or your muscles are weak because of poor conditioning or because of discomfort, the turn can become even more pronounced, which will cause even more pain and damage to the cartilage and tendons. The treatment for this entails bracing while you play to keep the wrist from turning. Other treatments include ice, anti-inflammatory medications, physical therapy, rest, or cross training. You may have to stay away from the racquet sports for a little while.

A painful wrist is a common racquet sport injury. The wrist may be sprained or sore from overuse. An overuse injury comes on gradually and gets progressively worse as you continue to play. A sprain causes sudden pain and is due to one specific move. A sprain is actually a tear of a ligament. Even if it's not necessarily a large tear—it can be on a microscopic level—the inflammation that accompanies it causes pain. (See Chapter 21.)

Pain in the fleshy part of the palm is usually a contusion or bruise due to an oversized grip on the racquet causing repetitive stress on this sometimes sensitive area. The obvious treatment is to reduce the size of the grip.

On the base of the hand on the same side as the pinky finger lies a small bone called the hamate (see Figure 21.3). Your hamate has a little hook on it that points toward the palm of your hand. Tennis players can sometimes fracture the hook by the repeated stress of the racquet butt against it. This can cause significant pain. One of my patients, an avid 28-year-old tennis player named Anna Marie, complained of pain in this area of her hand. She had seen a couple of doctors and was diagnosed with a bruise because her x-rays were normal. The pain continued for three more months despite rest. At last she came to see me. On her physical exam she had localized pain only at the hook of the hamate so I took a special-view x-ray that displays the profile of the hook. Sure enough the hook had broken and had never healed. It is not uncommon to miss the fracture with standard x-ray views.

Because Anna Marie's hook had not healed and was separated from the rest of the bone by scar tissue because it had been broken so long, she required surgery to remove the hook. If your doctor can identify the fracture early, a cast will generally allow the bone to heal without surgery. Once Ann Marie healed, she purchased a racquet with a smaller butt on the grip and is now back to playing tennis.

Pain in the fleshy part of the palm behind the thumb is usually due to an oversized grip on the racquet. The obvious remedy is to reduce the size of the grip. Also dry your racquet frequently because your sweat can cause excess friction and irritation in this area.

RACQUET SHOULDER

As I mentioned earlier, shoulder problems are very common in female tennis players. Fifty percent of professional women tennis players' injuries and 73 percent of the elite girl players' injuries have been those involving overuse to the shoulder. These injuries usually are due to strength imbalances. The external rotator muscles of the shoulder—which rotate the shoulder outward—often have less strength than the internal rotators—which rotate the shoulder inward—and therefore there is an imbalance. All racquet sports players can develop less flexibility in the internal rotators when they don't train specifically for their sport and do not stretch sufficiently.

The shoulder is the most mobile joint in the body. This is because the bones in the shoulder are made up of a large golf ball–shaped top of the arm bone, which fits into a flat, golf tee–shaped socket (the glenoid). The only reason your shoulder doesn't dislocate or come out of the joint is that it is connected and stabilized by a series of ligaments (connective tissue connecting bone to bone) and tendons (connecting muscles to bones). (See Figure 21.1.) Injuries to these structures can result from sudden trauma and cause your shoulder to become unstable. There also can be microscopic trauma that occurs over time with overuse. The combination of an unstable shoulder and ligament tears is common in female tennis players. Repetitive overhead actions in tennis can cause a shearing force in the ligaments that hold the shoulder together. Your shoulder will not generally come out of the socket, but pain, soreness, popping, and even catching or locking with overhead motion can occur. The pain can really be bad when your racquet contacts the ball in the overhead position. Certain structures in your shoulder become irritated and inflamed. The ligaments can tear enough to cause popping or catching as they get caught in the joint. A frequent finding in tennis players with this problem is tightness with internal rotation of the shoulder. As mentioned above, if you bring your arms behind your back and scratch as high as you can, you will determine if your internal rotation is less in your racquet arm compared to your other arm. This tightness of internal rotation causes your shoulder bones to pinch against your biceps tendon and ligaments, which may cause even more pain and popping.

A classic example was a patient of mine, Mimi, who came in with shoulder pain without any known injury. She was 48 and an avid tennis player. One morning she awakened with mild shoulder soreness. Over the next several weeks, the pain progressed and she had to modify her tennis game. She even stopped serving because raising the racquet over her head became intolerable. She didn't come to see me until the pain was so bad that it affected her sleep. If she rolled onto her shoulder at night, she would wake up and be unable to get back to sleep. She tried over-the-counter pain medication, which helped, but she couldn't play tennis anymore.

Her physical exam showed that she had some mild looseness in her shoulder (instability). Her rotator cuff was inflamed and painful while I was testing it, but I did not feel that there was a tear in the rotator cuff tendons. When I asked her to reach behind her back with her racquet arm, she could only reach the back of her pelvis whereas she could use her nonracquet arm to scratch between her shoulder blades. X-rays did not show any problem with her bones.

I sent her to physical therapy to help relieve the inflammation and work on a strengthening program for the rotator cuff muscles. After several weeks, Mimi had not responded very well so I ordered an MRI (magnetic resonance imaging). The MRI is a computer-generated image, which shows bone, muscle, tendon, ligaments, and fluid or inflammation (bursitis or tendonitis). This study is quite sensitive in diagnosing tears or fluid in structures where fluid doesn't belong.

Sure enough, she did have a rotator cuff tear and I repaired the tendons surgically. She healed and returned to tennis, but I warned her that she must continue to strengthen her rotator cuff in the future to prevent reinjury to her rotator cuff.

Imbalances in the shoulder are not the only cause of shoulder pain. You can also suffer indirectly as a result of weak muscles in your legs and buttocks. Generally speaking, women have weaker hamstring and gluteal (buttock) muscles than men. When you serve, your hamstring muscles in your thighs and the muscles in your buttocks are less activated than they would be in a male player. The result is that your trunk muscles work at higher levels of intensity than they would in a male player, while your hip and leg muscles work at lower levels of intensity—especially on your nondominant (nonserving) side. This can cause your trunk muscles to work harder and increase forces across the muscles in the shoulder producing overuse injuries there. Your performance may be affected because of the decreased functions of your shoulder and arm. If your shoulder hurts for more than a few days, see a doctor and begin a shoulder rehabilitation program.

TENNIS LEG

Tennis leg is a term used to describe a calf muscle or tendon tear that occurs when a player rushes the net. It occurs almost exclusively among tennis players. It feels as if you were hit very hard in the back of the leg by the ball. This injury can be prevented with an adequate warm-up and stretching program. The two major causes of racquet sports injuries are failure to warm up properly and overstressing joints and muscles. Many tennis players hit eight balls over the net and think they are ready to go. A cold unstretched muscle is just waiting to be torn.

Muscle weakness in the legs also may predispose you to lower leg problems by failing to provide a stable base for muscle activity and by not allowing stiffening of the entire leg to respond to flexion or rotation loads. (See Chapter 23 for leg strengthening exercises.)

RACQUET KNEE

Women athlete's knees, as I will continue to point out, are really the Achilles heel of their bodies. In other words, they are very vulnerable to injury.

Front-of-the-knee (anterior) pain is common in tennis players. Classic symptoms include pain, clicking and other noises (crepitus), swelling, weakness with flexion and rotation, inability to hit a shot that involves rotation, and occasional subluxation or dislocation of the kneecap. It more often affects the nondominant leg (opposite side from the racquet hand) and usually is associated with twisting, especially on the service motion. The most frequent cause of anterior knee pain is imbalance in the lower extremity.

Many racquet players complain of pain around the kneecap during and after playing. Some say they feel the pain deep in the knee or behind the knee. The pain usually comes on gradually, and the player may feel fluid from time to time. These are the signs of runner's knee. The constant bending of the knees playing racquet sports causes the kneecap to pull out of alignment if there are underlying imbalances. I see more and more tennis players wearing knee braces to support rehabilitated knees. A quick stop with a bent knee can cause the quadriceps muscle in the front of the thigh to pull or even tear. If your legs are not properly warmed up and stretched when you lunge for a ball, you may pull a hamstring in the back of the thigh.

If the outer part of your knee starts to hurt about 20 minutes into a racquet game and keeps getting worse, you may have iliotibial band syndrome. Once you stop playing, the pain usually disappears—until your next match, that is. Then it starts right up again in the middle of the match. The easy treatment is a good set of stretching exercises (see Chapter 23).

RACQUET FOOT AND ANKLE

Racquet sports are more running games than hitting games. Therefore, many racquet sport injuries are running injuries, such as arch pain, stress fractures of the foot, ankle sprains, runner's knee, thigh and hamstring pulls, and back strain. And you can tear up a knee playing a racquet sport as badly as you can in basketball by suddenly changing directions. You can avoid many foot problems by investing in a good pair of tennis shoes. Look for shoes with lateral stabilizing straps, a strong toe box, a midsole for cushioning, a heel stabilizer, and rubber soles with a pivot ball in front. Cheap, poorly built shoes can add to foot problems. Ankle sprains are common in tennis and badminton due to sudden side-to-side direction changes. They may get progressively worse if you continue to play. You should ice a sprain until the pain subsides and then rest for several days. Anything but the mildest sprain should be x-rayed to assure that the ankle is not in fact broken.

RACQUET NECK

Neck pain is common in racquet sports. You have to look up to hit an overhead shot or a serve, and you easily can pull a neck muscle. This injury, called wryneck, often results in an inability to turn your head in more than one direction. To treat wryneck, ice the affected side and then gently stretch your neck away from the stiff side. That is, if your right side is stiff, try to place your left ear on your left shoulder.

RACQUET BACK

If you suddenly twist your back, hit a ball off balance, or skid to a stop, you can strain your back. If you experience a severe shooting pain, you probably pulled a back muscle, and you need to rest and ice your back for a few days and take an anti-inflammatory medication such as ibuprofen. You should also begin a back stretching program as soon as recommended by your physician.

Chronic back pain may be due to a difference in the lengths of your legs. A small discrepancy in leg length can cause pain, usually on the side of the longer leg. A heel lift in the shoe of the shorter leg can correct this discrepancy. Do not permanently attach the lift inside your tennis shoe. Rather, use the lift in all of your shoes to relieve the pressure on your back.

RACQUET EYE INJURIES

Racquetball and squash players suffer more serious eye injuries than tennis players. The ball in these sports is smaller and harder than a tennis ball, so the blow to the eye is much more concentrated. Even tennis players should wear goggles or eye guards. Injuries also can occur from the racquet striking your eye. These injuries can cause severe permanent damage.

No one should step onto a racquetball or squash court without eye protection. Open-frame goggles are totally useless. When hit with enough force, the ball can compress and come right through the opening. Clear plastic goggles provide far better eye protection. Wearing eye guards can prevent virtually all serious injuries. Most eye guards or goggles completely cover the eyes with a pane of clear shatter-resistant glass or plastic.

If you are hit in the eye, apply ice intermittently for several days to reduce swelling. If your vision is extremely blurry, or if it remains even slightly blurry after one day, see an eye specialist immediately.

RACQUET BRUISES AND CUTS

Whenever I'm playing singles and hear my opponent yell, "Around!" I cringe, half-expecting the ball to hit me in the back of the head. The confined area of the court and the side-by-side struggle for the center of the court encourages banging, which causes cuts and bruises. Immediate first aid should take care of cuts, but you may need stitches if they are deep. Treat bruises with ice and rest.

TIPS TO PREVENT RACQUET SPORT INJURIES

If you want to prevent or treat a racquet sport injury, you should start by correcting any loss of flexibility or strength you have experienced. You should also try to avoid playing on hard-surface courts such as those constructed of cement, asphalt, or synthetic materials. To prevent lower back injuries when playing tennis on hard-surface courts, wear heel inserts to absorb the shock. Wear tennis shoes with good support to prevent ankle injuries. For added support, wear two pairs of socks or specially padded tennis socks. To prevent blisters on your hands, dry your racket handle frequently. When serving or hitting an overhead, do not arch your back unnecessarily. Instead, bend your knees and raise your heels, so your upper body weight is evenly balanced.

IMPROVING YOUR RACQUET SPORT GAME

Contrary to popular belief, the best way to improve your tennis game is not simply to play more tennis. You need a total-body strength-training program to help you move faster, hit the ball harder, and beat the players who are currently beating you. In tennis, muscle strength has to be accompanied by muscle stamina, which you can build using light weights and doing many repetitions. To avoid upper body muscle strains, incorporate calisthenics such as push-ups, pull-ups, abdominal crunches, and torso twists into your regular workout routine (see exercises in Chapter 23).

For more information about the various racquet sports, check out these organizations:

UNITED STATES TENNIS ASSOCIATION
70 West Red Oak Lane
White Plains, NY 10604
Telephone: (914) 696-7000
usta.com

UNITED STATES RACQUETBALL ASSOCIATION
racquetball.org

LADIES PROFESSIONAL RACQUETBALL ASSOCIATION
ladiesproracquetball.com

WOMEN'S INTERNATIONAL SQUASH PLAYERS ASSOCIATION (WISPA)
27 Westminster Palace Gardens, Artillery Row
London, England SW1P 1RR
Telephone: 44-20-7222-1667
Fax: 44-20-7976-8778
E-mail: wispahq@aol.com or psa@psacdf.demon.co.uk
wispa.net

6

LACROSSE AND FIELD HOCKEY

High-Speed Goals

LACROSSE AND FIELD HOCKEY are two high-speed field sports that require great cardiovascular fitness and endurance. Both sports require strength, speed, coordination, and technical skill.

Lacrosse is a fast game in which players are often in contact with each other, crosses (sticks), and the ball. As a result, players are required to wear basic protective devices such as helmets, facemasks, mouthpieces, gloves, shoulder pads, shin pads, and arm pads. Goalkeepers, who defend against oncoming players, must wear additional shin guards, chest protectors, and throat protectors; however, their hands are not afforded any more protection than a field player's hands, which makes their thumbs extremely vulnerable to injury. The only mandated protective equipment for women's field players is a mouthpiece. The other protective devices are optional.

Females play by the same general rules as males but female lacrosse rules limit stick contact and prohibit body contact. They require only mouth guards and optional soft head-protection. Checking—the method by which a player knocks the ball from another's stick—is prohibited for women when it is uncontrolled; directed toward the face; holding down the other's stick; and/or the checker's stick is too close to the head or face.

Girls' lacrosse has its own modified rules. Beginners, some as young as four years, are not allowed to use checking and use modified sticks and (often) soft balls instead of hard ones. Protective mouth guards are mandatory at all levels. Eye guards or goggles are permitted, as are close-fitting gloves, soft headgear (no hard helmets except for the goalie). Goalies must wear helmets, throat protectors, chest protectors, and goalie gloves. Some type of leg padding for the goalie is strongly recommended by U.S. Lacrosse, the national governing body of the sport. All protective devices used should be close fitting, padded where necessary, and as lightweight as possible.

HOW TO PLAY BETTER LACROSSE

Lacrosse requires skill and coordination. To prepare for it, you should strengthen your legs and arms and improve your endurance (see the exercises in Chapter 23). An overall well-conditioned athlete typically has success in this sport. Basic skills such as throwing, catching, and cradling are important to master. Proper conditioning is important not only for successful play but also for prevention of injuries, especially overuse injuries. Important qualities in a lacrosse athlete are speed, quickness, and explosive power.

Preseason conditioning focused toward the sport and team practice is essential. Stretching can prevent many noncontact injuries, which make up more than 30 percent of all lacrosse injuries. Quick stops, direction changes, and starts can cause muscle strains. Stretching should be performed before and after play and daily year-round for maintenance.

Strength training in women's lacrosse is important to build explosive power and coordination, not to produce bulky muscles. Power in the large muscles of the buttocks and thighs is most important. The muscles of the lower back and abdomen are also essential to transfer the strength from the legs to the upper body. Focusing on good technique with lots of repetitions rather than heavy weight is important for children and adolescents. In these cases weight training must be modified and well supervised to prevent injury.

Establish your cardiovascular fitness program during the off-season. Aerobic activity for 30 to 45 minutes three times a week at 65 to 80 percent maximum heart rate is the recommended program in the early conditioning phase. Once your endurance increases, you can increase the frequency, intensity, and duration of workouts as well.

Transfer training is somewhat unique to lacrosse. It consists of bounding and leaping exercises. Perform these exercises only after you've established good strength, flexibility, and endurance; otherwise they will shock your neuromuscular system. You should learn them from an experienced coach. Do not perform these exercises more than twice a week in the preseason. Continue once per week during the season.

As compared to soccer and gymnastics, women's lacrosse is a relatively safe sport. The injury rate for women's lacrosse is substantially lower than that for men's lacrosse. This proves that the women's game is more of a noncontact sport. In collegiate women, muscle strains make up 37 percent of injuries, joint sprains 18 percent, and bruises or contusions 8 percent. The lower extremities are the most commonly injured. Unlike in men's lacrosse, shoulder injuries are relatively uncommon in women players.

LACROSSE KNEE

Abrasions to the knee are common due to the lack of protective padding and the frequent falls and skids on the ground. Careful cleaning of the wounds is essential to prevent infection. A painful swelling on top of the kneecap (pre-patella bursitis) also can result from skids and falls. This occasionally requires drainage. I remember Tippy, a lacrosse player from our local college, who suffered both an abrasion and pre-patella bursitis from the same injury. One week later, she had developed an infected kneecap bursitis. She did not seek any medical treatment until she had a high fever and severe pain. By the time she came to see me, she needed emergency surgery to wash out the infection. She healed well and returned to the sport.

Sprains of the knee are not uncommon in any female noncontact sport. The high speed planting and cutting necessary in lacrosse can put the knee at risk for ACL injuries (see Chapter 22).

LACROSSE FOREARM AND HAND

Fractures and contusions of the hands and forearms are relatively common in lacrosse. Modern gloves can prevent finger fractures to some degree. Women's rules do not allow stick checking to the hands or handle area of the stick, yet contact does occur inadvertently. Gloves are not mandatory for women and do not necessarily prevent fractures but they can decrease the incidence of superficial injuries and bruises to the hands.

LACROSSE BALL–RELATED INJURIES

Direct contact of the lacrosse ball can be quite dangerous. The ball is made of a hard solid rubber and can be propelled at more than 100 miles per hour by male players. In women, ball speed is not as high, but injuries can still be serious if the ball contacts the face or neck. Since 1983, women goalies have been required to wear drop shields from their helmets.

PREVENTING LACROSSE INJURIES

Increased rates of head and face injuries among women players and the expanding number of children learning to play lacrosse—some as young as four years of age—is prompting emphasis on more protective gear. A University of Virginia study, published in the journal *Brain Injury* in 2001, showed that lacrosse injuries to the head and face were significantly more common among females (30.1 percent of all injuries) than among males (18 percent of all injuries), and often resulted from contact with the ball. The study went on to say that children aged four to eleven experienced the highest rates of injuries to the head and face of all lacrosse players.

A study in the *American Journal of Sports Medicine* by Hussein A. Elkousy in May 2000 pointed out that the thumb tip is vulnerable to fractures from direct impact of the ball and that this type of injury could be avoided through the use of better designed equipment to protect the digit, such as a glove with a more rigid thumb casing.

For more information, check these websites:

U.S. Lacrosse at lacrosse.org. This organization was founded on January 1, 1998, as the national governing body of men's and women's lacrosse. Although U.S. Lacrosse has only recently emerged within the national lacrosse community, it represents the past and the future of the sport.

United States Club Lacrosse Association at uscla.com. This is the oldest club lacrosse league in the world. It entered its forty-first season in 2002, with 20 teams competing in a four-conference format. Teams presently range from Boston through central New York and the mid-Atlantic states to southern Maryland. There are plans in the near future to expand into the Midwest and South with the hope of developing a true national club league.

FIELD HOCKEY

In terms of the number of players worldwide, field hockey is second only to soccer. In the United States, there are an estimated 100,000 participants.

The plastic balls used in field hockey travel at very high speeds, posing a risk to all players. Goalies are especially vulnerable, as they often have to use their entire bodies to prevent the opposing team from scoring.

Goalies once wore leather protectors but today these have been replaced by hard plastics and foam. A goalie's armor includes leg guards, kickers (to kick the ball away from the goal), chest pad, throat protector, helmet, and gauntlets. The gauntlets protect the hands and lower arms and are constructed from a combination of hard and soft plastic foam to absorb shock and protect fingers. To help prevent injuries, it is vital that protective equipment is fitted to the body properly. All players should use shin guards as well as mouth guards because runner's knee, shin splints, and tibial (leg bone) stress fractures are common in field hockey. The following are common female field hockey injuries, many of which can be prevented with good conditioning, a safe environment, and proper equipment. For more detailed information on each body part's injury and therapy, refer to Chapters 21 through 23.

The results in the 2001 NCAA Injury Surveillance System (ISS) reports show that the upper leg, lower leg, and knee were the top body parts injured in practice, while the head, upper leg, and knee were the top injuries during actual play, accounting for 42 percent. Strains, contusions, and sprains were the top three types of injuries, accounting for 54 percent of reported injuries in practice, while contusions, lacerations, and concussions accounted for 59 percent of the injuries reported during regular play.

If you suffer an ankle sprain while playing, treat it with RICE (see Chapter 22). When the swelling subsides, begin a range-of-motion ankle-strengthening program. A severe sprain should be x-rayed to check for a fracture. For bruises, rest and ice are usually the recommended treatments. An orthotic (shoe insert) can correct the foot strike in case there is any foot abnormality (such as flat feet) to relieve knee and back pain and help prevent stress fractures in some cases. Leg exercises can help prevent recurrence. Lower extremity balance is essential for preventing chronic knee overuse injuries such as inflamed tendons (tendonitis).

IMPROVING YOUR FIELD HOCKEY GAME

The constant running in field hockey and lacrosse and the use of the stick provide good aerobic exercise as well as increased arm and leg strength. You need strong legs and arms plus speed and endurance. You also need training in these sports to develop quick moves and quick reflexes.

Lacrosse and field hockey are great sports in many ways. They are two of the fastest growing team sports in the country. They offer a great way to condition and strengthen your body and are very challenging and exciting. With the proper conditioning and training, serious injuries are rare. Mild injuries such as scrapes and bruises are just part of the game.

For more information about field hockey, contact:

U.S. Field Hockey Association, One Olympic Plaza, Colorado Springs, CO 80909. You can reach the organization by phone at (719) 866-4567 or visit the website at usfieldhockey.com.

7

SKIING AND SNOWBOARDING

Hot Sports in the Cold

THE AIR IS COLD, the sun is bright, the powder is soft, and you are ready for the challenge of a winter sport. But are you *physically* ready?

There are many different types of skiing activities out there. Whether you do them just for fun or compete in events, you will experience thrills and spills. Injuries sustained during skiing can be serious or even fatal, so you want to avoid getting hurt.

GETTING IN CONDITION FOR WINTER SPORTS

Do not begin any snow- or ice-based activity without first conditioning yourself. That means you should build your endurance, strength, and flexibility. You can do it in many ways depending on what you enjoy. For instance, if you live in or near mountains, you can ride a mountain bike, swim, kayak, or climb. All of these activities help build endurance. If you are a flatlander, you can run, jog, take aerobics or dance classes, or swim—it doesn't really matter as long as it's an endurance exercise you enjoy that also elevates your heart rate.

If you live at sea level, for instance, and you're planning a ski trip, you should start conditioning at least four weeks before you go. If you do not live at a high altitude, when you travel to a ski mountain, be aware that altitude can be a factor not only for your endurance level, but also for your overall health. It is extremely important to keep well hydrated when performing a winter sport at a higher altitude. If possible, it helps to acclimate yourself for the first two or three days of a winter sports trip; drink plenty of water and avoid alcoholic beverages.

If you have had bad experiences at high altitudes in the past, such as headaches or dizziness, your doctor may prescribe a medication that eases the symptoms of altitude sickness.

Increasing Your Strength

Strong lower body muscles are important for skiing and snowboarding, so you should concentrate on strengthening your hips, thighs, and calves. People commonly ignore their hip abductor muscle because they are not aware of its importance in winter sports. Ankle strengthening is also essential to protect the ligaments, the tough fibrous cords that help stabilize your ankles. And if you are to maintain good posture during a winter sport you must strengthen your back as well. In addition to strengthening your back muscles, work on strengthening your abdominals. The abdominal muscles are often ignored in exercise programs, but they are essential for a healthy back and spine. If your abdominal muscles are fatigued, they will not support your lower back enough and you could hurt yourself. (See the strengthening exercises in Chapter 23.)

Flexibility is another important aspect of conditioning to prevent muscle and tendon strains and tears. Work to increase your flexibility, especially for your hamstrings and the calf muscles.

Choosing Your Equipment

In addition to preseason conditioning, you have to choose the right equipment to guard against injuring yourself and to enjoy your skiing activities. Several decades ago, skis were designed without releasable bindings and the risk of breaking a leg was high, although, by contrast, the risk of spraining your knee was relatively low at that time. Since the advent of releasable bindings, and the change in ski technology, you are less likely to break a leg but more likely to injure your knee ligaments.

If you are a beginner skier, be sure to have the bindings (devices that connect your boot to the ski) set at a low level that will release easier if you fall.

If your binding setting will not release easily, it may cause your knee to twist, especially if you are a beginner. Most ski shops will discuss your level of skiing with you and recommend the appropriate binding setting. The newer parabolic skis have changed the face of skiing altogether. These skis are designed to make the ski turn much easier on the skier.

BEFORE YOU HIT THE SLOPES

Have your skis waxed and tuned so that they will turn more easily and be less grabby in soft snow. Have the bindings checked by a professional to make sure they are set properly. Apply sunscreen on all exposed skin including your face, nose, and ears.

Stretch and warm up before skiing. After the long cold lift ride to the top, do 10 to 15 deep knee bends to warm up your quadriceps and knees. Stretch your hamstrings as well. There are two good ways to stretch hamstrings. One way is before you put your skis on. Sitting with your legs stretched out in front of you, slowly reach for your toes while keeping your low back straight. Feel the stretch behind your thighs. The second excellent hamstring stretching technique is good once you are on your skis. When you get to the top of the ski lift, get out of the way of other skiers and make sure you're in a safe place. Bend your knees slightly and reach for your ski boots. Then gently straighten your knees until you feel a stretch behind your thighs.

If you haven't skied in a long time, it's always a good idea to take a lesson to brush up on proper technique. Ski easy runs in the beginning of the season until your timing, strength, and coordination return.

Know your terrain. Even in the familiar ski areas snow conditions may change from day to day. The first run of the day should not be on the most difficult slope.

Dehydration may increase fatigue and potentially increase altitude sickness, so drink plenty of fluids. Carry a water bottle or other type of hydration backpack. Avoid alcohol before skiing. It can lower body temperature and decrease coordination.

Most injuries occur near the end of the day when skiers are tired. As the day goes on, ski progressively easier runs.

SKI WELL

Skiing well—with good technique—is also vital to reduce your risk of injury and enhance your skiing experience.

You should develop your technique to center your weight over the sweet spot—the region of the ski that allows you to use the least muscle energy and achieve the most efficient turns while skiing. When your body is positioned in this way, rather than being too far backward or forward, your skeleton can take some of the energy and your muscles work less hard. This will conserve your energy for a longer day of skiing.

When I was learning to ski, I can recall having severe burning in the quadriceps muscles in the front of the thigh by the time I got to the end of the ski run. It wasn't until I found the sweet spot of the ski that I learned how to ski most of the day without any quadriceps burning at all. Sweet-spot skiing also allows you to absorb stresses, such as bumps or uneven terrain, with less stress to your joints and therefore less risk of acute or overuse injuries. It permits you to ski powder more effectively. Your hands should be in the forward position, again to center your balance and to keep your body moving down the fall line of the mountain. In this position, your hips and legs are making the turns, but your upper body is directed down the hill with very little motion above the waist; this can prevent you from injuring your knees.

Timing is important in every sport. When you are tired, you become more vulnerable to injuries. In fact, the most common time of day for ski injuries to occur is between 1:00 and 3:00 in the afternoon when you've been skiing all day and your muscles are fatigued. Be smart; quit in time and head for your after-ski relaxation place.

SNOWBOARDING

Snowboarding is similar to skateboarding and surfing except that it is done on snow. The rider stands on the board with her left or right foot forward facing to one side. Her feet are attached to the board via high-backed or plate bindings, which are usually nonreleasable (one manufacturer now makes releasable ones). The history of this sport is controversial but most agree that it dates back to the mid-1960s or early 1970s. Whether the first snowboarder was the guy who bolted two skis together to make a board for his daughter or the one who was inspired to create a board by sliding on a cafeteria tray, remains a point of contention. In any case, snowboarding today is a multibillion-dollar business and an Olympic event for women.

The three basic boards are:

- *Race.* This type of board is used for downhill giant slalom (GS) and slalom racing. They tend to be stiff, narrow, and long. They are designed for high-speed use and feature long edges for turns.
- *Alpine.* This board is used in a manner similar to regular skis. In fact, it looks like a really fat ski.
- *All-around/free riding* (also called all-terrain or all-mountain). These boards are used in all snow conditions and most of them can be ridden in the half-pipe, a terrain built especially for snowboarders. The halfpipe is one of the Olympic events. Athletes are judged by how long they're able to stay in the air and by the difficulty of the tricks they execute during each successful air maneuver. Almost all the boards sold in the United States are all-arounds.

ACHES, PAINS, AND INJURIES DUE TO SKIING AND SNOWBOARDING

Snowboarders have about the same injury rate as skiers. If you are not careful during winter sports, you can suffer serious or even fatal trauma. You can do much to reduce your risk of injury if you precondition yourself. You should also purchase good equipment and maintain it well. If you follow the safety rules for your sport, use common sense, and listen to your body, you will likely avoid injuries. Take lessons if you are a beginner or a refresher course if you haven't done the sport in a while. It's important to know your limitations. Just because your friends want to ski the double black diamond run doesn't mean *you* should. Take an easier run and meet them at the bottom.

Of course, despite your best efforts, accidents *can* happen. The following information presented in this section is not a substitute for professional help but should allow you to become more knowledgeable about the prevention and therapies available for winter sport injuries. For more detailed information on each body part's injury and therapy, see Chapters 21 through 23.

SKIING AND SNOWBOARDING KNEE PAIN

Each winter activity has its own set of injuries; however, when it comes to overuse injuries there are some similarities. For instance, a very common complaint in all sports is knee pain. Women receive more stress to the knee than men do as a result of their anatomy. Overuse injuries from poor preseason conditioning or from overdoing an activity (or both) can cause pain in the front of your knee (tendonitis, plica syndrome, or patellofemoral syndrome; see Chapter 22).

I do see knee injuries in snowboarders, although they are certainly not as common as they are in skiers. Twisting injuries are rare with snowboarders because their boots are fixed to the snowboards and therefore their knee ligaments are not usually involved. With the right crash however, *any* body part can be injured. Snowboarders' menisci may be at more risk than their ligaments. The meniscus is the shock absorber of the joint and consists of two C-shaped cartilages in the knee. If the snowboarder takes a jump ("big air") and lands flat on her board, the compression in the knee can damage this cartilage.

Anterior knee pain and patellofemoral syndrome are two terms that encompass most causes of overuse knee pain. The most common causes of anterior (front) knee pain in female skiers are tight hamstrings (the muscles in the back of the thigh), weak quadriceps (the muscles in the front of the thigh), and weak hip abductor muscles. The hip abductors are the muscles that bring the leg out to the side of the body.

I often find more overuse injuries in the endurance sports, such as cross-country skiing, rather than the alpine skiing activities. This is because there is more repetition applied across the knee joint.

Telemark skiing, on the other hand, requires a lot of muscle strength to perform adequately. Telemark is an old, traditional way of skiing. The man known as the father of Telemark skiing is Sondre Norheim from the county Telemark in Norway (and hence the name). Traditionally, Telemark skiing is done with low leather boots and a binding that allows your heel to swing. This type of skiing has become very popular as more and more people realize the freedom you get when your heel is free. In Norway, about 50 percent of skiers at ski resorts are Telemarkers. These skiers generally have better knee balance and fewer overuse injuries because this sport develops their muscle strength.

ALPINE SKIING

The alpine skiers I see typically have more traumatic knee injuries than Telemark skiers, although most injuries are not the result of a high-speed crash. Women's ligaments are quite susceptible to noncontact injury. This may be due to many factors, including bone structure, hormonal changes, muscular strength and balance, lack of preseason conditioning, and faulty ski technique and equipment. Certainly if your bindings are too tight and the ski does not release during a twisting fall you're going to have a problem.

The typical skier who comes to me having just sustained a knee injury reports that her bindings did not release. Occasionally she will report that she felt or heard a pop in her knee. This pop can represent a ligament or the cartilage (meniscus) tear. There is not always severe pain associated with a ligament injury. If the meniscus—the shock absorber cartilage—of the knee is injured, however, that causes significant pain.

An injury to the anterior cruciate ligament (ACL) (see Chapter 22) may not cause severe pain. In fact, many of my patients say that after the injury they get up and continue skiing, simply to test out the knee. It is not until near the bottom of the run that they find that their knee just does not feel right and is not as stable as it should be. This—and the presence of significant swelling—is what prompts them to visit a doctor. In the older patient, sometimes a fracture (broken bone) can occur from a low-energy twisting fall. Unlike some ligament tears, a fracture usually causes significant pain to the point where the patient is unable to bear any weight on the leg.

If your knee is swollen (as it will be if you've torn a ligament or broken a bone), you will likely be in pain and should seek prompt medical attention. If you came to my clinic, I would look for swelling and tenderness on the front, sides, and back of your knee. I would then test your knee for stability. To do this I would gently place your leg in different positions to see if your knee moved in abnormal ways.

I would also need to determine whether the meniscal cartilages (crescent-shaped shields) had been injured. These cartilages are among the most important structures in the knee and they cannot be adequately replaced. Therefore, it's important to know if the injury has occurred and if a repair is necessary. If it's not treated early, the meniscus can be damaged to the point where there is no repair. A twisting fall or a compression can cause these injuries. Snowboarders can also suffer this type of injury because many snowboarders will take big air—or sometimes even "hospital air" (this is what I call the process of taking such big air that the snowboarder ends up in the hospital).

HAND AND WRIST INJURIES

Injuries to the hand are quite common in skiers. The most common hand injury I see is a ligament tear called a skier's thumb. This injury is much more common in cross-country skiers and Telemark skiers because of the increased pole planting in these sports—and the increased stress applied to the pole. It occurs in alpine skiers as well; however, it is extremely rare in snowboarders because they don't use poles. However, if they fall into the snow or ice or a rock and the thumb gets jerked out to the side, it can produce the same ligament tear skiers experience.

Karen, a 22-year-old on her honeymoon at a ski resort, is a good example of a victim of skier's thumb. She fell onto her right hand while holding a ski pole. Her thumb was pulled away from her hand, and she felt a pop. She got up and her hand was weak when she tried to grip her ski pole again. Her new husband accompanied her to my clinic. Karen's hand was mildly swollen. I examined it and diagnosed her with a torn ligament in her thumb. In her case, I was able to treat her with a cast with which she could still ski. She walked out holding her husband's hand with her left hand. After four weeks in the cast, she went through a course of physical therapy, and she regained all of the function in her thumb and still had happy memories of her honeymoon.

You can help to avoid this common injury that Karen suffered by holding your ski pole with the strap underneath your hand. Then when you fall your thumb won't be locked into that position at risk for injury. No matter how you hold your pole, however, some of these injuries cannot be prevented.

Another common problem is an overuse injury to the wrist. It is called bugaboo forearm syndrome, and it is simply an inflammation of a tendon sheath coming from the thumb. This occurs often in backcountry skiers, especially those who ski in deep powder. I have had several patients come back from a helicopter skiing trip complaining of bugaboo. It is simply treated with physical therapy and occasional bracing. Surgery is rarely indicated.

One of the most common injuries I see in snowboarders is wrist fracture. This is because snowboarders often fall toward their back, or rear, and in a reflex action, put their hands out to catch themselves. This fall on an out-stretched hand is the most common cause of fractures of the wrist in any sport. It is common in in-line skaters as well. For in-line skaters it is commonplace to wear wrist guards. Unfortunately, in snowboarding wrist guards are rarely used.

Jennifer, for example, fell on her wrist while snowboarding without wrist guards. She was a 23-year-old avid snowboarder who had the extreme snowboarding championships coming up in the next few weeks. After her injury she did have some swelling and a lot of pain, but she didn't want to stop snowboarding so she wanted to avoid visiting a doctor. She came to see me three weeks after her injury because her pain just wouldn't quit. Unfortunately for her she had a scaphoid fracture and it was displaced (the fracture line had moved out of place). If she had sought medical attention right away, a cast probably would have given her an excellent functional result. In her case, however, she required surgery with a bone graft from her arm and a screw into the bone. Her surgery went well and she healed her fracture. Because her treatment was delayed for three weeks and the bone position was poor, it is likely she will suffer some destruction of the bone (necrosis) in the future. (See Chapter 21.)

ELBOW AND FOREARM INJURIES

Elbow and forearm injuries are most commonly seen in snowboarders. Again, this is caused by falling onto an outstretched hand; the force travels up the arm. Elbow and arm fractures and/or dislocations can occur. Forearm fractures in adults generally require surgery with plates and screws to put the bones back where they belong. Elbow dislocations require a reduction (putting the elbow back in place) by a physician. Not only are elbow dislocations extremely painful (I know—I had one), but you can also develop nerve or vascular injury if you're not treated quickly. Fractures in the elbow can occur with a dislocation as well. These fractures sometimes require surgery so it is important to get professional care right away. There is no good way to prevent an elbow dislocation; there are no guards, splints, or braces to wear. The best prevention is good technique.

SHOULDER INJURIES

Shoulder injuries can occur with tumbling falls. Take the case of Tania, a fearless 18-year-old female who was skiing moguls (the bumps). She got her ski pole caught in some rotten snow, which kept her arm static as her body continued down the hill. She dislocated her shoulder.

She was in severe pain and could not move. She was brought to my clinic by the ski patrol. With some very gentle traction, I put her shoulder back into place. I put her arm in a sling for two weeks, and then I prescribed a very intense course of physical therapy. Unfortunately, because of the high recurrent rate of shoulder instability at her young age, she ultimately required surgery to repair torn and stretched ligaments in the shoulder.

Bursitis is less serious than shoulder instability but is quite painful and occurs frequently in skiers. Tendonitis of the shoulder is also common. It involves inflammation of the tough tissue that connects muscle to bone. Both bursitis and tendonitis are more likely to occur in cross-country skiers or endurance skiers, rather than alpine (downhill) skiers. This is because in alpine skiing, repetitive shoulder motion is not usually performed to the point of overuse injury. Backcountry skiers who carry heavy backpacks and have to climb through rugged terrain, however, can certainly develop overuse injuries, such as bursitis or tendonitis. As pointed out above, generalized shoulder strengthening can help prevent overuse injuries. When these conditions do occur, bursitis and tendonitis of the shoulder are usually treated without surgery. Instead, physical therapy and anti-inflammatory medications are prescribed. (See Chapter 21.)

FOOT AND ANKLE INJURIES

Ankle sprains are a common injury in many sports. Sprains are actually tears of ligaments (the strong rubber band–like structures that attach bone to bone). Ankle sprains are common in winter sports, particularly in snowboarders who wear soft-shelled boots.

By far the most common ankle injuries are those in which an inversion or rolling of the foot and ankle in a weight-bearing position occurs. Oftentimes this is associated with a pop over the outer side of the ankle and may indicate a torn ligament. A pop might also represent a fracture of the fibula—the smaller of the two bones in the leg. There may be immediate swelling making it difficult to walk. Just because you can walk on the leg doesn't mean your ankle isn't broken. The pain is usually over the outside of the ankle. In most cases, the other structures are intact.

Another common injury in skiers' ankles is a type of tendon (peroneal) dislocation. Unlike ligaments that connect bone to bone, the peroneal tendons are the ones that lie behind the ankle bone (lateral malleolus) on the outside of the ankle and they live in a tunnel that is created by a ligament called the extensor retinaculum. Sometimes, if the foot is turned to the outside in a ski boot with enough force, this ligament, which protects the housing of the tendons, can tear and the tendon then becomes free to move outside of its housing and over the ankle bone. This can cause a lot of pain and weakness in the ankle joint. Peroneal tendon dislocation is an injury treated with casting if it is diagnosed early.

Foot and ankle fractures are rare in skiers also because their boots are rigid. Ankle fractures and sprains are much more common in snowboarders because they often have less rigid boots. A particular ankle fracture is so common in snowboarders that it has been nicknamed snowboarder's ankle. Fractures do occur, however, when a skier has a major ankle twist while skiing. In addition, when snowboarders or skiers take hospital air, ankle fractures are often the result because these athletes land so hard on their feet. Ankle fractures can often be treated in casts, but some fractures do require surgery if the joint surfaces are not perfectly aligned. The surgery generally requires insertion of metal plates and screws to hold the bones in place. See the section on the ankle in Chapter 22 for further explanations of treatment.

Strengthening the muscles around the joint can do a lot to prevent ankle injuries. Part of your preseason conditioning should always include ankle work. Ankle ligaments are at high risk of injury, and therefore the stronger the muscles are the more protection the ligaments, tendons, and bones have against injury.

LEG INJURIES

It is quite common to sustain bruises or contusions to the leg when running into things while skiing or snowboarding. Cuts to the legs can occur from sharp skis during a fall. If these injuries are severe enough they can require medical attention. It is important to have this treated early to reduce the risk of infection.

Trees are obvious obstacles and can cause severe injuries, ranging from simple bruises to complex fractures. Sometimes there are unseen obstacles. For instance, Mary, 32, an expert skier, took a fall while skiing. Unfortunately there was a rock hidden under some light snow and she slammed into it. This rock caused a very severe bruise to her leg, which took several weeks to heal. If the bruise seems really large and the swelling is significant, see your doctor to make sure it's not a fracture. In addition, when there is enough swelling, just from a bruise, a very serious complication called compartment syndrome can occur. In this condition the pressure inside the leg rises because of bleeding from either a bruise or, more likely, a fracture. Consequently the blood supply to the foot and the nerves are at risk, which places the muscles in the leg at risk as well. Emergency surgery is often needed in these cases. It is a very serious injury if not treated appropriately.

Amy, an exuberant 16-year-old, is a patient who suffered a compartment syndrome. She struck a tree while snowboarding with a group of friends. She developed swelling, but at the emergency room x-rays did not reveal a fracture. She was sent home. Several hours later her leg was still swelling and her pain became so severe that it was unbearable and she returned to the emergency room. I was consulted and diagnosed her with a full-blown compartment syndrome and performed emergency surgery.

Leg Fractures

Skiing-related leg fractures typically involve the thick inner leg bone (tibia) and the smaller leg bone (fibula) because they occur at a point just above the rigid ski boot. This is a very significant injury that often requires extended treatment to recover. It takes about three months for the average tibia fracture to heal, whether it is treated with a cast or with surgery. Recovery time can be significantly longer for smokers because cigarette smoking may inhibit bone healing.

It usually takes high-energy trauma to cause a fracture of the tibia. Some women, however, have poor bone density, which places them at greater risk of this injury—and even low-energy twisting falls can cause a tibia fracture. The tibia is a bone that usually requires good positioning in either a cast or with surgery in order to heal. In contrast, the fibula, (the smaller bone in the leg) does not require perfect positioning for adequate healing, except at the ankle.

Sixteen-year-old June fell onto a hidden rock while skiing. Unlike Mary (mentioned earlier), however, June had a fracture of the fibula at approximately the midpoint of the leg. She did not require surgery or a cast because her tibia was not fractured. Therefore there was stability in the leg to allow this outer bone to heal. Nevertheless, this is a painful injury, and it can take two to three months to heal completely.

Thigh Fractures

Thigh (femur) fractures are fortunately uncommon in skiing and snowboarding. Most of the thighbone fractures I have seen are in young males who are extremely aggressive in their sport. They try to take big air off cliffs and sometimes land against immovable objects, such as trees. The snowboarders call this "hucking carcass." Hucking carcass means they find the steepest drop and the biggest cliff to take the biggest air. I call it taking hospital air. Most femur fractures are treated surgically by placing a large metal rod through the center of the bone from the hip down the shaft of the femur or sometimes from the knee up the shaft of the femur.

HIP FRACTURES AND DISLOCATIONS

Cindy, 37, was a very high-level ski instructor in Crested Butte, Colorado. She was using very short skis, a new fad. These short skis are drawing a younger population because they are less expensive. Unfortunately to keep the cost down, these skis have no releasable bindings and therefore the injury types that now occur often mirror those of the 1960s. Cindy's ski got stuck in some rotten snow and the rotational forces of her body combined with the fact that her bindings did not release resulted in a very severe hip fracture. The top of her thighbone, which is part of her hip joint, broke into four pieces. This is the type of fracture that I generally would see in an older woman with fragile bones, yet Cindy had very strong, healthy bones. It just demonstrates the incredible forces that can travel through our skeletons with this type of activity. It also demonstrates how important it is to have good, safe equipment. Cindy required emergency surgery during which I put in a plate and several screws to stabilize the bone and allow it to heal in the correct position. She healed and was back on the slopes by the next ski season. She went on to acquire a higher level of certification for professional ski instructors and has been healthy since. She never tried another pair of those short skis though.

Hip fractures usually occur from high-energy trauma in young people. I have seen, however, many female skiers older than 45 years who fracture their hips from rotational forces in a twisting fall at low speed. One patient, Nancy, 51, was simply getting off a chair lift and her skis traveled in two different directions, which caused one leg to rotate outward. Nancy fractured her hip. She did not have any idea that the quality of her bone was poor until this happened. I recommended a bone-density scan to evaluate her bone quality. The scan revealed that her bone density was low for her age. After her hip surgery, Nancy began taking medications to strengthen her bones and was eventually able to ski again.

Hip dislocations occur in women but are more common in male skiers. This is probably because men's bones are stronger, and therefore if the right force is applied to the lower extremity in a man, the soft tissues will fail first and therefore the hip will dislocate, or come out of socket. In women, the bones are not as strong and if the same force is applied, it will fracture the top portion of the bone in the hip joint (the acetabulum), rather than dislocate the hip joint. Hip dislocations do occur in some women today because, unlike 10 or 20 years ago, they are performing the same dangerous stunts as men.

FRACTURED PELVIS

Fractures of the pelvis are rare in skiing, but they can occur. When they do happen during skiing, they usually occur in non-weight-bearing areas of the pelvis, and therefore they do not require surgery. The few pelvic fractures I see in female skiers usually come about in women with low bone density with low energy falls right onto their rear ends or the sides of their pelvis.

FRACTURED SPINE

Spinal injuries rarely occur in skiing and snowboarding except in women with fragile bones. Women with poor bone density can suffer compression fractures of the spine but these mishaps are not associated with spinal cord injuries. Compression fractures generally require bracing and about two to three months to heal. Soft tissue injuries of the back are more frequent from falls or twisting injuries. The muscles in the back can go into spasm and become quite painful.

Fortunately, cervical (neck) fractures are quite rare. The ones I have seen in my practice have been elite snowboarders. One of my patients, 25-year-old Pam, was competing in the X-games in Crested Butte. She was doing the big air competition. This involves jumping off a ramp on a snowboard, taking as much air as possible, doing flips or twists, and then landing the snowboard on the slope below. Unfortunately for Pam, she landed on her head and despite the fact that she was wearing a helmet, she suffered a fracture of the cervical spine. This was an extremely scary injury because her spinal cord easily could have been damaged if the fracture had been a fraction of an inch over from where it occurred. If she had injured her spinal cord, she might have been paralyzed from the neck down. She was transferred by air ambulance to be treated by a spine surgeon. Fortunately, she healed without problem.

HEAD INJURIES

Head injuries do occur during skiing and snowboarding. They are actually quite common, especially when skiing around obstacles such as trees or when the ski area is crowded with skiers or snowboarders.

Several years ago there were two celebrities who died from head injuries while skiing. Neither was wearing a helmet. A couple of months after their deaths it was difficult to even purchase a helmet in the local ski shops because they could not keep up with the demand of helmet sales. The number of people wearing the helmets has continued to increase. The U.S. Consumer Product Safety Commission (CPSC) is urging skiers and snowboarders to wear helmets to help prevent head injuries from falls and collisions.

Skiing is one of the most exciting winter sports. Depending upon the type of skiing you do—whether you're cruising down beginner slopes or going down a 50 degree extreme incline—your level of conditioning is important. If you are going down a beginner slope, you should be in at least moderately good shape. If you are going down an extreme incline with trees and other hazards, however, you had better be in excellent physical condition or you will be very vulnerable to injury.

In any case, if you are injured during snowboarding, or skiing, see a physician promptly to determine whether treatment is necessary.

For more information, check out the following resources:

U.S. Ski and Snowboard Association
1500 Kearns Boulevard
Building F, Suite F200
Park City, UT 84060-0100

Telephone: (801) 649-9090

usskiteam.com

Information on rules, equipment sources, and major events for both competitive and recreational skiers and snowboarders.

SKI CENTRAL

skicentral.com

The primary gateway for accessing ski and snow sport-related sites. Skiers and snowboarders can use this free service to easily and quickly find information on the Internet related to their favorite sport.

AMERICAN CROSS COUNTRY SKIERS

P.O. Box 604

Bend, OR 97709

xcskiworld.com

Founded in 1998, the AXCS serves U.S. Master (age 30 and older) cross-country skiers with a wide range of education, promotion, and communication programs. It is the world's largest resource for information about cross-country skiing.

UNITED STATES OF AMERICA SNOWBOARD ASSOCIATION (USASA)

usasa.org

The USASA is an amateur competitive snowboarding association. It has spawned the likes of Ross Powers, Keir Dillon, and Kelly Clark. It aims to sustain the sport's growth and support the grassroots snowboarding program.

SNOWBOARD.COM

This represents the largest group of snowboarders in the world. As a member, you can communicate with snowboarders in your local area as well as around the world.

8

ICE SKATING AND ICE HOCKEY

Ice Maidens

SKATING INVOLVES COMPLETE control over every single muscle in your body. Learn to focus not on getting the trick, but on gaining a greater sense of awareness of your body and increased control. Physical talent may be required to be a high-level competitor, but anyone with a strong desire to improve can master all of the basic skills and learn at least some of the jumps. A lot depends on how regularly you can find time for practice and lessons—and your willingness to persevere in pursuit of your goals.

EQUIPMENT

Purchase your boots and blades separately. The length of the blade depends on the size of your boot and your age. Center of gravity varies from person to person, so the blade is not always going to be in the direct center of the boot's sole. Have the blade fitted onto your boot by an expert.

Your boots should fit snugly so that the tips of your toes just brush or can stretch to reach the toe of the boot. Good-quality beginner boots are moderately stiff to provide adequate support, and the more advanced boots get progressively stiffer. The advantage of stiff boots is that they last many years and provide good support. Their disadvantage is that they have a long and perhaps painful break-in period and they are more expensive. If you buy skates that are too stiff, you may find them virtually impossible to break in. Lighter boots on the other hand are more comfortable and break in faster. The downside is that they also wear out faster.

Whatever make of skating boots you buy, it is most important that the boots fit properly (your foot should be held firmly) and show first-class workmanship. Custom-fitted boots are not necessary unless your foot/ankle is shaped unusually or has been injured or if you require extra support for your weight or you're doing advanced jumps. When trying on boots, wear the same socks/tights that you will skate in. Thick socks are not a good idea, as they will allow too much movement of the foot within the skate. The construction of the boot tongue is important, as a relatively stiff padded tongue will stay in place and keep the pressure of individual laces from injuring your feet. Some tongues have padded lamb's wool linings, but tongues of higher level skates are generally padded with foam rubber. The foam rubber should be from ⅜ to ½ inch thick and fairly stiff with small pores.

Don't depend on your shoe size as the marker of your skating boot size. Skating boot sizes vary from one manufacturer to another. Ask to be measured by a competent vendor. They should have you sit and put a little pressure on the measuring board. Try on the boots before having the blade mounted, and don't hesitate to try others if you're not satisfied with the fit.

Breaking In Your Boots

Wear new skates around your home with the blade protectors on. The objective is to get your feet to sweat so the leather will warm up and mold to fit your feet. Breaking in the skates takes patience. But it's worth the extra time—the chances of injuring yourself are greatly reduced if your skates fit well.

Wear thin socks. Basically, you want the socks to slide against the leather. Thin polyester socks are good in this respect. Lace and unlace your new boots three or four times before skating. Skate for short periods at first paying attention to the way your feet feel. Stop if there is chafing or irritation. Never ignore discomfort because it can turn into blisters and infection.

If the top rim of your boots rubs your legs, buy some cloth medical tape and moleskin to protect the irritated areas. Bandages or round foam makeup pads can be made into pads to fit over the bony prominences of your ankles (malleoli) and over the Achilles tendon if there is direct painful pressure at these points.

Getting the Right Blades

There are three kinds of figure-skate blades.

- Freestyle blades have large toe picks for jumps, deep grind so you won't skid, and less rocker for more acceleration.
- Patch blades have the shallowest grind for maximum glide and tiny toe picks (only used for pushes and stops).
- Dance blades are shorter so you won't step on your own or your partner's blades. Compared to freestyle, they have smaller toe picks and more rocker to make turns easier.

You should get in the habit of inspecting your blades each time you dry them off. When they are dulled or there are a lot of nicks, get them sharpened. The usual test for sharpness is dragging a fingernail lightly over the edge—if it planes off a little sliver, they're sharp, if it just slides, then they're dull. It is not unusual for blades to wear unevenly. For example, the inside edges may wear more quickly than the outside edges or the fronts more quickly than the tails.

A good-quality pair of figure skates provides at least as much ankle support as a pair of hockey skates. However, you must select boots of adequate quality and correct fit to help your ankles stay erect as you condition them and balance to control the skates. Most cases of weak ankles are due either to cheap skates or to floppy, worn-out, or oversized rental skates.

LEARNING TO STOP

In skating, knowing how to stop is of course very important. The easiest stop is a snowplow, in which you turn your toes toward each other in a V and then put pressure on one of the blades (the right will probably feel better) so that it skids sideways along the ice (instead of gliding ahead). This slows you down. Try not to lean forward or tip onto your toes when executing this move. It may be helpful if you first bend your knees and think in terms of pushing your heel out, rather than turning your toe in.

IMPROVING BALANCE AND POSTURE

Almost every skater has a strong side and a weak side. It may be due to a difference in muscle strength or to a preference to do moves in one direction. Unfortunately, the tendency is to do the move on the leg that works and ignore the mirror image move on the other leg, without even realizing it. It is a good idea to do at least as much practice on the weak side as the strong side.

The most frequent cause of balance problems is poor posture. It is imperative that you keep your knees bent, torso upright, and head up. Keep your eyes at least over the top of the boards of the skating rink. There seems to be a natural defensive tendency to crouch down, bend forward, and look down at the ice. If uncorrected, this leads to chronic poor balance—and that's how noses get broken.

Try to keep your weight over the center of your skating leg, meaning the leg on which you are gliding at the time. There should be a direct line of pressure from the top of your head through your hip and down to your skating leg. Your free leg, the one on which you are not skating, should be relaxed. Any time you lean forward or let your head drop, you shift your weight toward the toes of the skates. The way skates are designed, the rear of the skate has a large curvature and is relatively stable, while the front has a smaller curvature and is relatively unstable.

Relax your shoulders. Tense shoulders tend to lift you off the ice and undermine the blades' ability to grab. Keeping your shoulders relaxed results in more stability and a better feel. You would do well to get an instructor or a more experienced skater to watch as you skate and as you prepare for the moves with which you're having trouble. Have them tell you the instant you start to lean or your head/eyes drop. Ask them to help you correct the position.

You can also do some exercises during your normal skating. Make a point of going around the rink with your eyes fixed on the top of the railing, the top of the hockey barrier, the intersection of the walls and roof, or even the lights. Get a feel for how your weight sits on the skates as you shift your balance and how much more stable and "in the groove" you feel when your weight is on the rear of the blade. Note what happens when you let it shift forward again. You can also follow another skater. Keep your eyes on this skater's head while you let your body match his or her stroke and body position.

Some lean problems stem from having your arms dangling with no clear idea of what to do with them. A good start is to hold the dance/figure skating position, with your arms out to the side and down at about a 45-degree angle, palms down and hands open. Imagine you're trying to levitate off the ice with palm power alone. Then move your hands around—from back to front and at different angles to feel how your balance shifts as the arms, shoulders, and head move around. The natural tendency is to compensate by shifting one part to offset the movement of another.

If your balance problem does have a posture component, the sooner you correct it the better. Bad habits die hard, especially when they're linked with early feelings of insecurity. The more you allow yourself to succumb to poor posture as a beginner, the more you will tend to do it as an experienced skater during moments when you feel uncertain or insecure.

Ice-skating injuries frequently are caused by overuse and lack of appropriate conditioning. Overuse injuries result from repetitive tiny traumas and can involve a variety of tissues at a number of different sites. However, contusions or bruises are the most common injury from falls onto the hard ice.

The bad falls are often the ones for which you are least prepared, while the falls resulting from various failed or incomplete moves are usually fairly predictable and are softened to some degree as a result. If you feel like you are going to fall, go ahead and do it. Fighting it often makes you fall harder and more awkwardly. We all know some of those falls are painful and some are very scary. However, after going down hard a few times, you will learn techniques for falling.

It's important to understand that you can fall and not hurt yourself. When you realize that you are losing your balance, get down and then roll off to either side. Avoid going over forward or your toe picks will catch. Bend your knees and get your body mass as close to the ice as you can so you don't have much farther to fall.

Practice falling. It is a skill like any other in skating. When you do fall, you want to change the force of hitting the ice from a direct impact to a sliding or rolling movement. Try to take the brunt of a backward fall with one of the cheeks of your butt. Roll the fall if you can to spread the impact. Slow down a forward fall with your outstretched arms, and absorb it with your chest (don't hit your knees or your chin). Remember that wrists are fragile—it's better to land on the muscle mass of the upper arm and shoulder. Wearing wrist guards may provide significant protection, but they are no guarantee against injury.

The basic principles of safer falls are to keep your head up and if you fall backward tuck your chin into your chest so you don't hit your head. Get your arms out of the way so you don't land on them. Try to land on your side or shoulders instead of an outstretched hand (which can cause a wrist fracture). Try not to fall on your tailbone, knees, or elbows. The best landing gear are the muscle masses of the thigh/hips and arms/shoulders.

Beginners should wear helmets, and experienced skaters should wear protective gear (mostly kneepads) when learning a new jump. If you wear eyeglasses, use a retainer or croakie. Ski or sporting goods stores usually have an assortment. Contact lenses may be a piece of equipment to consider if you need vision correction.

SKATING WELL

If you are afraid or timid, you will sabotage your chances of improvement. I subscribe to the idea that if you don't fall during a practice session, you are skating too defensively and thus are not pushing yourself to make real progress. Many skaters will tell you they don't feel loose until they have fallen once to get rid of the fear. Remember the cowboy in the movies who gets tossed from a horse and keeps getting back on? In skating, if you fall and don't get back on the ice, you may give up the sport. Don't worry if you're still afraid the first few times out. As long as you keep getting back out there, eventually you will get over it. Try wearing hip, knee, and butt pads. Even if you don't fall it will give you a sense of security.

Never skate with your hands in your pockets, and do not tuck your pants into the top of your skates because you can cut off circulation when your skates are laced too tight to accommodate the added bulk.

Do not wear a scarf because it can fall off and get caught under your skate blade causing you or others to fall. Don't tie your laces around your ankles because they can come undone and get caught under the blades causing you to fall. Do not tie your laces too tight so that you cut off circulation in your foot and cause skate bite, an inflammation of the sheath that covers the tendons of your foot causing pain and swelling.

Do not wear jeans because they get cold and stiff and they restrict movement when damp or wet. Running pants or sweatpants are better. Fleece vests, jackets, and pants are also excellent choices. Cotton is good next to your skin whether you are skating indoors or out—you will perspire even in cold weather and this fabric allows evaporation and keeps your body from overheating. Do wear clothing that is lightweight, allows freedom of movement, and is warm but not too warm. To that effect, layer outerwear so that you can remove a layer when you start heating up but wear light gloves or mittens to keep your hands warm and to protect your hands when you fall.

ICE HOCKEY

This sport is gaining tremendous popularity among women athletes since the USA women's team won the gold in their first Olympic competition in 1998. At last count, there were 39,345 females registered members of USA Hockey, the sport's governing body. Of that number, three-quarters are younger than 16.

As with any winter sport, proper gear is essential for enjoyment and safety. You should wear a helmet with foam lining, a securely fitted chinstrap, and a full-face mask; a mouth guard; pads for your shoulders, elbows, hips, knees, and shins; and hockey gloves. Some leagues now require neck guards. All the equipment should be certified by HECC (Hockey Equipment Certification Council), the Canadian Standards Association (CSA), or the American Society for Testing Materials (ASTM).

Make sure your equipment fits properly. Your helmet should fit snugly with a strap that gently fits around your chin when it is fastened. Helmets and face protectors are not mandatory for many adult recreational players, but that doesn't mean you should not use a helmet. It is vital to your safety.

Figure skates should not be used for playing hockey. The blades protrude more and can cause injury. Hockey skates can be used for figure skating (even for jumping) but your progress will be limited. Hockey blades are short and highly rockered, especially at the ends; they are designed for maximum agility. Blades for goalies aren't as rockered. Hockey skaters tend to skate more hunched over and are much more concerned with quick stops, starts, and changes of direction. Figure skaters tend to skate more upright and have more fluid movements.

As emphasized throughout this chapter, precondition yourself. In hockey, exercises that strengthen the neck, back, and legs and increase flexibility will help prevent injuries. You should also warm up and stretch before playing.

Knowing how to stop in hockey is probably even more important than in recreational or figure skating because you are in competition and usually skating at a fast pace with other skaters coming at you. Hockey stops involve an up-down movement and a slight forward shift of weight to the part of the blade under the balls of your feet. With both skates together and on the ice, rise up, which will cause your weight to rock forward a bit. Quickly turn your skates 90 degrees to the side, which will cause them to skid, and then sink down again, leaning slightly away from the direction of travel, which will press the edges into the ice.

After you have completed a hockey stop, your upper body—head, shoulders, and torso—will still be facing in the original direction of motion. Your arms may not be exactly perpendicular to that direction; in fact, the back arm (the one that corresponds to the trailing skate) may be slightly forward to assist in the twist and help you maintain balance. Your lower body, however, will be 90 degrees from the original direction of motion. Your knees, toes, and hips will be pointing toward the side.

This position, in which the upper body is twisted approximately 90 degrees from the lower body, is very common in various skating moves, so you might as well get used to it. While gliding forward on one skate, bring the free skate in toward the heel and turn the skate perpendicular to the one on the ice all in one smooth motion without lifting the free skate more than an inch or so from the ice. The first thing to remember is that it's the outside edge of the braking skate that touches the ice. You want your foot far enough back that you don't step on the blade of the skating foot (disastrous results will ensue if you do), but close enough so that you can comfortably, gradually shift your weight onto that braking skate's outside edge.

Don't forget to practice with the other foot as well. Go slowly until you get a feel for the balance, and then pick up speed gradually.

I see many shoulder injuries such as acromioclavicular (AC) separations in ice hockey players. This is an injury to the ligaments on top of the shoulder due to a direct impact on the shoulder. In ice hockey, this occurs from falling onto the ice or "slamming into the boards" (the walls surrounding a hockey rink). Collarbone breaks (clavicle fractures) are also very common when a hockey player lands hard on the ice on her shoulder or when she slams into the boards leading with her shoulder. Both AC separations and clavicle fractures are often treated without surgery, but there are exceptions. (See Chapter 21.)

FOOT PAIN

Probably the most common cause of foot pain in skating is boots that are laced too tightly over the instep. The lacing should be snug but not so tight as to cut off circulation or pinch the foot. If your boots feel too tight (e.g., at the ball of the foot) even when the lacing is loosened, you should have the fit checked at a competent skate shop.

Many skaters (especially beginners) have a tendency to clench their toes while skating, which can lead to foot cramps. The tendency to do this can stem from boots that are too loose, weight too far forward on the blade, or just bad habits. Another cause of foot pain is excessive tightness of the Achilles tendon (see Chapter 22). You can do wall push-ups to stretch the tendon (see exercises in Chapter 23).

If your feet continue to hurt after you've stopped skating and taken your boots off, if you cannot skate at all without pain, or if you have continuing problems with stiffness and soreness in the feet, you should stop skating and consult a sports medicine specialist. You can risk serious damage otherwise. The common foot ailment that afflicts skaters is called plantar fasciitis, and it's a condition in which the fibrous tissue (fascia) underlying the skin of the bottom of your foot is inflamed and shortened. (See Chapter 22.)

Bumps on your feet while you're breaking in a new pair of skates could reflect a temporary reaction—swelling, bruising, or callus formation (injuries of only cosmetic significance)—or continuing distress to underlying tissues, vessels, or nerves. Some of these things can be ignored; others may become points of chronic irritation if the source of the problem isn't removed. Be sure to consult your doctor if these bumps do not go away after a couple of weeks of rest or after boot modification.

SKATING STRAINS AND SPRAINS

Lower body injuries account for about one-third of the injuries in ice hockey—including sprains, strains, and bruises to the thigh, knee, and ankle. Facial lacerations and head injuries are also common, although incidences of these injuries can be markedly reduced by wearing a helmet. Catastrophic injuries such as spinal cord damage may occur but are very rare.

Bodychecking—contact between players—is the most commonly reported cause of injury and is associated with the more severe injuries. Many of the players injured by bodychecking collide with goalposts and the boards. Bodychecking is associated with 46 percent of all minor injuries and 75 percent of major injuries. The women's hockey league I played in was a no-check league. But this was just a name. Everyone was checking anyway—it's hard not to when you are skating very fast and your opponents just seem to get in the way. This kept me busy in the game, not only as a left wing, but also as the team doc.

Ice hockey is a great sport for women, but to prevent injuries you have to wear proper equipment and avoid carelessness with blades and sticks.

There is nothing more fun and thrilling than winter sports. I hope I haven't discouraged you by describing injuries and treatments. I practice orthopedics in mountain medical clinics and am a physician for the Crested Butte Mountain Resort, which is the home of the U.S. Extreme Ski and Snowboarding Championships. I love winter sports and I want you to enjoy them. To be able to do so, you have to perform preseason conditioning, avoid unnecessarily dangerous exploits, and use your common sense by listening to your body. If you do, you can stay healthy and happy on the snow and on the ice.

For more information, take a look at these websites:

USA HOCKEY, INC., at usahockey.com. This is the national governing body for the hockey in the United States. Its mission is to promote the growth of hockey in America and provide the best possible experience for all hockey participants by encouraging, developing, advancing, and administering the sport.

UNITED STATES FIGURE SKATING ASSOCIATION at usfsa.org. This website features news, competition results, ticket information, and athlete biographies. It is visited monthly by an average of three hundred thousand skating enthusiasts.

9

SWIMMING

Wet and Wonderful

SWIMMING IS A SUPER SPORT because not only does it provide aerobic bene-fits, but it can be done by young and old alike, new mothers, asthmatics, female athletes in top shape, or women who have physical problems ranging from arthritis to major injuries. Swimming is less stressful on the joints than land-based athletics. It can be performed in a variety of ways—and it's fun.

In the water we females have an advantage over our male counterparts—and it's called fat. This is one of the rare times when we can appreciate hav-ing more body fat than they do. It adds to our buoyancy. We also are built better for endurance so we can usually swim longer and farther than they can. But both sexes can benefit from this sport because it's the only one that strengthens nearly all the major muscle groups.

Aerobic exercises such as jogging and biking increase the efficiency of your body's intake of oxygen. Swimming, although more gentle, also can be an aerobic exercise because repetitive movements of large muscle groups in water require a continuous supply of oxygen. But here's an interesting fact: even though your heart rate is down while swimming compared to other sports, your oxygen consumption is up. Called the "diving reflex," it causes your heart to slow down automatically when your body is immersed in water due to pressure and cooling. Your heart will beat 10 to 15 beats per minute slower than normal. If you want to reach your target heart rate to obtain the aerobic benefit of swimming, you have to consider this. If you calculate a target heart rate during exercise, subtract 10 to 15 beats per minute and you can still obtain the same aerobic benefits from swimming as from aerobic sports on land.

For aerobic benefits, you should swim at least three times a week, but start slowly and increase duration and intensity gradually. If you have any preexisting injuries or medical conditions, be sure your physician evaluates you before beginning a swimming program. Just because swimming is gentler on our bodies than other sports does not mean injury is out of the question. Sometimes our bones, muscles, and joints cannot keep up with our enthusiasm to try a new sport.

Take the case of Joy, 42, a high-powered, single careerwoman. She decided she was spending most of her time sitting in front of a computer and therefore needed to get in shape. She joined the local health club, jumped right into the swimming pool, and started doing a lot of laps every day. Two weeks later, she could hardly lift her arm over her head and she was having trouble sleeping because of shoulder pain. She had developed swimmer's shoulder.

Should you develop a problem while swimming or just exercising in the water, early diagnosis by a physician usually can get you back to enjoying yourself. Let's go over some of the most common swim-related problems I see and the therapies I recommend. For more detailed information on each body part's injury and therapy, refer to Chapters 21 through 23.

STROKES AND STRAINS

Whether you are a competitive swimmer or swimming just for fun, you should be aware of the possible harm that can result from moving through water improperly. There are four strokes in swimming: breaststroke, backstroke, butterfly, and crawl (freestyle).

When you swim, your stroke consists of: the pull phase (the underwater portion of your stroke) and the recovery phase (the above-water portion of your stroke).

In the butterfly stroke, a dolphin motion is produced with your whole body to relieve stress on your shoulders and to allow you to move faster through the water.

st of the swimming strokes and it relies heav-
hrough the water. Your arms move together
the arms are not pulled below the waistline.
e is underwater and the legs are used more
p kick places a tremendous stress on the knee
the inside of the knee, especially in women
able knees than men.

200 to 1,500 times every mile while a major
ler may rotate only 1,000 times in a week.
ter arms and less muscle power than males,
have to use more strokes to propel their bodies through the water. This may lead to shoulder problems.

Joy, mentioned above, who got into trouble when she started doing laps without proper conditioning is a prime example of someone with swimmer's shoulder or impingement syndrome. It is usually an overuse injury and begins as pain in the front of the shoulder and arm weakness. If it is not treated, it can eventually lead to a tear of the rotator cuff (a band of four tendons that moves and stabilizes the shoulder). Swimmer's shoulder occurs most often during the freestyle, backstroke, and butterfly strokes. These strokes can cause repeated rubbing of the rotator cuff muscles and the biceps tendon against the bony ceiling of the shoulder (acromion).

Swimmers generally have strong internal rotators of the shoulder. They often have weak external rotators, which allow further friction of these tendons against the acromion (see Figure 21.1). Strengthening the rotator cuff muscles is important for preventing this syndrome and treating it if you do develop it. These strengthening exercises are easy to perform and can be done at home without any fancy or expensive exercise equipment. It is also important to keep the internal rotator muscles stretched out to keep balance in the shoulder.

I recommended Joy enter a physical therapy program that included stretching and rotator cuff muscle strengthening. I also recommended a short course (10 days to two weeks) of a nonsteroidal anti-inflammatory medication (NSAID) such as over-the-counter Advil or Aleve. In more chronic cases, a cortisone injection into the shoulder may be necessary. This will reduce the inflammation causing the pain, which will aid in the rehabilitation efforts. See other therapies for impingement of the shoulder in Chapter 21.

Joy continued to have shoulder symptoms for about two weeks. Once she got over the acute discomfort of her swimmer's shoulder a coach identified some major flaws in her technique. She observed that Joy brought her elbow too high over her head, which loaded stress on her rotator cuff. The rotator cuff muscles, which hold the shoulder in the joint, can be overstressed with the arm at an angle above parallel to the ground. All swimming strokes, except the breaststroke, place the arm in this over-the-head position and stress these muscles as the arm is pulled through the water. The stress on the rotator cuff muscles is similar to that imposed by throwing a baseball or serving in tennis.

While the sport of swimming has a low injury rate, Joy's swimmer's shoulder is one of the most common physical problems related to the sport. The majority of swimming injuries are from overuse and poor swimming technique, as Joy found out.

If you are overtraining, the ligaments around your shoulder may become stretched and cause the bone at the top of your arm (humeral head) to slip around the shallow socket in your shoulder. As it slips, it may catch the biceps tendon and the bursa (small sac in the shoulder), pinching them and causing pain. In addition, Joy's rotator cuff muscles were so weak that they could not keep up with the stress of swimming. While her coach worked with her to correct her faulty strokes in the pool, her physical therapist helped her strengthen her shoulders with stretching, weights, and rubber bands.

In the more competitive swimmer, overtraining is also a common cause of injury. Most successful competitive swimmers train five to seven days a week for 10 to 11 months per year. Many train twice a day and their workouts can be compared with running 45 miles per day. Your shoulder joint is the most mobile joint in your body and has very little bony stability or protection. Therefore, it pays to take care of it.

Shoulder Instability

Repetitive forceful stretching of the joint capsule caused by shoulder motions during swimming can cause chronic shoulder instability. This doesn't mean your shoulder will dislocate (come out of the socket), but it can move around enough to change the biomechanics of the shoulder joint and cause pain. If you are a backstroke swimmer, you are particularly prone to instability in the front of your shoulder.

The pain of shoulder instability can be difficult to distinguish from swimmer's shoulder and they often coexist. It usually takes a shoulder specialist such as an orthopedic surgeon to make the diagnosis and recommend the appropriate treatment. The pain tends to be worse at the midway point of the pull phase of the stroke; there can be a click in certain positions. Occasionally the patient will complain of the shoulder "going out."

Twenty-year-old Sandy, for example, had tremendous pain in her shoulder for a year. She ignored the discomfort and continued to train until one day she felt the shoulder come out of joint. It popped back into place right away, but she was left with soreness and fear that the shoulder would come out again. I examined Sandy and felt that her shoulder was extremely unstable with very loose ligaments. Actually she had been born with loose ligaments—many women are—and the stresses being applied with the swimming strokes were too much for her shoulder to handle. I put Sandy on an aggressive rotator cuff strengthening program to compensate for her instability. She also needed some medication to reduce inflammation of bursa and tendonitis that had developed over a year of abuse. Sandy was able to resume her swimming pain-free in about three months.

Initial treatment is conservative with rest, ice, and anti-inflammatory medications. A strengthening program to compensate for the instability is central to the treatment's success. If you have this problem and you start swimming again, you may have to modify your stroke to prevent recurrence. You may have to avoid certain strokes, such as the backstroke and butterfly. If you do not respond to conservative therapy after one year, you may need surgery to tighten your shoulder joint and make it more stable.

I want to point out that swimmer's shoulder and shoulder instability may be aggravated by the use of hand paddles, which some people use for training. Use swim fins while training to increase the power and speed generated by the kick and thereby reduce strain on the shoulder muscles while they are healing. A kickboard may be used in order to maintain cardiovascular and lower extremity fitness in cases where the shoulder problem is quite chronic and will require a longer rehabilitation time. It is important that the kickboard is held with the affected arm slightly flexed at the elbow and shoulder, as the standard kickboard position with the arm straight out essentially reproduces the aggravating position of the shoulder.

Prevention of Swimmer's Shoulder

You may need a dry-land strengthening program for the rotator cuff (especially external rotators) and scapular muscles and stretching of the internal rotators. First have a coach or swim instructor check your technique for proper stroke mechanics. As in most sports, warm up and cool down. Start each workout with 5 to 10 minutes of gentle swimming (at least 10 percent of your total time or yardage), followed by 5 minutes or so of on-deck flexibility exercises.

Gradually increase your training distance. If you are just starting to swim, try to go continuously for at least 10 minutes. Once you can do that comfortably, increase your swim time by 2 minutes every third session. Then try to add a set of 10 sprints of about 50 yards each. Rest for about 30 seconds in between.

COLLARBONE PAIN

Continuously placing your arm in the full overhead position compresses the two ends of your shoulder bones together where your collarbone hooks into your shoulder (AC joint). This may cause the bone ends to become irritated and painful, and the small cartilage between the two bones may degenerate or tear. In severe cases, the outer end of the collarbone decreases in bone density.

The management for this condition is to change your training program. Stay out of the water for a short time until your pain is reduced. Use a kickboard for conditioning, but continue to rest the arm until the pain is gone. I recommend ice and over-the-counter or prescription anti-inflammatory medications during this time. If these treatments are unsuccessful, your joint may respond to a direct injection of cortisone. This will cut down on the inflammation. In severe cases surgical widening of your joint may be necessary.

ELBOW INJURIES

Believe it or not, you can get tennis elbow from swimming. The arm pull in the butterfly stroke and the breaststroke may cause stress across the elbow. A high elbow position during the first part of the pulling phase (like reaching over a barrel) sends stresses through the bone on the outside of the elbow where many of the tendons from the top of the wrist originate. This can cause the same kind of inflammation as tennis elbow. It's not just the elbow that can be a problem—it is also the wrist. The major muscles that extend the wrist originate at this portion of the elbow and can also become painful with swimming when overused.

If you have swimmer's tennis elbow and/or wrist problem, I would initially recommend rest, ice, stretching, and muscle and tendon strengthening as well as medication. Physical therapy techniques such as ultrasound may also speed recovery. Stroke modification may be necessary to prevent recurrence. Occasionally, corticosteroid injection into the elbow becomes necessary. In rare cases, surgery may be indicated to remove chronic scarring of the elbow tendon.

SWIMMER'S BACK INJURIES

Although serious injury is not common in swimming, the sport at times can stress or strain parts of your body.

Low Back Strain

There are several stresses that may be applied to your lower back during swimming. The most commonly occurring stresses are flip turns, striking the water while extended during a dive start, and providing body roll in the freestyle and backstroke. To maintain body position and motion with the butterfly and breaststroke there can be tremendous stress on the lower back. Treatments of the symptoms of low back strain generally include rest, heat, and medication such as over-the-counter Aleve or prescription drugs such as Bextra. Stretching your back and hamstrings and strengthening your abdominals are important for both treatment and prevention of these injuries. Young female swimmers with scoliosis (a curved spine) may find that their condition worsens when they swim without the proper conditioning.

Stress Fracture/Spinal Bone Slippage

A stress fracture in your lower spine (spondylolysis) can occur without a specific trauma. The pain is typically at the belt line (spine) and may radiate into the hamstrings. It can occur with regular swimming strokes but is worsened by starts and flip turns. Hamstring tightness is frequently associated with a stress fracture in the back. Treatment begins with rest and activity modification (avoid flip turns and aggressive starts). The butterfly and breaststroke should also be avoided. If the condition doesn't improve, it may require treatment with a rigid brace or, more rarely, with surgery.

KNEE INJURIES

Though swimming is a relatively low-impact sport, women's knees may once again be susceptible to injury.

Swimmer's Knee

Lilly, a 27-year-old homemaker who was about 30 pounds overweight, came into my office complaining of significant knee pain. Her doctor had recommended swimming because he said it would help her lose weight and would be good for her joints. Upon examining her, I found that Lilly had an old ligament injury to her knee from playing tennis in high school. Ligaments are fibrous bands that connect bones at a joint. This subtle instability did not present any problem with walking and other normal daily activities but it was causing her pain when she swam the breaststroke. Lilly simply needed some muscle-balancing exercises to overcome the problem. Until she was able to do them, however, I recommended she focus on other strokes besides the breaststroke to allow her knee to recover.

If you are a breaststroker, your knee may be vulnerable. The syndrome known as "swimmer's knee" that primarily affects breaststrokers is similar to "runner's knee" (see Chapter 13). When you whip kick, you suddenly snap your knee as your leg straightens out. The whip kick causes your kneecap to shift and to rub on the side of the groove, which can cause pain under your kneecap. This knee problem is usually due to improper technique. The ligament on the inside of the knee may be sprained. Since there may be some instability during the whip kick, treatment of symptoms is usually recommended. You need to rest, avoid whip kicking, and use ice and anti-inflammatory medications.

Another common problem in breaststroke swimmers is joint stress. While you are bending your knees, your legs push against resistance. If you combine this with pushing off the wall with your legs, you can cause significant stress on your knee joint. Treatment is the same as for the breaststroker's ligament sprain. In addition, you may need to wear a neoprene kneecap-stabilizing brace during workouts. To reduce pain on land, treat the problem as you would runner's knee: Use an arch support or orthotic device in your shoe and do thigh and hip muscle-strengthening exercises.

Unpleasant Plicas

Breaststrokers aren't the only swimmers who are vulnerable to knee injuries. Knees are wrapped in a synovial capsule—a protective, fluid-filled bag. You may have been born with extra small folds of synovial tissue—called *plicas*—on the inside of your knee. When plicas rub against the thighbone they can become inflamed and cause considerable discomfort and even snapping. (See Chapter 22.)

FOOT AND ANKLE INJURIES

The most common cause of foot and ankle pain in swimmers is inflammation (tendonitis) of the extensor tendons. These are the tough cords that attach your muscle to your bone. They flex your ankle and bring your foot up toward your head. Swimmers strive to point their toes down (plantar flex) to place their feet in a better position to push water backward and then move back to neutral. If you repeat this movement often enough, tendonitis can occur. If you have this condition, you will have pain and occasionally crepitation—a squeaky or crunchy noise and sensation—in the front of your ankle. You will need rest, ice, anti-inflammatory medication, and stretching. In severe cases, to reduce inflammation, you may require a corticosteroid injection in the area around the tendon (but not into the tendon itself). You can continue to swim with this condition but you will need to kick less forcefully until the pain recedes.

Swimming, as I have pointed out, is a great sport for all ages and most bodies. I want you to have fun and avoid injuries. That means proper conditioning, good technique, and expert instruction.

GOOD INSTRUCTORS

Even if you have been swimming for years, a good swim instructor can help you improve your technique and refine your skills. The instructor can accentuate your strengths and minimize your flaws, which can help prevent many of the injuries associated with swimming. All parts of your stroke are linked, including your head position and how high you kick in the water. The timing of your breathing affects your alignment and the path of your arms as you swim. You can usually find a swim coach at your local Y, fitness center, or municipal pool. Try for an instructor that is certified by The American Swimming Coaches Association (see page 114).

There are two freestyle drills that coaches use and have been found useful for all swimmers—the on-your-side drill and the fist drill.

- **On-Your-Side Drill.** This drill helps you maintain and establish a good body position, reducing drag, improving body rotation, and lengthening your stroke. It is best performed with swim fins. You kick six to ten times on a side before rolling over to the other side. Try to have one goggle in the water and one out to help you position your head properly. Remember to rotate from your hips. Do 200 to 300 kicks per session of the on-your-side drill.

- **Fist Drill.** Swim with your hands in a fist. This one helps you learn to bend your elbow at the beginning of the stroke, giving you more power with every pull. The lack of pulling surface promotes bending your elbow, which uses your forearm and the strong muscles of your back.

You might opt for a water aerobics class with a certified instructor. You can learn basic techniques and then practice them between classes. There are many different water exercises that can help you strengthen your body and make it slimmer. Here are some of them:

- *Water walking or jogging.* You can dance, trot, or just amble in chest deep water. The benefits are similar to such movements on land but there is less impact on your joints.
- *Water aerobics.* You perform rhythmic moves for 20 minutes or more in shallow or deep water to get your heart rate up and your lungs inhaling and exhaling deeply.
- *Water strength training.* Movement of upper and lower body using water resistance and/or equipment strengthens, firms, and sculpts the muscles.
- *Flexibility training.* Large moves using full range of motion and full body stretches. Very therapeutic if you are suffering from arthritis.
- *Water yoga and relaxation.* Gentle, easy movements in the water help your stresses float away.
- *Deep-water exercises.* You run and jog but your feet do not touch bottom. Flotation belts and other devices are used with various exercises.
- *Wall exercises.* Using the pool wall for support to isolate various parts of the body.
- *Lap swimming.* Start with a few laps and gradually increase them.

SWIMMER'S EAR

For swimmers, most of the medical problems associated with the sport are not terribly serious. However, it pays to get treatment promptly should you experience any of these maladies. Swimmer's ear, or otitis externa, is an infection of the external auditory canal. It can come on gradually and often occurs after some type of minor trauma to the ear canal. The most common cause is the swimmer using her index finger to remove water from her ears. The ear canal may swell and become tender to the touch. The pain worsens and the swelling may cause temporary hearing loss. There may be discharge from the ear, and, in extreme cases, the bones, cartilage, and nerves of the ear may become involved. Once diagnosed, your doctor may place a cotton or gauze wick into your ear canal for a couple of days. Eardrops and antibiotics may also be necessary to treat the infection.

You can prevent swimmer's ear by carefully cleaning the ear if water or material enters the ear canal. Avoid sticking anything (fingers included) into the ear canal.

RED EYE: CONJUNCTIVITIS

Excessive exposure to chlorinated pool water may result in swelling of your cornea (the protective covering of the eye). This can cause mild blurring of vision and a halo effect around lights. Your eyes may be red and sensitive to light. These symptoms will generally resolve without treatment over several hours. Using goggles may help prevent this problem. Infections rarely occur because germs that cause infections in the eye usually can't survive in the chlorinated environment of most pools.

GERMS

Chlorine is the most common germ-killing chemical in pools. Although it does a pretty good job, it does not kill all germs. Germs in a pool can cause gastrointestinal problems such as stomachaches and diarrhea. These germs can be especially dangerous in young children, pregnant women, and people with weakened immune systems.

Germs can also cause skin problems such as granulomas. These are reddish bumps that may enlarge into purplish lumps. A granuloma is a localized infection that may develop when water containing an organism contacts an area of traumatized skin. Granulomas appear approximately six to eight weeks after exposure to the germ and usually pop up on the elbows, fingers, back of the hands, and knees. The granulomas may disappear over a period of months or last more than a year. Treatment with tetracycline (an antibiotic) is effective. This should not be used in children however because it can cause discoloration in developing teeth. Whether or not an antibiotic is prescribed most people can expect a complete recovery from granuloma.

One final caution, swimming is a super sport, but don't swim alone. Drowning is the ultimate danger, especially for young swimmers.

For more information, refer to these resources:

U.S.A. SWIMMING
One Olympic Plaza
Colorado Springs, CO 80909
Telephone: (719) 866-4578
usa-swimming.org
This organization is the national governing body for the sport of swimming. It provides competitive swimming programs and services for members, supporters, affiliates, and the public.

UNITED STATES WATER FITNESS ASSOCIATION
P.O. Box 3279
Boynton Beach, FL 33424
Telephone: (561) 732-9908
uswfa.com
The USWFA provides national certification courses for water fitness instructors and personal trainers.

THE AMERICAN SWIMMING COACHES ASSOCIATION
swimmingcoach.org
This organization offers leadership in American swimming through education, certification, and cooperation. It is dedicated to creating and enhancing programs to strengthen the coaching profession.

CLUB SWIM
clubswim.com
This is a portal to facilities and memberships for both experts and amateurs who indulge in the sport.

DIVERS ALERT NETWORK (DAN)
The Peter B. Bennett Center
6 West Colony Place
Durham, NC 27705
Telephone: (919) 684-2948, (800) 446-2671
diversalertnetwork.org
This nonprofit medical and research organization is dedicated to the safety and health of recreational scuba divers. It is associated with Duke University Medial Center.

SCUBACENTRAL.COM
This is a search engine for those interested in scuba diving.

10

SCUBA DIVING

Exploring Another World

IF THERE IS ONE SPORT WHERE the differences between female and male bodies are controversial as far as participation and safety are concerned, it is scuba diving.

Scuba is an acronym for "self-contained underwater breathing apparatus." Although scuba diving was originally developed for military tactics and commercial construction purposes, the number of females diving today is increasing and, in fact, 50 percent of newly certified divers are women.

Mandy Huber, for example, was a 22-year-old recent college graduate when she began scuba diving. After taking an open-water course, she decided to train to become a Divemaster.

"I had always wanted to try scuba diving, and I immediately fell in love with the sport," Mandy says. "Underwater I feel like an astronaut. The weightlessness gives me sense of freedom I don't experience on land. I think one reason I love diving is because it's a whole different world underwater.

"It took me about six weeks to become a working dive professional conducting underwater tours for tourists. It's a fun lifestyle, but it also includes a lot of responsibility. You are accountable for your clients' safety, which is sometimes a challenge because you can't talk underwater. You learn to communicate in other ways and to always be aware of what's going on. You need to be prepared for any situation that might occur."

Mandy maintains scuba diving is a good sport for women of all ages and backgrounds: "My clients ranged from teenagers to a 65-year-old woman with a bad back. One reason diving is such a great sport is that anyone who enjoys diving can choose a role to fit his or her needs. You can just dive for fun and be a follower, or you can take a leadership role and plan and navigate dives."

Scuba diving is a lot of fun and a great sport for physical and mental fitness. There are, however, many female body factors that may or may not keep you out of the water. There is controversy over whether women are more at risk than men while scuba diving because of the composition of their bodies.

DECOMPRESSION SICKNESS (DCS)

Your scuba tank is filled with compressed air that is 79 percent nitrogen and 21 percent oxygen. The oxygen is metabolized by your body tissues and therefore does not accumulate. The nitrogen, an inert gas that you exhale on land as a waste product, acts differently when your body is under increased pressure underwater. Nitrogen dissolves in your bloodstream and body tissues. When you ascend from a dive, you are traveling from a higher to a lower surrounding pressure, and the gas decompresses in your body. If you ascend too quickly, the nitrogen will come out of solution at an increased rate and form bubbles in your tissues and blood vessels, which may lead to decreased blood flow that may cause painful tissue damage or even tissue death. This condition is called decompression sickness (DCS).

Fat tissue can hold five times more nitrogen than muscle. Because women have on average 10 percent more subcutaneous fat than men, it has been suggested that females might be more susceptible to DCS than males. Lawrence Martin, M.D., author of *Scuba Diving Explained* (Best Publishing, 1997), has studied some of the physiological gender differences in scuba divers. A number of his observations are included below. There are two types of DCS.

- **Type I Decompression Sickness:** This is the "pain only" DCS, which causes a throbbing or tearing pain in large joints such as the hips or shoulders. It is commonly called the bends, a name that aptly describes the body contortions divers experience in severe cases. It can also cause skin marbling and intense burning or itching of the skin (skin bends). Type I sickness will generally occur within 12 hours of the dive and very often isn't recognized early on. If symptoms do not resolve within 30 minutes or worsen, a more severe form of sickness is likely and you must get immediate help.

• **Type II Decompression Sickness:** This is a more serious condition, which can occur in the spinal cord and, less commonly, in the brain. The syndrome can begin with back pain, leg numbness, and weakness. If your brain is involved, you may have double or blurred vision, headaches, ear problems, seizures, or weakness of one side of the body. Type II DCS may appear quite rapidly with 50 percent of symptoms occurring within 10 minutes after the dive and 85 percent within an hour. Immediate expert care is vital—a medical doctor or team that has access to a hyperbaric (oxygen under pressure) chamber if necessary.

The best prevention for DCS is to plan your dive and stick to the plan. Although decompression stops are not necessary in recreational diving, which has a 130-foot depth limit, you should always plan a three-minute safety stop at the depth of 15 feet to allow your body to begin releasing nitrogen. This stop allows some of the excess nitrogen in the tissues to diffuse into the bloodstream and be expelled by the lungs (which is called off-gassing) thereby minimizing risk of decompression sickness.

Conditions That Increase a Diver's Risk of DCS

• **Dehydration:** Because you are breathing compressed air, your body is already at risk of dehydrating at a faster rate. Dehydration causes a reduction in the amount of blood available for nitrogen release from the bloodstream and tissues. Because many dive destinations are in warm climates, you will already need to drink more water than you usually do. Make sure to drink at least three liters per day.

• **Altitude:** At higher elevations there is less atmospheric pressure, so you must adjust your dive plan to accommodate this difference.

- **Cold water:** Cold water slows blood circulation resulting in slower off-gassing/nitrogen release rates. Make sure to adjust your dive plan for this.

- **Flying after diving:** Wait at least 12 hours, or up to 24 hours if you have had multiple dives for multiple days, before flying. Wait at least 24 hours if any dives required decompression. If you fly too soon, you will increase your risk for DCS because the nitrogen bubbles will not yet have been eliminated from your bloodstream.

DIVING BEFORE OR DURING YOUR PERIOD

Will your blood in the water attract sharks? Don't worry about this myth. Menstrual flow is increased during diving but it is too little to interest sharks. You might experience decompression problems, however, because of fluid retention, abdominal cramps, and tissue swelling that occur during menstruation. This might make it more difficult for you to get rid of dissolved nitrogen. While there is no definitive proof, it might be advisable to make fewer, shorter dives in shallower water. The same holds true if you suffer from premenstrual syndrome (PMS), which can include mood swings, irritability, decreased mental alertness, fatigue, depression, bloating, swelling, breast tenderness, and joint pain.

Endometriosis: Escaping Tissue

Endometriosis is a condition in which cells lining the uterus escape to various locations outside the womb. During menstruation, these rogue cells bleed but have no way out of the body. As a result, blood collects in the surrounding tissues, causing pain and discomfort. If you have endometriosis, you may not be at greater risk of diving-related illness, but you will likely be more comfortable if you skip diving while you're menstruating.

Oral Contraceptives and Diving

If you practice birth control with oral contraceptives or an intrauterine device, are you at greater risk when scuba diving? Some physicians who treat divers believe that oral contraceptives may increase the likelihood of developing DCS or worsen the severity of tissue damage by promoting more rapid and profound activation of clotting after an accident. So far, no definitive studies have been reported. IUDs have also not been associated with any problem. Scuba diving does not dilute spermicide in the vagina used for birth control.

DIVING WHILE PREGNANT

As you will read in Chapter 18, the American College of Obstetrics guidelines cites scuba diving as a sport that pregnant women should avoid because the fetus may not be able to off-gas (release nitrogen) at the same rate as the expectant mother, thus making the fetus more susceptible to decompression sickness. Furthermore, no one knows how to treat a pregnant woman safely if a diving accident does occur.

How soon after pregnancy can you begin or resume scuba diving? A lot depends on how fast you get back in condition. After a vaginal delivery, many women can resume light activity after one to three weeks. Of course, this depends on whether she was in good condition *before* delivery and whether she has any aftereffects such as anemia, postpartum fatigue, or an infection. Generally the recommended wait time is four weeks after delivery. But to be safe, you should check with your obstetrician. You need to allow time for your cervix to close to decrease the risk of introducing infection into the genital tract. If you have had a cesarean delivery, you should stay out of the water until your obstetrician gives you the go-ahead.

Breastfeeding your baby when you begin diving again is safe. The nitrogen absorbed by your body during diving is expelled from the body during respiration, and is not expressed in breast milk.

DIVING WITH BREAST IMPLANTS

Are you afraid your breast implants will flatten if you dive? Silicone and saline implants are used for cosmetic reasons or to replace breasts that were removed because of cancer or trauma. Dr. Richard Vamm, vice president of research at Divers Alert Network (DAN), placed implants in the Duke University

Medical Center hyperbaric chamber. The study did not simulate the implant in human tissue. Three types were tested: silicone filled, saline filled, and silicone/saline filled.

The least affected were the saline-filled implants. The silicone/saline–filled implants showed the greatest volume change but the researchers concluded that if gas bubbles do form in implants, they resolve over time and the increase in volume would not burst the implant or harm breast tissue.

DIVING AFTER A HYSTERECTOMY

If you have had a hysterectomy in which your entire uterus was removed either vaginally or through your abdomen, you can follow the information in the pregnancy section on page 119. There is no reason not to dive after a hysterectomy, although it is usually recommended that you wait six to eight weeks before you take the plunge. Check with your physician.

DIVING WITH OR AFTER BREAST CANCER

Chemotherapy and radiation treatments can have toxic effects on the lung and surrounding tissue and on body cells that have a rapid growth cycle such as blood cells. Chemotherapy and radiation treatments also can have unpleasant side effects such as nausea, vomiting, and fatigue. If you are experiencing these side effects, diving is of course not a good idea. An evaluation to establish the safety of your diving should include an assessment by your physician to ensure the damage may not predispose you to a blood clot or collapse of a lung. Any wounds would have to be completely healed so that immersion in salt water would not contribute to infection.

DIVING WITH OVARIAN TUMORS

A tumor on your ovary may be cancerous or benign, solid or hollow. Ovarian cysts are sometimes filled with fluid. As with breast cancer, the major concern with regard to diving is the effect of therapy. To dive, your wound should be healed and your strength returned. You should have an evaluation by your physician before you begin or return to diving.

GOOD INSTRUCTION IS VITAL

You can't just put on a wetsuit, strap on a tank, and dive into the water. There are potential hazards not only from decompression sickness but also from air embolism, chilling, exhaustion, injuries from marine life and discarded waste, boating accidents, and equipment failure. Therefore, you have to be reasonably fit (see the list of those who should not dive at the end of this chapter) and you have to have good instruction.

To be really knowledgeable and certified for the sport, you should complete a basic open water course—it's about 30 hours of instruction—at your local Y or dive shop. About a third of the time is usually spent in the classroom and the remainder in a supervised pool or body of water. You will learn that you must always scuba dive with a buddy. You should also use equipment with a secondary regulator, called an octopus, in case of primary regulator failure or as an air source if your buddy runs out of air. Buddies can summon help for each other in case one of you gets into trouble.

OTHER POSSIBLE DIVING PROBLEMS

Deep water is a tricky element, and plenty can go wrong while you're down under. Here are a few more examples of hazards to keep in mind.

Rapture of the Deep

Rapture of the deep (nitrogen narcosis) is a nervous and mental condition resembling alcoholic intoxication. Although the exact interaction between nitrogen and the body that causes narcosis is unknown, nitrogen narcosis is caused by nitrogen inhaled under pressure. Nitrogen in air begins to have intoxicating effects at depths lower than 100 feet. The greater the depth, the greater the effect. Nitrogen narcosis is also often called martini's law, because for every additional 33 feet descended below 100 feet, it feels as if you have had one more martini. Everyone reacts differently to nitrogen, which means you may be more or less susceptible to its effects. Symptoms include loss of judgment and skill, false sense of well-being, lack of concern for safety, difficulty in accomplishing simple tasks, and foolish behavior. Treatment is to get the diver to shallower water.

The Air in There

Any cavity in the body that holds air can be affected by pressure and can result in pain, discomfort, or injury. For example, increased pressure can cause:

- **Outer and middle ear squeeze** due to the compression of the membrane (tympanic) in the ear from increased pressure. If pressure cannot be equalized, the pressure imbalance may lead to the ear membrane rupturing. Pain, severe dizziness (vertigo), panic, vomiting, and too rapid ascent may be the result. The way to equalize is by using a valsalva maneuver (trying to exhale with your nostrils pinched and your mouth shut, which forces air into the eustachian tubes in your ears) and a timed gentle ascent. You will learn how to do this from a certified instructor before you take your first dive.

- **Tooth squeeze**, which can occur when a small pocket of air becomes trapped between a dental filling and the tooth's nerve root. Upon ascent, the air expands and places pressure on the nerve root, which results in a sharp pain. Check with your dentist. You may have to have one or more fillings repaired.

- **Mask squeeze**, which may occur as the pressure increases with your descent. If you do not equalize the pressure for your mask as you do for your ears, the increased pressure on the mask will put pressure on your eyes. Common effects are very red eyes, and sometimes bruised skin around the eyes or cheeks.

- **Stomach squeeze**, which may develop as you ascend from a dive. The gas in your stomach and intestines will expand and put pressure on the linings and walls of these organs, which can cause pain. The best way to avoid this problem is to know which foods and drinks give you gas and avoid them before diving.

Breath holding is a problem if you ascend too rapidly due to panic or poor training. The small air pockets (alveoli) in your lungs may become hyperdistended and may even rupture. This can even cause a pneumothorax (collapsed lung). *Never* hold your breath while diving!

Bone damage (osteonecrosis) is a type of decompression sickness that generally occurs in professional and naval divers but may also affect recreational divers. The most common joint affected is the hip, although I have also seen patients suffer shoulder and even knee osteonecrosis. In fact, whenever I see a patient with a large joint pain with suspected osteonecrosis, the first question I ask is "Have you ever been scuba diving?"

When You Are Too Cold

Because water conducts heat away from the body 20 times faster than air, you can expect body heat loss occurs when your skin is in contact with the water. It can occur in warm water but it is more common in cold-water dives. You can become fatigued and weak. You may begin to shiver uncontrollably and lose your judgment. Don't let this happen to you. Prevention means wearing some type of body suit or wetsuit, which retains some of your body heat at the skin's surface. The colder the water or longer the dive, the thicker the suit you need.

Calf Pain or Cramps While Diving

It takes a while to get used to wearing fins no matter how good they are or how much they cost. Before a dive trip, practice with your fins in the pool. A good conditioner for the dive season is to swim with fins and snorkel with enough weight to make you struggle to stay up. One exercise to strengthen your legs is to stand with both feet on the stairs— without the fins—then move back so only the front half of your feet are on the step. Then practice raising your body using your feet (toe raises). Try to increase the duration next training session.

If these cramps occur during a dive, simply grab the toe of the fin and pull it up toward you keeping your leg straight to stretch out the calf muscle and relieve the cramp.

Nosebleeds While Diving

Nosebleeds during diving are common. If they don't stop when you leave the water, place decongestant nose drops on a piece of cotton and place the cotton in your nose where the bleeding is and press gently. If you continue to have nosebleeds, check with your physician. Do not take oral decongestants before a dive.

Seasickness

If you get seasick on the boat or on the surface of the water, *do not* take over-the-counter antiseasickness medications. They all have a side effect of drowsiness, which can add to the effects of nitrogen narcosis once you're underwater.

Trouble Clearing Your Ears

A common problem divers experience is a difficulty equalizing pressure in the ears during descent. This can occur at different depths depending on your size. As soon as you feel pressure in your ear, you should equalize. On descent, try to go down feet first, never head down. Try to clear or equalize about every five feet. Be gentle. If you have trouble clearing, pinch your nose through your mask and try to breathe out your nose. This will force air into the ear to equalize the pressure inside the ear. If you still are not able to equalize, ascend a few feet and try again. Another technique is to lift the tongue against the roof of the mouth and swallow. If you continue to descend without equalization, the pain will increase and it will become more difficult to equalize. Again, *do not* take decongestants before a dive. The medication can wear off during your dive, resulting in additional equalization problems once you are at depth.

If you fail to equalize, you should abort your dive and return to the surface. Severe pain or even a ruptured eardrum can occur if you don't listen to your body. No pain, no gain doesn't apply here. Ear pain while diving can come from several sources, including ear infections, water against your ear, and a rupture of the ear drum. Seek professional advice if you continually have ear pain or equalization problems.

WHEN YOU SHOULD DELAY SCUBA DIVING

Some health problems should signal you to put off diving until they are resolved. Do not dive if you have

- Temporary anemia (low blood count)
- Sinusitis or sinus infection
- Ear infection of any type
- A cold
- A continuous cough
- An acute orthopedic or muscle problem that impairs underwater movement such as a broken arm or tendonitis
- Any acute impairment of vision such as an eye infection or injury
- Significant fatigue, which can increase your susceptibility to nitrogen narcosis

You should avoid diving if you use antianxiety or sedative medications. Diving is not recommended for those who have just consumed alcohol or who smoke cigarettes. There is also a danger for those who dive following or preceding heavy exercise, as such activities may change normal off-gassing.

WHEN YOU SHOULDN'T SCUBA DIVE AT ALL

You should avoid scuba diving altogether if you suffer from any of these health problems:

- Heart problems such as angina (pain), heart failure, irregular rhythm
- Chronic asthma
- Lung problems including emphysema, a history of a lung rupture or collapse, diffuse scarring, or smoking

- Serious ear problems
- Psychiatric or emotional instability
- Epilepsy requiring drug treatment for prevention of seizures
- Diabetes requiring insulin (unless your physician gives you permission and detailed instructions)
- Alcoholism or other dependency on mind-altering drugs
- Sickle cell disease
- Hemophilia or other severe bleeding and clotting disorders

Scuba diving is an exciting and challenging sport, but for your enjoyment and safety, caution and preparation are everything. It is essential that you have a physical examination by a physician knowledgeable in the sport and the science of scuba diving before you take the plunge. You must then be knowledgeable and vigilant while indulging in the sport.

For more information, contact:

Divers Alert Network (DAN)
Telephone: (800) 446-2671
diversalertnetwork.org
DAN is a nonprofit medical and research organization associated with Duke University Medical Center. It has served as a lifeline for the scuba industry by operating diving's only 24-hour emergency hotline.

11

BIKING

Popular Pedal Pushing

CYCLING IS A FANTASTIC SPORT and a great way to get into shape. Just about anyone can take up cycling for fun and recreation and/or as a way to train aerobically for other sports. It is also a super way to cross train or rehabilitate from lower body injuries. Whether you like to cycle on the road or in the dirt, there are limitless places to ride. Cycling is also kind to the environment; using your bike as a mode of transportation is a wonderful way to cut down on pollution while at the same time being good to your body.

Mountain biking has become a very popular form of cycling. The tires are wider and have swept or flat handlebars. A mountain bike is grand for riding on loose gravel or the grass. Off-road bicycles now account for 62 percent of new bicycle sales in the United States and are popular on both city streets and rough trails.

Janine Latus, a Columbia, Missouri, mother of three whose writing appears in *Parents, Woman's Day*, and many other popular magazines, is another enthusiast of mountain biking.

"I mountain bike in the woods because if I didn't, I'd go nuts from stress. I'm a single mother with three kids. I can only bike at dawn, when the older ones watch the younger, or if my youngest is at her dad's house," Janine says. "When I'm outside, it's nearly spiritual. When I'm riding my bike and my heart pounds in my ears and I'm sweating and breathing hard—that's when I feel most alive. It invigorates me."

There are no buts about it—female butts are different from male butts and so is what is in front of them. That means that gender differences should be taken into consideration when choosing a bike saddle and when riding a bike.

A big fuss was created in the late 1990s when the media quoted Irwin Goldstein, M.D., a Boston University impotency specialist, as saying: "Men should never ride bicycles. Riding should be banned and outlawed. When a man uses a standard bike seat, his weight flattens the main penile artery, temporarily occluding the blood flow required for erections."

Once the male potency problem was made public, bike manufacturers rushed to redesign seats so that pressure would not be put on the main penile artery. But what about female bicyclists? We can develop vulvar abrasions, lacerations, bruising, swelling, boils, blisters, and contusions from sitting on the saddle. We may develop skin chafing, ulceration, irritation (saddle sores), bone pain, benign tumors of fibrous tissue, nerve damage, and trauma to our urinary tracts.

There has been little media focus on the genital trauma in female bicyclists, perhaps because we are reluctant to talk about it. The area between the ischium bones at the bottom of the pelvis and the vulvar tissue in front of them suffers the most, especially if the handlebars are in the low position. Female saddles should support female bone structure but not interfere with vulvar tissue.

When you ride a lot of miles without your skin being acclimated to the stresses of riding, saddle sores on the buttocks or inner thighs are a likely result. To ensure quick healing treat the wounds early. Well-padded cycling shorts and ointments or powders to reduce friction are the best prevention.

Each woman's physique is different, so you'll have to test some saddles before you choose the one that is most comfortable for you. Study the possibilities with great care, and look for saddles especially made for women. These are soft at the nose end of the saddle; they may be split slightly in some way allowing the pelvic bones to rest correctly. If you're a racer, you'll use a different position on the saddle, so it has to be longer—similar to a man's racing saddle. If you're not racing, choose something larger and comfortable. Tractor seats offer a good alternative.

Saddles come in one of three materials: leather, synthetic leather, or other synthetic fabric. Leather products are strong and durable and provide relatively good resistance against abrasions and tears. They are less flexible than synthetics and may not do well in wet weather or in extreme cold and heat. Synthetic leather is less expensive and usually a bit more weatherproof. Some people feel that synthetic leather is less comfortable than leather. The remaining fabric materials are used for cushy padded and gel-filled seats and are pliable but not particularly durable. The end result is that saddles tend to be grouped into several categories.

- *The comfort saddle:* If you are a casual rider, this large, padded, and sometimes strangely shaped seat will allow you to sit high on a padding of polymers and nearly suspended from your bicycle. The greater width of these saddles tends to make them uncomfortable for long-term use.
- *The general-purpose saddle:* This type of saddle may be for you if you ride your bike one to five days per week. Prices vary widely, and to a certain point, the more expensive the saddle, the greater the comfort and lower the weight.
- *The racing saddle:* Racing or sport saddles are those from which you pilot your bicycle to the finish line. Lightness and stiffness are valued above comfort and support, but the high price of these saddles doesn't necessarily mean they are better-made versions of more comfortable saddles.
- *The ergonomically designed saddle:* There are an increasing number of designs for females. You have to try them out individually; though they are specially designed, they may not be comfortable for you.

FITTING YOUR BICYCLE

You cannot control a bicycle that is too large. You should be able to straddle the bike and stand with both feet flat on the ground. When it comes to finding the right frame, you should find a bike that is as small as possible vertically, while being long enough horizontally so your knees are not under your chin. When you stand astride the frame there should be clearance between the bike and your crotch: one to two inches for sports/touring bicycles and three to six inches for mountain bicycles. A mountain biker should have two or three inches of clearance to allow for changing terrain and increased maneuverability.

Your saddle should be properly adjusted for your height. The knee flexion of your extended leg should be at 25 to 30 degrees when your pedal is at the six o'clock position. The saddle is generally lower in mountain bikes to maintain stability and maneuverability. If you experience knee pain, your seat may be too low. If you have hip pain (see page 178, "Iliotibial Band (ITB) Friction Syndrome"), your seat may be too high. Saddle tilt should be level or slightly downward for women.

The saddle should be adjusted forward and backward as well. The crank arm is the piece of metal that attaches to the pedal. With pedals at the three and nine o'clock positions, the front of your knee should be directly in line with the front of the crank arm.

Your handlebar height should be at least one to two inches below the top of the saddle (or three to four inches if you are tall to allow for longer torso and arms). Mountain bikers should stick with the one- to two-inch rule to have more maneuverability and stability in rugged terrain. Be sure to adjust seat height first before handlebar height.

Placing your elbow on the tip of saddle, your extended fingers should reach the transverse part of handlebars. The width of the bars should be the same as the width of your shoulders—the exception being mountain bikes, which have wider handlebars.

The length of the crank arm is important in relation to your height. Your foot on the pedal should be in a neutral position with the ball of your foot sitting over the pedal axis. You don't want your foot to toe in or out.

TYPES OF BIKES

There are a wide variety of bicycles available, including sport/touring, racing, motocross (BMX) stunt bicycles, and, of course, stationary bicycles. Now more than ever bikes can be customized. If you want a really good workout, check out the road bike. On this bike you will be bent forward and you get a better workout than you would riding recreation or touring bikes. Touring bikes are similar to street bikes but with fatter tires.

You have a choice of whether you want to sit upright or lean forward on your bike. You may even wish to lean back and low—in that case, you should get a recumbent bicycle. There are now 18-speed bikes made of carbon or titanium for racing. There are carbon Trek bikes made with titanium that are reportedly very comfortable to ride but very expensive.

Whether for competition or for exercise or leisure, you can typically find good cycling areas both on and off-road. Cycling competitions take place on road, track, or dirt courses. Performance bicycling competitions use halfpipe ramps. There are many different events from individual sprints and team sprints to relay type races.

COMFORTABLE BIKING HINTS

There are a number of things you can do to make the experience more comfortable and enjoyable—from wearing the right clothing to making sure your bike is properly maintained.

Cycling Shorts

Whether you ride through rough mountainous terrain or on a paved road, shorts with a padded crotch will save you from pain. Cycling shorts provide protection from vibration and chafing. They're designed so that the seams don't fall in places where they might chafe. The more technologically advanced the shorts, the more expensive they tend to be.

Cycling Gloves

Wearing gloves can reduce superficial hand injuries (especially in off-road cycling), provide insulation in cold weather, and supply padding to help prevent nerve compression in the hands.

Cycling Shoes

Specialized cycling shoes use toe clips or sole cleats to attach the stiff shoes to the pedals (clipless pedals). A correct fit can prevent foot and ankle problems. It is very important to adjust the clipless pedals to your experience and comfort level. Similar to skis with tightly adjusted bindings, if the clipless pedals are too difficult to snap out of, you could injure yourself. I have treated several meniscus tears in the knees of cyclists who had their clipless pedals too tight.

You can also have the cleats on the shoes modified with spacers to help correct the biomechanics of flat feet or high arched feet. It's important to check your shoes regularly for breakdown. You need shoes with a rigid sole.

Eye Protection

Glasses made from polycarbonate provide protection against weather, foreign bodies, and ultraviolet light. Eye protection is extremely important for many reasons. Besides protecting the eyes from long-term damage from the sun, foreign bodies such as dirt, rocks, or insects can cause significant damage, not only to your eyes, but also to the rest of your body if you crash because your vision has been temporarily impaired. If you do get dirt or insects in your eye, flush the eye out with saline solution (if available) or cold water to remove the debris. Don't use your fingers because this can cause a corneal abrasion (scratched cornea). Until you can get medical help, cover the eye with a patch or a bandage to protect it after you have flushed it out.

If you crash, a direct blow to the eye can cause retinal detachment, an orbital fracture, or a collection of blood in the front chamber of the eye. All of these conditions require immediate evaluation by an eye specialist. A retinal detachment may be painless. If you see specs or spots or if you have blurry or clouded vision or a sensation of flashing light, see an ophthalmologist.

An orbital fracture is a break in the bony socket of the eye. This is very painful and can result in severe swelling in the eye region. See a specialist immediately.

If a collection of blood in the front chamber of the eye is not treated as an emergency by an ophthalmologist, permanent eye damage can result.

Cycling During Menstruation

Most female cyclists recommend using a tampon when cycling. Some women cyclists find their period comes more than once a month and others skip their period after a strenuous trip or race. If you have a problem with your menstrual cycle, seek the advice of a gynecologist, preferably one who indulges in sports or at least knows about the effects of exercise on menstruation.

CYCLING HEAD INJURIES

Although the most common bike injuries involve scrapes and strains, head injuries are responsible for the majority of fatalities and long-term disabilities. More than 1,000 people die each year while cycling—three out of four die as a result of head injuries. In fact, if each rider wore a helmet, an estimated 500 bicycle-related deaths and 151,000 nonfatal head injuries would be prevented each year. Unfortunately, estimates suggest that only 10 percent of all cyclists wear helmets, and only 2 percent of children under age 15 wear them when riding. The percentage is close to zero when looking at teenage riders. Falling and hitting your head on a paved road can cause a concussion or even a skull fracture. This can potentially lead to bleeding inside your skull, which can be fatal. A concussion can be mild or severe, depending on how hard you fall. If you lose consciousness or become disoriented after a fall, a physician should examine you. If you are dizzy or you experience headaches, vision changes, nausea, vomiting, or difficulty remembering your fall, seek medical attention immediately.

When biking, wear a helmet at all times, even for a short trip. In the event of a crash, a bicycle helmet reduces the risk of serious head injury by as much as 88 percent. Helmets have also been shown to reduce the risk of injury to the upper and middle face by 65 percent. Be sure the helmet you buy has been approved by the American National Standards Institute (ANSI), the Snell Foundation, or the American Society for Testing and Materials (ASTM). The helmet should fit comfortably and snugly. It should sit on your (or your child's) head in a level position and not rock from side to side. It should have a chinstrap and buckle to keep it in place. The helmet should have a hard outer shell and an absorbent inner liner at least one-half inch thick.

OTHER CYCLING INJURIES

As an orthopedic surgeon living and working in the mountain-biking paradise of Colorado, I have had firsthand experience with many injuries that can occur from the sport. Treating these injuries has certainly made me a more cautious and prepared rider. I hope that once you read the recommendations in this chapter, you will become a more cautious and responsible cyclist as well.

Although injuries to mountain bikers of all ages account for only 3.7 percent of bicycle injuries overall, up to 51 percent of recreational and 85 percent of competitive mountain bikers sustain injuries each year. The injury rates are particularly high among 20- to 40-year-old mountain bikers who hit an obstacle in the trail and lose control of the bike, often while riding downhill at excessive speeds over unfamiliar terrain. Parts of the bike itself can cause injuries; the saddle and seat-post may cause genital and rectal injuries if the rider crashes, and landing on the handlebars in a crash can cause abdominal and vascular trauma. Most crashes involve striking the ground; in these cases, multiple fractures can occur.

Many city bike accidents are the result of a bicyclist riding on the wrong side of the street. Often automobile drivers, when turning at an intersection or entering traffic from a driveway, are looking to the left. They may not see a bicyclist approaching from the right.

Most minor and major injuries, however, involve just the rider and her bike. The following are examples of common female cyclists' injuries, many of which can be prevented with good conditioning, a safe environment, and proper equipment. For more detailed information on each body part's injury and therapy, and refer to Chapters 21 through 23.

CYCLING SKIN PROBLEMS AND INJURIES

I'll now discuss some of the more common skin problems associated with biking.

Road Rash

Skin and soft tissue abrasions (road rash) are common in cycling. Indeed, road rash can encompass anything from superficial scrapes to major wipeouts that necessitate removal of embedded debris.

I was a physician at the Track Cycling World Championships in Bordeaux, France, with the U.S. team in 1998. The velodrome track was made of wood. When one of our cyclists crashed, a large piece of the track lodged in her thigh. I had to remove the fragment and sterilize the area—then she was off racing again. If you do get debris embedded beneath the skin, you should seek medical treatment to reduce the risk of infection. Mild skin chafing will respond to talcum powders or lubricating ointments such as petroleum jelly, whereas more severe or ulcerating sores may require rest, sitz baths, and appropriate ulcer management.

Lacerations

Many crashes result in open wounds with uneven edges. These wounds are most common on the hands, arms, head, face, and legs. I have seen many lacerations result from bodily contact with the gears, which can cause a nasty cut. I had a patient who was simply walking her bike and the gear bit into her leg. The cut was deep and required stitches. Lacerations should be treated by a physician to make sure the wound is cleaned out appropriately and to determine whether suturing is necessary. It is also important to have a tetanus injection every seven years.

Bruises

Bruises or contusions occur when there is compression to the soft tissues. Bleeding that reaches the superficial tissues underneath the skin often makes for some lovely colors. Contusions are most common over bony prominences such as the hip (greater trochanter), elbows, shoulders, and knees. Contusions are extremely common in cycling, especially mountain biking. Most contusions are treated with RICE (rest, ice, compression, and elevation; see Chapter 22) and gentle stretching. Anti-inflammatory medications are often helpful as well, especially if you continue riding the next day. Protective gear is the best way to prevent severe contusions.

Sunburn

When you're cycling outdoors, sun and heat can prove hazardous. Wear high-quality sunscreen and protective clothing.

Cycling Thirst

Cyclists are susceptible to dehydration problems. Make sure to drink plenty of fluids before you go out for a long ride. Carry a full water bottle with you. During training or an event, you should drink eight ounces of water every 20 minutes to maintain hydration for maximum athletic effort. If you are planning a mountain bike trip in the backcountry where there is no place to refill your water bottle, consider a hydrating system that you can wear on your back. These systems can hold a lot of water in case you get lost or delayed by weather in the backcountry. Take a drink every 15 minutes or so. For rides longer than two hours, you may want to mix an electrolyte drink with the water. Many people also carry energy bars to replenish their glucose and electrolytes.

Cycling Neck and Shoulder Pain

Neck and shoulder pain are common among cyclists. The horizontal position your body must assume on a bicycle with dropped handlebars is often the cause. When riding in this position you have to extend your head up to see in front of you. You also have to support your weight with your arms, which may lead to muscle fatigue. This combination of strains on your back and neck generally affects the trapezius muscle and the levator scapula muscle. The trapezius is a large muscle that starts at the base of the skull and extends out to the shoulders and then down the back. If this muscle goes into spasm or becomes inflamed, it can result in debilitating neck and shoulder pain as well as upper back pain (see Chapter 21). To avoid this, you can raise the handlebars to allow you to sit in a more upright position. Regularly changing your hand and arm position on the handlebars can also help. Remember to keep your elbows slightly flexed while riding.

Cycling Backache

In addition to causing neck and shoulder pain, cycling with your body in the horizontal position may lead to pain in your lower back. Again, stretching and strengthening exercises and a higher handlebar position should alleviate the pain.

Cycling Hand Problems

Elbow and hand symptoms usually resolve rapidly if you stop cycling. But often you can experience irritating numbness and tingling. There may be several reasons for this sensation. Does it happen only when you are on your bike or does it continue when you are off it? You may have a common condition among mountain bikers, which may require you to alter your technique. Are your elbows locked? If they are, then the problem may lie there. Ideally, you should keep your elbows flexed and your arms and wrists as relaxed as possible while still maintaining a secure grip on the handlebars.

Riding mountain bikes downhill can be an adrenaline rush but it can also be uncomfortable. If your elbows are locked and your grip is too tight, you can experience numbness and tingling and discomfort in your arms and hands. This is generally treated by modifying your biking technique. I remember when I started mountain biking. My boyfriend (now my husband) took me to Moab, Utah, one of the most awesome places in the world for technical and challenging mountain bike riding. I was still learning, and when we went down some of the steep descents I recall my upper body and arms were as stiff as could be. This caused tremendous discomfort in my arms and hands and I didn't feel very safe either. My boyfriend told me: "Relax your arms and grip a little. Let the elbows flex to absorb some of the shock, and enjoy the ride." Well, it worked. My grip was secure yet I wasn't clenching.

You can experiment with different grips on the handlebars. Softer grips and better padding on your gloves may also remedy the problem. Balance is key. Having a well-trained technician fit a bike to your anatomy will help you avoid many of these problems.

CYCLING BOTTOM PAIN

Cycling puts pressure on your butt and your vulva. Hopefully, you will have enough padding in your shorts and in your properly shaped saddle to avoid most of the problem. Still, on long rides, you may experience a sore bottom.

Use talcum powder or a lubricating ointment to lessen friction between your bottom and your bike. Staying off your bike for a while may be the answer if nothing else helps.

Vulvar abrasions, lacerations, or contusions usually respond to symptomatic measures such as sitz baths and correction of saddle fit. If the problem continues or gets worse, see your gynecologist promptly.

CYCLING FOOT PROBLEMS

You may experience foot pain if improper seat height is causing excessive pressure on your foot or you have ill-fitting shoes. If there is too much pressure applied to the ball of your foot, you can develop metatarsalgia. This is an overuse syndrome in which the tops of your foot bones, which make up the ball of your foot, become inflamed and irritated. The treatment is modification of your seat position, pads in your shoes, and rest if necessary. Tight shoes (or toe clips that have been applied too tightly) can cause numbness and pain in the foot due to swelling and nerve compression. The best treatment for this is new shoes that are fitted appropriately to your foot. Make sure that the toe box is wide enough to allow comfortable forefoot and toe spreading while the foot is exerting pressure on the pedal.

If the saddle is too low, repeated stresses to the Achilles tendon can cause an overuse syndrome called Achilles tendonitis. (See Chapter 22.) The pain occurs in the back of the ankle just above the heel and is exacerbated when going up steep hills on the bike while standing on your toes on the pedals. The best treatment is adjusting the seat height before the tendonitis becomes chronic. Stretching, ice, and anti-inflammatory medications can help treat the problem, but sometimes physical therapy is necessary.

Plantar fasciitis, or heel pain, can be a problem because of a low saddle height, but it is also caused by a worn-out bicycle shoe that allows too much flex in the sole. You can treat the condition with new shoes, saddle-height modification, stretching exercises, ice, and by taking anti-inflammatory medication.

CYCLING KNEE

Knee pain in cycling is very common, especially in women. It is often due to imbalance of muscles and flexibility, a poor-fitting bike, poor seat position, poor foot position, and/or overuse when underconditioned. The most common knee pain occurs in the front of the knee due to the imbalance of the kneecap.

A plica is a band of synovial lining of the knee that some people (not all) are born with. If this band becomes thick from overuse in an unbalanced knee, the pain can be severe. There can also be swelling or catching inside the knee. Plica syndrome is very common in cycling, especially in athletes who log a lot of miles. I treated one of our U.S. cyclists who had been suffering with plica syndrome pain for a year and a half. I had just started taking care of the team. She had seen numerous doctors. She'd had several negative MRIs and months of physical therapy. No one had entertained the diagnosis of plica syndrome, but upon examining her I thought it was obvious. She had a tender band on the inside (medial) aspect of her knee. Because the problem was so chronic and physical therapy was not working, I took her to surgery for an arthroscopic procedure where I cut the plica out. She was back on the bike rehabbing in a week and competing in a month. She's had no further problems with knee pain since.

If the saddle is too far forward or too low, knee pain can become a problem. In addition to treatment, you should have your bicycle fit evaluated by a professional. You should also begin aggressive balancing of your lower body muscles and kneecap. The most important components include strengthening and stretching of the thigh and hip muscles. Until you can get your muscles balanced (and, believe me, it won't happen overnight), you should have a physical therapist teach you how to tape the kneecap to allow it to track correctly. If you have flat feet, this can exacerbate the problem. Therefore inserting orthotics in your shoes or posting your bicycle cleats may be necessary. Rest or cross training may be a good alternative to biking until your pain subsides. Since this is an overuse syndrome, the last thing you want to do is ride while you are in pain. Instead, remove the stress that caused the pain in the first place. Riding with a lower gear and higher cadence may be sufficient rest until the pain resolves. If refitting the bike does the trick, by all means ride—this will help build your quadriceps muscle.

CYCLING HIP PAIN

For cyclists hip pain generally occurs in the tough fibrous band called the iliotibial band (ITB). This begins at the outer hip region from a muscle called the tensor fascia lata and attaches just below the knee joint on the outer side. Errors in training, a too-high saddle height, and/or lack of flexibility of the ITB can cause hip pain. With the repetitive movements of the hip and knee during cycling, the ITB can become severely irritated and inflamed. If the ITB is tight, it can also rub against the top of the thigh bone in the upper outer thigh and cause a swollen bursa in this region. It often takes 20 minutes of cycling for the pain to appear, and if you get off your bike the ache sometimes disappears immediately.

The treatment for all these problems is to lower your seat, ice, stretch the ITB aggressively, and take anti-inflammatory medications if necessary. Orthotics or cleat adjustment may be helpful in cyclists with flat feet. If you continue to have bursitis that does not respond to the above measures (including formal physical therapy), a cortisone injection may be necessary to cure the problem. (See Chapter 22.)

CYCLING FACE INJURIES

Contusions, facial fractures, dental fractures, and foreign bodies in the eye may all cause a problem when you are riding. If you crash and have a facial bruise or, worse, a fracture, get to a doctor fast. Don't just put an adhesive bandage on your face. You will very likely be disappointed with the cosmetic result.

BROKEN BONES

Janine, the mountain biker described at the beginning of this chapter, knows the perils of injury from bicycling. "I was riding a mountain bike when I flipped over the handlebars jumping an erosion log (a log sunk sideways into the path to reduce erosion) and smashed everything. I had huge contusions on my thighs, a broken finger, and third-degree separation of my left shoulder, which had to be surgically repaired. I walked out of the woods with every ligament in my shoulder on my left side ripped, so my arm was hanging by muscle and skin. It had dropped nearly two inches by the time the doctor saw it. I had to have it reconstructed."

Janine has young children at home but she still mountain bikes today. "The benefits outweigh the risks," she says. "Every mountain-biking ride is a wild experience. You're pushing as hard as you can uphill and then riding the roller coaster down. The uphills can be excruciating, but the sense of accomplishment is great. And the downhills can be pure guts."

You can read from Janine's story how devoted females are to this sport, despite its injury potential. Fractures in the upper extremities are very common in cyclists. When a rider crashes, she often has a reflex reaction to place her hands in front or to the side to break her fall. If this occurs, the wrist or hand is at risk for a fracture. If you crash while riding in a pack of cyclists, your hands and arms are also at risk of being run over by another rider. This could cause not only fractures, but also serious soft-tissue injuries. All potential fractures of the hand and wrist must be evaluated and treated by a physician as soon as possible. Most often, a cast is recommended; however, if the fracture is more severe or if there is bad soft-tissue damage, surgery may be necessary. (See Chapter 21.)

If the bike suddenly slips out to one side, on gravel or a wet surface, your elbow may be the first part of your body to contact the ground. This can cause a fracture of the olecranon, the bony point of the elbow that is visible when you bend your elbow fully. If you suspect a broken elbow (because of swelling and pain), you must seek medical attention. Just because you can move your arm doesn't mean it isn't broken.

In mountain biking, especially downhill, it is easy to fall forward off of your bike over the handlebars. In this case, your shoulder may impact the ground before your hands can come forward to break your fall. When this happens, shoulder injuries occur. Shoulder injuries are by far the most common serious injuries that I see in my practice as a result of cycling. When you fall on your shoulder you can either fracture the collarbone (clavicle) or injure the acromioclavicular (AC) ligaments and cause a separation. Most of these injuries are treated without surgery. A clavicle fracture will keep you off the bike for 6 to 12 weeks (with the exception of a stationary bike, which you can use for training if you don't use your hands). AC separations vary in their severity and may keep you off the bike for two weeks to three months. Severe types of AC separations do require surgery. (See Chapter 21.)

Shoulder dislocations can occur with cycling crashes as well. I treated 22-year-old Micki, a mountain biker who had a recurrent dislocating shoulder after multiple ski accidents. She needed surgery to stabilize the joint. Micki chose to wait to have her surgery until after ski season so that she wouldn't miss out on any skiing. She didn't care much that she kept dislocating her shoulder every time she made a bad pole plant. She underwent surgery and was strongly advised not to get on her mountain bike until I cleared her for this activity. I told her that she could ride a stationary bike, but that was it during her early healing and rehabilitation phases. Unfortunately, Micki did not listen. She was out on an aggressive downhill mountain bike trail seven weeks after surgery. She crashed, flew over the handlebars, and landed with her arm out to the side and rotated outward. This position puts a normal shoulder at risk for dislocating not to mention a postoperative shoulder that isn't healed yet. Sure enough she dislocated her shoulder and had to repeat the surgery.

If you do get a shoulder dislocation, you'll know it. Your shoulder will appear deformed. You will be unable to rotate or raise the shoulder, and you'll have severe pain. Get immediate professional medical attention. Most first-time dislocators can be treated without surgery and with aggressive rehabilitation. However, if you dislocate recurrently, as Micki did, then surgery will be necessary.

OVERUSE INJURIES

Overuse injuries may occur if you ride your bike often, especially if you race. Overuse of the muscles in your neck and back can cause strains and pains and bone aches. Overdoing it can also cause compression nerve injuries and perineal and genital complaints. You may need the advice of your physician and a coach to adjust various components of your bike, such as seat height and handlebars to avoid overuse injuries.

RIDING WELL

The first part of training—whether you're racing, touring, or riding recreationally—is mostly about going slow. Riding long distances at a moderate pace within your limits—known as base mileage training—develops your aerobic endurance, the basic element of cycling fitness. Anaerobic activity happens when you deplete the glycogen (sugar) in your blood for an immediate burst of quick energy and then must turn over into aerobic metabolism to keep going. The length of your base period depends on your specific goals, but a rule of thumb is to do base training for about one-third of your full season.

You develop your aerobic endurance by riding just above 60 percent of your maximum heart rate. (A heart rate monitor will help you stay on target.) A strong aerobic base allows your muscles to operate for long periods of time without building up lactic acid, giving you increased stamina and endurance.

While training, it's important to work consciously on your pedal cadence (revolutions per minute). Think about the physics for a moment. You are moving yourself and your bicycle a certain distance (therefore expending a certain amount of energy) every minute. If your pedal cadence is twice as great (keeping the total distance and time to cover it the same) the amount of energy imparted to the bicycle/rider combination per revolution of the pedals is half as much—and the strain on the knees and ligaments of the legs is less per revolution as well. Most regular riders use a cadence of 80 to 100 revolutions per minute on level terrain. If you are having knee pain, you may need to increase pedal cadence from your current 50 or 60 per minute (a favorite for occasional riders).

At higher cadences, it is much easier to accelerate (rapidly increase revolutions per minute). Becoming comfortable riding at higher cadences is an important part of training for recreational riding as well as for competition.

CYCLING PERFORMANCE TIPS

For most cyclists the trunk, which includes the back and abdominal muscles, is a weak link. How many times have you heard of elite riders having to pull out of competition because of back problems? Why? Because they don't have the torso support to resist the tremendous forces their powerful leg muscles can generate. Any force directed into the pedals also goes up into the torso. If the trunk is weak, that force *doesn't* go into the pedals; rather, it is dissipated in the flexing of the torso. Look at tired riders. Every stroke generates an S-curve in the back. This effect causes fatigue and, eventually, overwork and spasm of low back muscles. In fact, a rider will never get stronger by pushing pedals as long as her torso absorbs the forces she creates. That's because she's negating the resistance of the pedals. Most riders give away significant pedal power because they don't possess adequate torso strength.

Back muscles alone are not adequate to supply the needed torso rigidity. Abdominal musculature can aid in torso support. These are the muscles that contract the body to enable a running animal to bring its legs forward. The quads straighten the leg. The hamstrings bend it at the knee. The abdominal and groin muscles pull the leg over the top of the pedal stroke. But they also provide stiffness to the torso to support and reflect the force of the legs, whether pushing, away against the ground (as in running) or pushing against the pedals (as in riding a bicycle).

If your only strength work is on your abdominals, this alone will vastly improve your riding. Strong abdominals are the foundation of strength for a rider; they are also the key to preserving a healthy back. Riding with undeveloped abdominals can be compared to riding a bike with a cracked frame. All the energy gets dissipated in flexion, which doesn't move you down the road.

Squats are a good exercise to strengthen the torso. (See Figure 23.29.)

Training Program

There are as many cycling training programs as there are trainers, but certain basic rules of thumb can be used to help you develop your own personal program. Before beginning a regimented training program, develop a base of at least 500 miles of easy rides. (If you have a good winter or off-season training program, you can pare down this recommendation.)

Once you have your training base, calculate your average weekly mileage, and then plan to increase it by no more than 10 to 12 percent per week. This includes both total weekly mileage as well as the distance of your long ride. (This percentage was developed from marathon training to minimize muscle and bone injuries. Bicycling is easier on the joints and muscles, which means that this figure can be pushed.)

It's important to ride at least five days a week, and take at least one day off. Depending on your level of training (or evidence of overtraining) the seventh day is an additional intermediate mileage day or an additional rest day.

If you are training for a single-day event or ride, your longest ride should be 10 to 14 days before the event. Then cut back on your rides during the three days immediately before the event. During those three days take short, low-intensity rides to keep your muscles from tightening up. This recommendation is not as important for multiday endurance rides, but common sense suggests that taking a few days off (or taking it easy with short spinning rides only) immediately before the event will facilitate maximum muscle recovery and glycogen repletion. Be flexible and adjust your program to your lifestyle. A rigid program is destined to fail.

For more information, contact:

NATIONAL BICYCLE TOUR DIRECTORS ASSOCIATION at nbtda.com. It offers information on a network of bike organizations that offer excursions.

AMERICAN BICYCLE ASSOCIATION, P.O. Box 718, Chandler, AZ 85244. You can reach the organization by telephone at (480) 961-1903 or visit the website at ababmx.com/index3.html. It has current safety standards for bicycle helmets and information about safety products and recalls.

12

ROCK CLIMBING

Upscale

ROCK CLIMBING IS ONE of the most difficult sports. You make your way up a rock face, gym wall, or mountainside by finding handholds and footholds. You put great demands on your back, shoulders, legs, hips, and arms. Experienced climbers can hang from a crack by two fingers. While strength is important, a climber's overall flexibility, balance, and strategy are equally valuable. But the biggest factors of all are desire and determination to climb—no matter what. Letha Albright is a perfect example. By day she is an editor at the Missouri State Teachers Association, but on weekends, she writes mysteries. Her novel *Daredevil's Apprentice*, recently published by Avocet Press, features a great rock-climbing scene. Here's her story in her own words:

"In October 1997, my then 15-year-old daughter and I took a one-day women's climbing clinic. I was instantly hooked. Climbing is something I'd always wanted to do. Growing up in Colorado, I'd always loved scrambling up rocks, but I never had a chance to learn how to use equipment to do it safely. Unfortunately, I was a 45-year-old woman with multiple sclerosis—and my upper body strength was abysmal. So my first goal became getting into shape. I began a weight-lifting, strength-building regimen so I could become a better climber. And I worked on my forearm strength at the local indoor climbing gym.

"I love the challenge of moving up a vertical face. I love the gritty feel and the dusty smell of the rock. I've always been an outdoors person, and I've always enjoyed exercise. Rock climbing satisfies both.

"I've learned that rock climbing is a perfect antidote for stress. When you're climbing, there's no room in your head for anything other than the next move. It requires total concentration, and all the worries and stresses of the day melt away.

"In June 1998, I fell about 30 feet and broke several bones, including two vertebrae in my back. Both lungs were punctured by broken ribs. I was in the hospital for two months, underwent several surgeries, and was in rehab for six months. I had to rebuild my muscles from nothing.

"I almost died, and I had to ask myself some hard questions. 'Should I continue climbing?' 'Is it fair to my husband and two children to ever chance putting them through such an ordeal again?' My daughter answered that one for me. One day she was at the hospital when my doctor made his rounds. 'Mrs. Albright,' he said. 'I'd recommend that you give up climbing. We may not be able to put you together a second time.'

"My daughter jumped to my defense: 'Is that what you tell people who've been in a car wreck?' she asked indignantly. 'That they should never drive again?'

"So by April 1999, I was back on the rock. The first time, as I was driving toward the local climbing crag, I wondered how I would feel when faced with the prospect of climbing. I had a tight feeling in my chest. But it was something I had to try. Kind of like getting back on a horse after it bucks you off. The minute I tied into the rock and said to my belayer, 'Climbing,' I knew it was what I had to do. I was flooded with happiness and a feeling of coming home.

"Most of my climbing partners are women. And many are better climbers than I am. Women encourage one another, and climbing becomes a community thing. Unfortunately, a lot of the men I've climbed with are charged with testosterone, and it's all a game to outperform each other. Women challenge one another, but we also empower each other.

"Most of the climbing I do is top roping, but I'm learning to lead climb. My favorite local climb was the two-pitch Andromeda Sprain, along the Missouri River bluffs. It's a 5.8 climb. [The easiest climb is rated 5.0.] I was following the local legend up the route, cleaning the protection he had set [removing the safety equipment while climbing upward]. I was afraid of failing, of not being able to make the climb, of making the local legend regret his choice of climbing partner. But I walked right up it.

"A couple of years ago, two other women and I were climbing on a route way out in the country. A local man about my age sat at the top of the bluff and watched us. When I started climbing, he called down, 'How old are you, anyway?' I was concentrating on climbing and yelled back, '48.' 'This I gotta see,' he said. The route was a tough one—rated 5.9—and I didn't think I'd be able to top it. But with that challenge thrown down and the implication that a woman my age couldn't possibly climb such a hard route, I made it all the way to the top. That may have been the most satisfying climb I ever made.

"At my age, training is an ongoing necessity. I work out six days a week, alternating a day of upper body work with a day of legwork. I also walk a strenuous, hilly route three or four times a week to improve my endurance.

"I would advise women who want to start rock climbing to take classes if they can. Read books on technique and watch climbing videos. Join a climbing club or rock-climbing gym and observe the other members. Find people you like to spend time with, work on your skills, and take every opportunity to climb. This isn't an easy sport, but it offers lots of personal rewards."

Letha Albright has literally overcome mountains despite her age and handicap, so you can understand how great the lure of climbing must be. An increasing number of women are challenging themselves to reach the top. A decade ago there were two climbing gyms in the United States. Today, there are more than 2,500.

How difficult is "difficult"? Ultimately, you want to hold on the whole way up the rock. However, most climbers prefer to go out and climb to compete against themselves. Females do climb differently than males. Men rely more on their upper body. Females carry more of their weight around the hips. Women rely more on technique than men do and often they are more graceful climbers.

Rock climbing, once the extreme sport of a few, is being embraced by more and more women and with this increase comes a correspondent increase in injuries.

ROCK CLIMBING BASICS

On climbs that last only one day, experienced climbers attempt to reach the summit by noon, before afternoon thunderstorms, lightning, hail, and rain increase the danger of the climb. Climbers also make sure they have enough daylight to rappel (slide down in a controlled fashion using climbing ropes) back to the mountain's base and reach base camp before dark. On rare occasions climbers are caught in the dark and must resort to headlamps or flashlights to find their way. On ascents that last more than one day, an early start gives climbers enough time to set up their next camp on the mountain before nightfall. If there is snow on the route, starting early usually ensures that the frozen surface will not melt before the climbers cross it. Because mountain climbers surmount dangerous terrain by using ropes and other equipment, they almost always climb in teams. The basic team is composed of two people, the leader and the second. Each has one end of the climbing rope tied to his or her climbing harness, a device that secures the climber to the rope in case of a slip. The leader's job is to lead the climb by following a natural line or path to each successive ledge or resting spot. The leader also places climbing equipment (called hardware) in cracks, snow, and ice at various points along the ascent. When attached to the climbing rope, the hardware becomes a series of anchors that hold climbers in the event of a fall.

Rock and mountain climbers use many different tools. The most basic of these are climbing harnesses, climbing ropes, ice axes, and crampons. Climbers also use a variety of types of hardware to anchor themselves to the mountainside. A climbing harness is an adjustable set of straps that buckle around a climber's waist and thighs. Most harnesses also come with special, easy-to-reach loops for attaching hardware and other tools. The harness serves as an anchor for one end of the climbing rope. In the event of a slip, the anchors set in the mountainside halt the climber's fall, and the harness holds her tight but does not restrict movement or breathing. Climbing ropes are specially made lines of a high-strength nylon called Perlon.

Ice axes have either a metal or fiberglass shaft. One end of the shaft is a pointed metal spike. The other end has a metal pick with serrated teeth on one side, and a straight, flat metal blade on the other. Ice axes have many uses. One of the most common is to help the climber stay balanced on steep slopes. The climber swings the axe with a short, quick movement to lodge it in snow or ice, creating a secure anchor. If a climber should slip and begin sliding down a snowfield, she can perform a self-arrest by turning face down on the snow and burying the pick in the snow surface. The climber's weight over the pick and firm grip on the ice axe usually stop downward movement. Mountaineers also use the axe to chop steps in snow or ice. Longer axes are used as walking sticks and for probing crevasses during glacier climbs. Alpine climbers gain a foothold on steep and snowy slopes by using crampons—frameworks of sharp metal teeth fastened to mountaineering boots that grip the snow and ice. They attach to the boots with straps that lace around the ankles or by snaps that connect to the boot sole.

Most sensible mountain climbers also carry several other items: a compass; topographic maps that indicate elevations, place names, and geographical formations in the area; and an altimeter, which calculates altitude above sea level and sometimes includes a barometer to anticipate weather changes.

Safety precautions include planning your route in advance and traveling with others. If you are going to climb mountains, you need to be in excellent physical shape. You may train for rock and mountain climbing by running, hiking, and bicycling. You have to be able to remain calm and focused in tense situations, such as when you are having trouble discerning the correct route up or down a mountain, when a storm is approaching, or when night is falling.

If you're a beginner, you should first learn safe climbing skills—whether you are going to scale a rock wall in a club or climb a mountain. Today, beginners may go the apprenticeship route or learn their climbing skills from a qualified friend or from climbing schools or guide services certified by organizations such as the American Mountain Guide Association (AMGA). (See page 166.)

Rock climbing and mountaineering are hazardous sports. We will now look at some of the common injuries associated with them.

CLIMBING WITH YOUR HANDS

Climbing is naturally hard on your hands, which have to grip rocks and crevices and haul your body up. If you want to rock climb, you have to rely predominantly on your finger and arm strength and know when and where to use any of four grip techniques depending on your situation. There are four basic grip techniques.

- **Open grip** is used when grasping wide or large handholds. This grip frequently turns into a cling grip as you pull yourself upward.

- **Cling grip** (also called the crimp) is when the distal interphalangeal (DIP) joint hyperextends as force is exerted downward and you pull your body upward. The DIP joint is the one closest to your fingertip. Each finger has three joints, the DIP, the PIP (proximal interphalangeal), and the MCP (metacarpal-phalangeal). (See Figure 21.3.) If your fingertip is wedged between two rocks and you hyperextend the DIP joint, you probably can imagine how painful it could be if your fingers are not conditioned for this type of force. The cling grip is regarded as the most painful. It places significant compression and shear on the fingertips and strain on the finger tendons. Climbers practice the cling grip by doing one- or two-finger pull-ups on doorjambs or training boards. In moderation, this exercise can strengthen the fingers and prevent injury, but it can also lead to injuries.

- **Pocket grip** involves placing one or two of your fingers into small holes. It is a particularly demanding grip because during climbing the small flexor tendons in your fingers support most, if not all, of your body weight.

- **Pinch grip** is used to grasp a projection of rock between the thumb and fingers.

The muscles that produce wrist and finger flexion originate from the inner portion of the elbow—the part of the elbow closest to your body if you have your arm to the side with your palm facing forward. All four of the grip techniques transmit extremely high forces through the tissues of the fingers, hands, and forearms, potentially resulting in a variety of acute and chronic injuries. Even a minor injury to your hand may become a major one because it can compromise your climbing ability and safety.

What type of climbing are you interested in? Most rock-climbing situations fit one of the following classifications.

- **Bouldering.** If you like to climb over large rocks, this is for you. It is usually done, however, to develop strength and to practice difficult maneuvers. This type of climbing results in fewer hand injuries than other types of rock climbing.

- **Face climbing.** This refers to the use of small edges, pockets, and knobs of rock for footholds and handholds.

- **Crack climbing.** If you want to ascend flat rock faces using your fingers, hands, and feet as wedges, you will be a crack climber. When you push and twist your fingers until they are wedged into a crack, the torque forces on your finger joints can get very high. This type of climbing is associated with joint dislocations and finger tearing amputations following a sudden slip or fall.

COMMON ROCK-CLIMBING HAND INJURIES

In general, hand and wrist injuries depend upon your climbing techniques and the duration and frequency of your climbs. All a professional has to do is look at your hands for scrapes and scars to determine the amount of climbing you do.

If you familiarize yourself with the causes and frequency of hand injuries, you should be better able to focus on preventing them by adjusting your training schedules to emphasize strength, conditioning, and flexibility. Most climbers' hand injuries are relatively minor and can be treated with rest, anti-inflammatory medication, splinting, and taping. Certain injuries, however, require a physician and sometimes surgical intervention because if neglected or not recognized, hand injuries may have serious consequences for movement and function.

Soft-Tissue Damage

Among the relatively minor hand injuries are soft-tissue traumas, including fingertip injuries, abrasions on the back of your hands and fingers (called gobies), and scarring. Fingertip injuries, not surprisingly, are the most common rock-climbing hand injuries, but climbers rarely seek evaluation or treatment for them. Fingertip injuries include bruising, severe abrasions, and splitting of the skin on the finger pads due to prolonged pressure and abrasion. Both mechanical factors and lack of blood flow cause skin breakdown called maceration. Scar tissue forms on the top of the hand in response to repetitive abrasion and wear that usually occurs with crack climbing.

Treatment for soft-tissue injuries includes rest, appropriate local wound care, and preventive measures such as the use of thin rubber pads or sleeves for protection when climbing or training. Gloves are not recommended because they interfere with a climber's critical need to feel the rock she's climbing and to obtain a secure handhold.

Finger-Bending (Flexor Tendon) Injuries

Several studies describe a spectrum of rock-climbing injuries involving the tendons that flex the fingers. Injuries to these tendons include inflammation of the tendons and sometimes the sheaths that house them. The tendons in these thin soft-tissue sheaths are supposed to glide easily as you bend your fingers. If fluid or inflammation builds up within the sheaths, your tendons cannot move smoothly, and this can become an extremely painful situation. You may also develop strains (microscopic tearing of the tendons) and rupture or tear off the tendon. If there is sudden traumatic force, the tendon can pull a tiny piece of bone off with it. This is called an avulsion fracture. Your finger-bending tendons are particularly susceptible to injury during the cling and pocket grips. These maneuvers place excessive stress on your tendons and surrounding structures.

An inflammatory response occurs because of repetitive stress. You may have pain and swelling along the underside of your fingers, which may extend into your palm or forearm. When you try to move the affected fingers with your other hand, it may be painful if the tendons on your holding hand are inflamed. You may also tear the sheath, which can cause a lot of pain and inflammation as well. If you suffer inflamed tendons and tendon sheaths in your hand, rest and anti-inflammatory medication are the best treatment as well as range-of-motion exercises.

When you strain the tendons that bend your fingers (flexor tendon strain), you feel a sudden onset of pain during a difficult cling grip. This is often referred to as climber's finger. If you have acute tenderness on your palm in line with your middle finger and it gets worse as you use your other hand to straighten your finger, you may have a tendon strain. If you have a flexor tendon strain you will probably need to rest, take an anti-inflammatory medication, and do range-of-motion exercises. When your pain has subsided and full range of motion has been restored, you can begin a progressive strengthening program, followed by a gradual return to climbing. You may need to tape your finger as a preventive measure. Many climbers wrap their fingers to help prevent flexor tendon and sheath injuries.

Trigger finger is a common condition in people who stress their flexor tendons repeatedly. I recall one patient, Kerri, an elite rock climber who came in complaining of her ring finger triggering, or locking up on her, when she would get up in the morning. She told me it was very painful to unlock it. She was only able to unlock it by forcefully extending her finger. She would feel a painful pop in her palm and then she could move the finger again. The problem was that she was so afraid of it locking again she had to modify many of her activities to accommodate this finger. She came into the clinic with these complaints, which had become progressively worse over the past three weeks. She had a painful swelling in her palm at the base of her ring finger. She was very apprehensive when I wanted to flex her finger. This was a classic example of trigger finger. When the flexor tendon becomes irritated, a nodule forms at the base of the finger and becomes trapped underneath a ligament called a pulley. There are a series of pulleys along the flexor tendons of the finger, which are strategically placed to hold the tendons down when we bend our fingers. If the nodule becomes large enough, eventually it may not pass beneath the pulley, which results in a locked finger that cannot be extended actively. Treatment includes injection of a corticosteroid (an anti-inflamatory) and lidocaine (a numbing medicine) preparation into the flexor tendon sheath. It is very important that the injection is into the sheath and not into the tendon itself. Tendon injections—especially multiple injections—can cause rupture.

If triggering continues even after two injections given a minimum of six weeks apart, or if your finger is locked, surgery to release the A1 pulley may be necessary. The A1 pulley is fortunately not needed and can be sacrificed to cure the trigger finger. The other pulleys in the finger are much more important. The surgery is very simple and fast and can be done as an outpatient procedure under local anesthesia. Once the A1 pulley is cut, the tendon and its nodule are free to glide back and forth without interruption.

The A2 pulley is similar to the A1 pulley except that this one is really important and must be intact for good finger function. It is located next to the A1 pulley. Rupture of the A2 pulley is a relatively common injury and has been reported in up to 40 percent of professional climbers. Rupture occurs as a result of the excessive stress on the A2 pulley during a cling grip. The long and ring fingers are most commonly involved. Pulley rupture can be acute or it can develop insidiously. If you have an acute pulley rupture, you will feel pain in your palm and in the finger bones closest to your hand. Minor A2 pulley injuries or partial tears can be treated with either firm taping around the pulley or with a ring splint, worn full-time for two to three months to permit healing. A hand surgeon should evaluate and treat complete tears of a pulley and the tendons affected. Surgical reattachment or repair may be required. If you have had the injury for more than three weeks, you may need a variety of surgical and nonsurgical methods.

If you suffer any injury to the pulleys or tendons, you should take time off from climbing.

Joint Contracture

Many rock climbers become unable to unbend their middle finger. The contracture is usually mild and is thought to be the result of repeated stresses of climbing. The joints can become swollen or fill up with fluid. The swelling occurs in the lining of the joints (synovium). Inflammation of the synovial linings is called synovitis. Treatment includes rest, stretching exercises, anti-inflammatory medication, postexercise icing, and a dynamic PIP joint extension splint. This is a device with springs on it, which gradually forces the joint to become straight again. Severe fixed contractures that compromise hand function may require surgical correction. Consult an orthopedist. He or she will often recommend less invasive treatment by a hand therapist before recommending surgery.

Ligament Injuries

Ligaments in the fingers and thumb are at risk for many types of rock climbing injuries. The ligaments can be sprained (microscopic tears); they can rupture (complete tearing or pulling off the bony attachment); or just become stretched over time (chronic attenuation). These injuries most often occur at the PIP joint but can also occur at the thumb joint to the same ligament that is injured in skiers. The ligaments injured at the PIP joint are collateral ligaments, which are on the sides of the joint. They most commonly affect the long or middle finger and occur during a maneuver known as dynoing, meaning rapidly ascending a rock face. As the climber ascends past a pocket in the rock in which she has placed her fingers, a finger can become trapped and bent, which can stretch the ligament awkwardly.

If you have a PIP injury, you will have mild to moderate joint swelling, tenderness, and pain with motion. Your physician may need to numb your finger with Xylocaine in order to examine it thoroughly. A joint that opens up widely while the physician moves it most likely has a complete rupture of the ligament.

If you have a PIP joint sprain and the ligaments surrounding the joint are partially torn, the joint is not completely unstable. This injury may be treated with therapy including rest, icing, swelling control, continued range-of-motion exercises, and taping the affected digit to the adjacent finger (a procedure called buddy taping). Persistent pain and swelling are common and may take months to resolve, but you may still be able to climb during that time.

If you have a complete tear of the PIP collateral ligament, there are both surgical and nonsurgical treatment options. Get the advice of a hand specialist.

Partial tears of the thumb MCP joint collateral ligaments are treated with a thumb spica splint for four to six weeks. This is a plastic splint that goes around the hand and includes the thumb. Certain tears absolutely need surgical repair within 10 days of the injury. A third-degree tear of the ulnar collateral ligament is one such tear. See a sports medicine orthopedic specialist or hand surgeon.

Chronic injuries with joint instability that impairs hand function usually require either reconstruction or joint fusion. This treatment usually is reserved for severe arthritis. Joint fusion is rarely done because when you fuse a joint, it no longer moves. If you have chronic instability, arthritis will eventually develop because the cartilage will continue to wear away.

Carpal Tunnel Syndrome

The finger tendons pass through the wrist in a narrow tunnel—the carpal tunnel. The median nerve also lives in this tunnel and can become compressed as a result of a rock climber's repetitive wrist flexion. (See Chapter 21.)

I had a patient, Merrill, an avid climber who complained of severe pain at night. She didn't have much discomfort during her climbs, but at rest or while trying to get to sleep, she experienced terrible pain. Even more disturbing to her was a strange sensation of burning and tingling that she just couldn't relieve with position, medication, ice, or any other treatment. On examination, I found Merrill had moderate carpal tunnel syndrome with a slight loss of sensation in the thumb, index, and long fingers. The affected hand had a weaker grip than normal and she had evidence of muscle atrophy in part of the hand.

I treated her with splinting and nonsteroidal anti-inflammatory medications. She also avoided climbing for a while. She responded well to this treatment and was back climbing in six weeks.

OTHER COMMON CLIMBING MALADIES

Rock climbing can be a dangerous sport, and there are a variety of things—both large and small—to watch out for.

Climber's Dehydration

The thing to remember about dehydration is that if you're thirsty, you're probably already dehydrated. A good rule of thumb is to drink a quart of liquid on the drive in, then take regular drink stops every 30 to 45 minutes, or carry a personal hydration system that you can sip from as you walk. If you have a headache, immediately try drinking some water. Try to keep your urine nearly colorless.

Climber's Blisters

Spare no expense when it comes to footwear. You'll rely more heavily on your feet when climbing than on any other part of your body, and blistered feet can ruin a long trip. Climbers who rent plastic boots or who buy new hiking boots should give themselves plenty of time to break them in. Preferred mountaineering footwear is either heavy-duty stiff-soled boots made of leather or synthetic material or lightweight plastic boots that are completely waterproof. Before going on any long hikes, get your feet used to the added wear and tear by taking shorter hikes earlier in the season on different kinds of terrain. Experiment with sock layering. You may feel that wearing only one pair works for you; some claim that two ultrathin liners and a pair of midweight wool socks do the trick. Finally, if you feel a hot spot developing on your foot, stop and take care of the new blisters so they don't get worse.

Climber's Conks

Mountaineers wear fiberglass or extra-strength plastic helmets to protect their heads. If you ride a bike, you probably wear one so why not wear a helmet to protect your head in case a falling rock, tree branch, or ice chunk hits you? If you slip and fall, a helmet may protect your head from serious damage. It depends, of course, on how far you fall—but chances are good that it can increase your chances of survival.

Climber's Scrapes, Cuts, and Abrasions

When using sharp instruments like a knife or an ice axe, be sure to cut away from you, and do *not* have the item you are cutting resting on your legs—use another rock, table, or otherwise sturdy surface that won't bleed if the knife slips. It's also a good idea to wear at least a thin layer of clothing over your entire body, including gloves, when crossing icy or rocky slopes, in case you slip and scrape yourself.

Climber's Shoulder

Climbing, by its very nature, puts your shoulders at risk. Shoulder injuries can occur if you fall during rock climbing but fail to release soon enough, causing you to wrench your shoulder; they can also occur when self-arresting with an ice axe, if you allow the axe to get too far away from the center of your body. To help prevent shoulder injuries, strengthen your arms and shoulders before and during the season. Practice self-arrests annually before you need to stop a fall on steep snow. Listen to your body and learn when to fall to save your fingers, elbow tendons, and shoulders. Make sure you get over the ice axe as quickly as possible and use your body weight to stop yourself, not the smaller muscles in your shoulder with your arm fully stretched overhead.

Two other common shoulder problems that I have seen in rock climbers are labral tears and shoulder instability.

Labral Tears. The glenoid labrum is made of fibrocartilage and lines the socket of the shoulder. It is extremely important for shoulder stability and function. It is commonly injured in rock climbers both acutely (with a specific pulling or compression injury) or chronically from overuse. I have taken care of several elite rock climbers from Telluride who all had the same injury. Three of them were actually climbing buddies and over a two-year span they all ended up needing surgery. All three are now back on the rocks and good as new.

All three of these women had complaints of shoulder pain, including pain only in certain shoulder positions while performing maneuvers on the rocks and occasional clicking and catching in the shoulder. They felt as if something was out of place at times; then it would pop back into place and the pain would disappear. They had no pain with most activities, yet climbing was hindered for them and this was their love in life.

Each of them underwent a similar physical examination. They had full range of motion of the shoulder and excellent rotator cuff strength. They did have some discomfort when I tested their biceps tendons and specific provocative tests were positive for a labral tear (where the biceps attaches in the shoulder).

A common location for labrum injury is at the top of the shoulder socket where the biceps tendon attaches. (See Chapter 21.)

Shoulder Instability. I have seen countless climbers with occult instability of the shoulder. By "occult" I mean that they don't dislocate their shoulders out of the joint; there is, however, a loosening of the ligaments in the shoulder (capsule), which causes a subtle instability. The mechanism of injury is often repeated hanging. To conserve energy when hanging, rock climbers often use the skeleton and its ligaments (static components) rather than the muscles (dynamic components). Over time this can stretch the ligaments and result in subtle or occult instability. You can also stretch these ligaments with an acute injury such as sudden traction force on the shoulder, which can cause a dislocation or a subluxation (a near dislocation).

The patients do not come in complaining of instability. They complain of pain. This is because the subtle instability causes some biomechanical changes in the shoulder, which makes the rotator cuff work harder, and in a disadvantaged position, which can cause impingement and tendonitis. (See Chapter 21.)

Climber's Muscle Aches

Some muscle soreness especially after a big climb should not keep you from continuing your sport. However, you must use common sense. If you are truly in pain in a specific muscle group, you are likely to cause more damage if you continue to climb. A muscle strain is a microscopic tear that can become inflamed. Torn and inflamed tissue is at increased risk for further tearing. Continued stress to the muscle will mean an overall longer recovery time. It can also be dangerous. If you are out on a climb with moderate pain in you calf, and you need your legs for balancing and ascension, you are putting yourself at risk for further injury if your calf cannot go the distance. If you have moderate pain, give the muscle some rest. Ice, stretching, anti-inflammatory medication, and cross training are a good idea. If the pain is more chronic or severe, you should seek out a medical opinion.

Climber's Knee and Ankle Injuries

Again, I emphasize the need for sturdy, comfortable, well-broken-in hiking boots that provide ankle support. Use trekking poles to assist you on climbs or descents; learn leg-saving techniques such as glissading—sliding on the ice using your shoes as skis. You can also do it on your buttocks and slow down or stop with your ice axe.

Climber's Fractures

Hand and collarbone (clavicle) fractures are common in rock climbers. These are injuries that can be splinted in the field and the climber can usually get back to civilization for treatment with the help of her climbing partners. Fortunately fractures to the legs (tibias), thighs (femurs), and hips are uncommon but I have treated several in my mountain practice. These types of fractures often require a helicopter rescue because the climber is at great risk of serious complications from her injuries. Rock climbing can be extremely dangerous if all possible precautions are not taken. Even so, accidents do happen—equipment may fail and human error also can be a factor.

Climber's Contusions from Falls and Slips

Injuries from falling can be related to exposure at high altitude, which can affect not only judgment, but also hand-eye coordination. You can also fall from not paying close attention to your (or your buddy's) climbing. Fractures of the ankle and shinbone are common in climbers who have fallen. In some cases, falling can cause severe injuries to the head, neck, and back. Such injuries can result in impairment or even death. Scrapes, bruises, and cuts from slipping and falling on ice, snow, or rock can be prevented by being sure of your footing—this involves practice on talus, boulders, and scree slopes.

Wear thin gloves, leggings, and a long-sleeved shirt when crossing snow or ice fields, to add a layer of protection for your hands, legs, and arms in case you slip or have to throw a hand down to catch yourself. Know how to climb using an ice axe in self-arrest and belay positions. Practice getting into position repeatedly—and quickly—to stop a fall. Belaying generally involves two people, the climber and the belayer. The belayer stays below as the climber ascends. The belayer doles out slack in the rope so the climber can ascend. Once the climber gets to a certain height she secures her ropes and the belayer becomes the climber and is protected from above.

Sunburn

Sunburn is one of the most common maladies among climbers and hikers. It's also one of the most preventable. Carry sunscreen with you on every outing, rain or shine, July or December, at high altitude or low. You can burn even on a cloudy day. If you are traveling across glaciers at high altitude, the burning effect of the sun will be magnified. Use glacier goggles, a hat, a bandana, and lightweight gloves to protect your face and hands. If you've misplaced or forgotten your glasses, you can create an eye protector by making two small slits in cardboard and securing it in place with a bandana. Snow blindness is exceedingly painful—it feels like sand scratching the eyeballs. Save yourself the agony and take appropriate precautions.

Climber's Chill

When your body temperature drops below 95°F, you are suffering from hypothermia. Even on a fairly warm but breezy day, if you sweat profusely and then stop moving, the wind can quickly cause you to get chilled. Proper clothing is essential. Alpine climbers avoid cotton clothing because once wet, it conducts heat away from the body. Instead, many mountaineers use synthetic underwear; fleece hats, jackets, and pants; and outerwear and snow pants made of waterproof-breathable material such as Gore-Tex. These materials allow sweat and water vapor to escape from the skin through the clothing. By keeping warm and dry, mountaineers avoid the dangers of severely chilling their body core, which can lead to hypothermia.

Unexpected weather conditions represent some of the most common and dangerous situations in mountain climbing. In the high county, rugged landscapes and high winds interact to make weather unpredictable. A sunny July day can suddenly deteriorate into a violent thunderstorm leaving a dusting of fresh snow on the summits. Just as quickly, the storm may clear returning the day to its previous peacefulness.

Altitude Sickness

If you are going to climb a mountain, you must be able to recognize and if possible prevent altitude sickness. Upper altitudes are defined as:

High altitude .... 8,000–14,000 feet
Very high altitude .... 14000–18000 feet
Extreme high altitude .... above 18,000 feet

To increase oxygen delivery to your cells and improve efficiency of oxygen use, your body undergoes numerous changes at these elevations. Normally, oxygen diffuses from your lungs into your blood because the gas pressure is greater in your lungs. At high altitudes, air pressure diminishes and reduces the pressure in your lungs as it decreases the amount of oxygen diffusing in your blood. For example, in a healthy person at sea level, blood is 95 percent saturated with oxygen. At 18,000 feet the same person's blood is only 71 percent saturated.

As the supply of oxygen goes down, the body makes an effort to compensate for the changes. Your heart will beat more quickly. Blood flow to your brain will increase in an attempt to deliver more oxygen. The blood vessels in your lungs will constrict, increasing resistance to flow through the lungs and raising lung blood pressure. Dangerously high blood pressure in the lung (pulmonary) artery may cause fluid to escape from the blood vessels and leak into the lungs making it hard to breathe (pulmonary edema).

Why some people become ill and even die from altitude illness is unknown. Most people who become ill, however, do so within the first few days of ascending to altitude. The only sure treatment is to descend.

The factors that affect the incidence and severity of altitude illness:

- Rate of ascent: The faster you climb the greater your risk.
- Altitude attained (especially sleeping altitude): The higher you climb the greater the risk.

- Length of exposure: The longer you stay high the greater the risk.
- Level of exertion: Hard exertion, without rest or fluid intake, increases the risk.
- Inherent physiological susceptibility: Because of specific physical factors some people are more likely to become ill than others.

The signs and symptoms of acute altitude sickness include headache, malaise, loss of appetite, nausea, vomiting, fluid retention (especially in the face and hands), disturbed sleep, and skin changes (including turning blue).

You should limit your activity during the first three days at altitudes higher than 8,000 feet. It may take three or four days to adjust. Drink lots of fluids. If you suffer from headache, over-the-counter medications may ease the pain. If symptoms worsen—or if you have loss of balance, difficulty breathing, or a change in consciousness—descend a few thousand feet. Drink fluids and rest. If symptoms continue to worsen or fail to improve, descend to the place where you began your climb.

PREVENTING CLIMBING INJURIES

You may be able to prevent finger injuries with skin protection, exercise, and thin rubber pads or sleeves applied to the finger or wrapped (taped) around the finger. Participate in an exercise program that includes stretching and range-of-motion exercises for the wrist and fingers to help prevent flexor tendon and pulley injuries. Include strengthening exercises; these are best accomplished by progressively increasing the duration and intensity of weight resistance.

Pay attention not only to your arm and shoulder muscles, but also to those of your quadriceps, hamstrings, calves, hips (including glutes), and core (abdominals and lower back). If these muscles are strong, it will help protect your knee and ankle from injuries. I have treated several climbers who sustained ACL tears after they lost control going down a scree field. (See Chapter 22.) I have also seen many climbers break their ankles upon descent.

Climbing should be invigorating—both physically and mentally. It should also be fun. Reaching the top may be your goal, but it is not worth your life.

For more information, check out these resources:

AMERICAN SAFE CLIMBING ASSOCIATION
P.O. Box 1814
Bishop, CA 93515
safeclimbing.com

AMERICAN ALPINE CLUB
710 10th Street, Suite 100
Golden, CO 80401
Telephone: (303) 384-0110
Fax: (303) 384-0111

AMERICANALPINECLUB.ORG
The AAC, founded in 1902, is a nonprofit organization dedicated to promoting climbing knowledge, conserving mountain environments, and serving the American climbing community.

AMERICAN MOUNTAIN GUIDE ASSOCIATION
710 10th Street, Suite 101
Golden, CO 80401
amga.com
This is a nonprofit organization that seeks to represent the interests of American mountain guides by providing support, education, and standards.

13

WALKING AND RUNNING

On Your Feet

WHETHER YOU WALK, race walk, jog, or run, you not only exercise your body, but you also enhance your self-image and mental health.

Walking, by definition, means "to go on foot." If you move your feet at a slow pace, you are walking. If you move them at a fast pace, you are running. There are lots of variations—each has advantages and disadvantages.

Race walking, both a competitive sport and a personal exercise, is a form of walking in which you must keep your feet in contact with the ground at all times. This means that before you lift your rear foot off the ground, your lead foot must touch the ground in front of you and be straight. The aim is to maintain a constant speed of your body's center of gravity without excessive up-and-down or side-to-side movements.

Jogging is running at a leisurely, slow pace, usually as part of an outdoor exercise program.

Running means moving your body forward in such a way that at some point in your stride both your feet are off the ground at the same time. Females run for many reasons—whether it is to compete in track and marathons, to become physically fit, to condition themselves for another sport, to lose weight, or just for fun and relaxation.

Running for the sake of running has become much more popular since Jim Fixx wrote *The Complete Book of Running* in 1977. Studies about the health benefits since then have shown that habitual runners when compared to couch potatoes:

- Live two to seven years longer
- Have 30 to 40 percent lower risk of developing heart disease
- Have 50 percent lower risk of developing Type 2 (adult onset) diabetes

A Harvard University study found that women runners produce a less toxic form of estrogen than their more sedentary counterparts. As a result, they cut their risk of developing breast and uterine cancer by half and their risk of contracting the form of diabetes that most commonly affects women by two-thirds.

It must be emphasized that exercise cannot entirely prevent these conditions, but the study points out that women can reduce their risk of and delay the progression of these illnesses.

The President's Council on Physical Fitness has concluded that when compared to 13 other popular forms of exercise, running is the best activity for heart and lung fitness, muscle growth, weight loss, and relaxation.

Many runners do run for relaxation. Carol Milano, for example, is the Brooklyn, New York, health and fitness writer and author of *Hers: The Wise Woman's Guide to Starting a Business on $2,000 or Less* (Allworth Press, 1998). She reveals: "I often get my best ideas while jogging. When I'm stuck for a good lead, one will invariably come to me as I'm loping along, hearing birds instead of phones."

When did she start to jog?

"In March 1981, I'd been taking an aerobics class at the local YWCA and finally realized that my favorite part was when we jogged around the gym to 'The Gambler.' One early spring day, I thought: 'I can do that outside at the track right down the street.' I put on a pair of sweatpants and a pair of sneakers, did the quarter-mile track four times, and was hooked. I got up to three miles a day very easily, and was doing five-mile runs by Memorial Day."

Carol now also race walks. "I'd heard that five times a week is often enough to jog. On my days off from running—or if I have a lot of business appointments and can't fit in time to jog that day—I wear my heavy-duty walking shoes (between meetings) and race walk around town, making sure I do a total of about three miles or more. Depending on how many appointments I have, and how far apart they are, I might end up covering four or five miles in a day. I'm religious about the daily activity because in reporting on osteoporosis I've learned that frequent weight-bearing activity is an excellent way to forestall it.

"When I lived in Manhattan, I belonged to the New York Road Runners Club and I ran in races regularly, in Central Park—usually 10K or thereabouts. Since relocating to Brooklyn at the end of 1985, I run in the annual Turkey Trot five-miler on Thanksgiving morning. ('Compete' is not the right verb in my case—I take part. I'm no threat to the front runners.)"

There are many controversies about female as compared with male runners and walking as compared with running. First of all, if you have watched the marathons, the men always seem to come in first. The reason for this most likely has to do with the male hormone, testosterone. Because of it, men have stronger muscles, denser bones, less fat, and proportionately larger hearts and lungs, as well as more oxygen in their blood. This doesn't mean that women can't run well in a marathon, but it's clear that men have the advantage. Statistically, women run approximately 10 percent slower than men at all distances (based on the average difference between men's and women's world records). And although a University of California analysis showed that elite women have been improving twice as fast as elite men over the past 30 years, women are not going to "catch up" to men. The improvement, according to the Road Runners Club, can be traced, among other things, to the greater number of women competitors, more opportunities to compete, and better coaching. Of course, the organization points out, certain individual women can far outpace most men. Ingrid Kristiansen's marathon world record of 2.21:06 is faster than what 99.9 percent of the world's men are capable of achieving.

If you take a brisk walk rather than a short high-speed run, will you be better off with a consistent lower level of intensity? You will be moving almost every part of your body. When you move your body over the same distance—five miles—instead of running, you will have done the same work and used the same amount of energy (calories) to do that work. The missing factor is time. If you walk five miles in one hour, you may run the same distance in half that time. So running does take more power.

By one estimate, a 150-pound person who runs at six miles an hour for a full hour can expect to use 720 calories. Walking at four miles an hour for 90 minutes would spend 486 calories. The total utilized, and the proportion of fat calories to carbohydrate calories burned, depend upon the time you spend exercising, the intensity, and the underlying conditioning of your body. For example, exercising at a lower intensity burns more fat; harder effort burns a bigger share of carbohydrates.

Nancy Williams of Penn State University's department of kinesiology endorses both forms of exercise, but she points out that running has the advantage of intensity, which triggers certain beneficial heart and lung responses that walking does not. But, she adds, both forms of exercise are good use of your time.

Just walking, in fact, may actually keep your brain more youthful, according to research presented during the American Academy of Neurology's annual meeting in Philadelphia in 2001. Author and neurologist Kristine Yaffe, M.D., of the University of California, San Francisco, reported that women who walk regularly are less likely to experience memory loss and other declines in mental function that can accompany aging.

For the study, Dr. Yaffe and her colleagues tested the mental functioning of 5,925 women once and then again six to eight years later. The least active women walked an average of about a half-mile per week, while the most active group walked an average of nearly 18 miles per week. This included walking for exercise and as part of daily activities.

"But we also found that for every extra mile walked per week there was a 13 percent less chance of cognitive decline," Yaffe said. "So you don't need to be running marathons. The exciting thing is there was a 'dose' relationship, which showed that even a little is good but more is better."

Physical activity was measured by the number of blocks walked per week and also by the number of calories used in walking, recreation, and stair climbing. According to Yaffe: "Examples of moderate activities that would reduce risk of decline would be playing tennis twice a week or walking a mile per day or playing golf once a week."

WANTING TO WALK

If you walk briskly, the consensus is that you will improve your circulation and respiration, increase muscle and bone strength, and calm your nerves. You should try to take a 20-minute walk each day. Here are a few hints to help you obtain maximum benefits:

- Set a comfortable pace and develop an easy unbroken stride.
- Keep your feet pointing straight ahead.
- Let your arms swing freely.
- Walk to work or, if that's too far, get off the bus or park your car several blocks away and walk the rest of the way. Make sure you are wearing good walking shoes, not pumps or heels.
- Go to the store on foot if you can. If not, walking around a mall window-shopping for half an hour is good—and you can do it in all kinds of weather.
- Climb the stairs instead of riding the elevator or escalator.
- Carry a backpack (three to five pounds), or carry light weights in your hands.
- Arrange to walk with a buddy who can help motivate you to get out there and move.

JOGGING/RUNNING PROGRAM

You shouldn't just jump into a jogging or running program without checking with your physician. Once your physician approves, be prepared to make your jogging or running program a priority. Here is a sample program.

- *First week:* Jog or run 40 seconds (100 yards); walk 1 minute (100 yards). Repeat nine times.
- *Second week:* Jog or run 1 minute (150 yards); walk 1 minute (100 yards). Repeat eight times.
- *Third week:* Jog or run 2 minutes (300 yards); walk 1 minute (100 yards). Repeat six times.

- *Fourth week:* Jog or run 4 minutes (600 yards); walk 1 minute (100 yards). Repeat four times.
- *Fifth week:* Jog or run 6 minutes (900 yards); walk 1 minute (100 yards). Repeat eight times.
- *Sixth week:* Jog or run 8 minutes (1,200 yards); walk 2 minutes (200 yards). Repeat twice.
- *Seventh week:* Jog or run 10 minutes (1,500 yards); walk 2 minutes (200 yards). Repeat twice.
- *Eighth week:* Jog or run 12 minutes (1,700 yards); walk 2 minutes (200 yards). Repeat twice.

By the eighth week, you should be in good enough condition that you can set your own jogging pace, but do avoid rapid mileage increases. Running should be at a speed and over a distance that causes *slight* breathlessness only. A simple heart rate monitor is invaluable in limiting undue exertion. While it is impossible to lay down strict rules as to how high your pulse should be allowed to rise, your physician can work with you to set a level. Keep close to those limits.

If you experience *any* of the following symptoms, stop jogging immediately, and do not jog again until you have consulted your physician:

- Pain or exertion under the breastbone (This can feel as if something is pressing against your rib cage. The pain may move or radiate to other areas of the upper body, such as your neck, cheek, shoulders, arms, or back.)
- A choking sensation during exertion
- Severe pain in the front portion of your shins or ankles when walking or jogging/running

The following are some further safety precautions for joggers/runners developed by USA Track and Field, Road Runners Club of America, and American Orthopaedic Society for Sports Medicine.

- Plan a progressive running program to prevent injuries.
- Perform a five-minute warm-up (which should raise your temperature by one degree) followed by stretching exercises. This is essential before starting a run. Following the run, stretching again is important.

- During hot weather run in the early morning or evening to avoid overheating.
- Do not run (or walk) when pollution levels are high.
- Start your run with your body feeling a little cool; body temperature will increase as you run.
- Drink 10 to 15 ounces of fluid 10 to 15 minutes prior to running and every 20 to 30 minutes along your route. (You can lose between six and 12 ounces of fluid for every 20 minutes of running.) Weigh yourself before and after a run. For every pound you lose, drink one pint of fluid.
- Run in the shade if possible to avoid direct sun. If exposed to the sun, apply at least 15 SPF sunscreen. Wear sunglasses to filter out UVA and UVB rays, and wear a hat with a visor to shade your eyes and face.
- In high altitudes, gradually acclimate yourself to lower oxygen levels by making slow, steady increases in speed and distance.
- Choose the right running shoes.
- Heavy clothing can produce sweating, which causes the body to lose heat rapidly and can increase the risk of hypothermia. Instead, dress in layers. The inner layer should be material that takes perspiration away from the skin (polypropylene, thermax); the middle layer (not necessary for legs) should be for insulation and absorbing moisture (cotton); and the outer layer should protect against wind and moisture (nylon).
- To avoid frostbite in cold weather, do not leave gaps of bare skin. Wear gloves, a jacket, and a hat, and cover your neck. Petroleum jelly can be used on exposed areas, such as the nose.
- Do not run at night, but if you run at dusk or dawn, wear reflective material.
- Don't wear a headset while running. You won't be able to hear cars, cyclists, or an attacker. With headphones on, you're a target.
- Run with a partner. If you run alone, carry identification, or write your name, phone number, blood type, and medical information on the inside sole of your running shoe.
- Let others know where you will be running. Stay in familiar areas away from traffic.

- Have a whistle or other noisemaker or carry a cell phone or change in case of an emergency.
- Whenever possible, run on a clear, smooth, and reasonably soft surface. Avoid running on hills, which increases stress on the ankle and foot. When running on curved surfaces, alternate which foot is on the uphill side frequently so that you have equal pressure on both feet during the run.
- Increase your time or mileage by 10 percent per week.
- If you're running three times a week, make no single run greater than 50 percent of your weekly mileage.
- If you're running five times a week, make no single run greater than 33 percent of your weekly mileage.

Injuries occur when repetitive running is performed too intensely, too frequently, or for too long at a time. Even the clumsiest people usually can avoid injury if they are careful to advance their training changes slowly. A medical practitioner should evaluate pain that does not improve after a few days' rest.

Despite all your precautions and preparations, using your legs and feet to walk or run may lead to injuries. The next sections of this chapter are devoted to the more common injuries. For more detailed information on each body part's injury and therapy, refer to Chapters 21 through 23.

WALKING AND RUNNING INJURIES

When you walk you don't lift your feet as high off the ground as you do when you run. As a result, walking causes less impact or force and therefore fewer injuries to bones and joints. But whether you walk or run, your legs and feet bear the brunt of your weight. Studies have shown that females are much more likely than males to suffer ankle sprains, shin splints, stress fractures, and hip problems. They are also more likely to suffer knee pain caused by lower body imbalances. On the other hand, females are less susceptible to Achilles tendonitis, plantar fasciitis, and quadriceps injuries although these injuries do occur.

Shin pain accounts for an estimated 10 to 20 percent of all injuries in runners and up to 60 percent of all overuse injuries in the leg. The term *shin splints* describes a symptom of exercise-induced shin pain; it is not actually a medical diagnosis. Most shin pain from running is a stress reaction within the bone called medial tibial stress syndrome (MTSS). (See Chapter 22.)

If you run or walk enough miles on the road, you will undoubtedly develop lower leg pain at some time. If you have pain from stress fractures in either of the two bones in your lower leg, you may say you have a shin splint. Stress fractures result from overuse. Repeated stresses on the bones can cause tiny, almost invisible breaks in the bone structure called microfractures. Normally, the body has time to heal the microfractures before they start to cause problems. However, overtraining and poor conditioning can aggravate microfractures and render them unable to heal. The microfractures become larger (but still very fine) stress fractures. A stress fracture of either of the lower leg bones—the tibia or fibula—is potentially very dangerous. A blow to the compromised bone, even a mild one, may shatter it. If the injury site is not rested, the stress fractures can continue to increase in size. Sometimes a chronic and recurrent stress fracture of the tibia may require surgery if it won't heal with nonoperative measures, although this is rare. Stress fractures have two primary causes:

- Excessive bone strain resulting in tiny traumas to the bone coupled with an inability to keep up with appropriate repair of the bone. This occurs most often in otherwise healthy female athletes.
- Depressed response to normal strain at the cellular and molecular levels where bone remodeling occurs. This is likely to occur with other physical problems, such as osteoporosis (fragile or brittle bones).

Stress fractures occur more often in female athletes. The risk of stress fractures in female recruits in the U.S. military, for example, is up to 10 times higher than for men undergoing the same training program. Many factors contribute to this higher frequency. Male athletes tend to have greater muscle mass, which helps them absorb shock better. In a study of female athletes, decreased calf girth was a predictor of stress fractures of the tibia. The larger width of male bones may also absorb shock better. Bone mass and bone mineral density can vary widely in females due to several factors, including hormonal influences and menstrual irregularities. Low calcium intake and eating disorders may contribute to the development of stress fractures. Conversely, oral contraceptive pills appear to help prevent stress fractures in female athletes.

A rigid high-arched foot absorbs less stress and transmits greater force to your leg bones, which may increase your stress fracture risk. Other risk factors for stress fractures include:

- *Training regimen.* Higher weekly running mileage has been shown to correlate with increased incidence of stress fractures. A sudden change in frequency, duration, or intensity of training also affects the risk of stress fractures.
- *Training surface.* Uneven surfaces, or hard surfaces such as cement, may also increase stress fracture risk.
- *Footwear.* Research has shown that training in athletic shoes older than six months increases the risk for stress fractures. Shoe age, rather than shoe cost, is a better indicator of shock-absorbing ability.

If your pain keeps getting worse as you increase your mileage, or if the pain becomes more intense each time you walk or run, trot off to your physician. You may need an x-ray or a bone scan to determine whether or not you have a fracture. Sometimes the stress fractures are so fine that they don't show up on normal x-rays. A bone scan is extremely sensitive and can even distinguish between a tibial stress injury and an actual stress fracture. In either case, you will have to stop the pain-provoking activity—usually for six weeks—to allow the bone to heal; otherwise you risk the three months of immobilization or potential surgery that could follow a subsequent complete fracture.

Once your doctor tells you that your stress fracture is healed, you must get into the habit of more aggressive stretching and strengthening. Return to your running *gradually.* The initial intensity, duration, and distance should be 50 percent of what you did before your injury. You can gradually increase your training by 10 to 15 percent per week if there is no recurring pain.

Stress fractures in the feet of runners are not uncommon. They generally occur in the metatarsals (the bones that attach to the toes). These fractures must be treated with rest from running and cross training. Working out in a pool, for example, can help you stay fit while you're healing.

Stress fractures of the hip are rare but they do occur. In my many years of treating college cross-country and track athletes, I have diagnosed dozens of stress fractures in the legs and feet but only two patients with a hip stress fracture. Both of these women had some underlying risk factors including an eating disorder (bulimia) and cessation of menstrual period for longer than six months (amenorrhea). One woman healed her hip stress fracture after four weeks on crutches and another four weeks of rest without crutches. The other woman, however, required surgery—with large screws placed into the head of the femur (top of the thigh bone)—to get her fracture to heal. If this particular stress fracture had become a complete fracture (with the bones moving out of place), it could have caused disastrous results for the young woman.

TENDONITIS

If you are in a hurry to develop your running, jogging, or walking activity, you may not have conditioned your muscles properly to get in shape. This can result in injury to the tendons, muscles, or bones in the lower leg. Tendons are tough, dense, cordlike bands of tissue that connect your muscles to your bones and transmit the force a muscle exerts. Inflammation of the tendons is called tendonitis. If you have been inactive for a period of time and then you overtrain, you are a prime candidate for tendonitis in the shin area. Usually, stresses and strains in the leg cause tendonitis but in the shin area, it can also be due to problems with the way your foot strikes the ground while running, poor conditioning, or a strength imbalance between two muscle groups that normally work together.

When tendonitis strikes, take a break from the activity that caused it. This often clears up the condition. To help prevent the pain from recurring, apply heat before stretching the tendon in question. Apply ice after the activity. Use an over-the-counter anti-inflammatory medication to relieve symptoms if your physician recommends it.

If the tendonitis results from a muscle imbalance you'll need to exercise and strengthen the weaker muscle to correct the problem. Many of the runners I have treated in my practice develop tendonitis in their lower extremities as a result of foot alignment problems and other muscle imbalances. If you suffer from recurrent tendonitis, have a sports medicine–trained physician evaluate your feet and your footwear. A simple pair of orthotics (shoe inserts) can often cure the problem.

MUSCLE PULLS

Brooklyn's Carol Milano has several times suffered a pulled or strained groin muscle from race walking. She had to refrain from the activity until it healed (about a week). "I still made sure I walked three miles a day, but I did it more slowly. I've never had a running-related injury that prevented me from doing it."

Muscle strains can be caused by lax ligaments or excessive ranges of motion at the joints. It is possible to have both hypermobile joints due to lax ligaments and tight muscles. This combination can create problems. Muscle strains can also be due to rotations in the wrong direction at the wrong time. These can be corrected by proper mechanical control. For instance, if you are running on an uneven surface or downhill, a sudden twist in the knee or ankle can stress a muscle and cause a microscopic tear. This is a muscle strain. Maintaining proper leg mechanics with each heel strike can help you prevent these injuries.

ILIOTIBIAL BAND (ITB) FRICTION SYNDROME

Iliotibial band friction syndrome affects the outer side of the hip or knee. Pain can occur either at the hip area or at the knee. The iliotibial band (ITB) is a wide, thick strip of fibrous tissue that is attached above to the iliac crest of the pelvis and below to outside of the leg bone just below the knee joint, and to the capsule of the knee joint. As the knee flexes and extends during running, your ITB repeatedly rubs over the lower outer part of your thighbone, which may cause inflammation. A sharp pain comes on gradually with each run or walk. You may run a mile or two before you feel the pain, but then it becomes progressively worse. You may hear a popping sound. Therapy is usually rest, ice, aggressive stretching, and muscle balancing. Orthotics are often necessary to get rid of chronic ITB syndrome. I take care of a lot of runners who have ITB syndrome; it can be very difficult to treat if it becomes chronic. Therefore if you think you may have it, please see your sports medicine physician sooner rather than later.

BACK PAIN

Low back problems can stem from many different causes. Therefore, it's important to make as accurate a diagnosis as possible. Sciatica is a condition where the sciatic nerve is irritated. The sciatic nerve is a very large nerve made up of five nerve roots that exit the spine in the lower lumbar and sacral regions. This nerve travels down through the buttock muscles and into the thigh supplying many muscle groups and areas of skin sensation. This nerve powers the muscles that make your reflexes work such as the knee-jerk reflex that is activated when your doctor strikes your knee with a rubber hammer.

There are two major causes of sciatica in runners. One is a herniated disk in the spine. The other is called piriformis syndrome.

The disks in your spine are fibrocartilaginous structures that sit between your vertebral bodies (the bones of the spine). If there is degeneration or injury to one of them, the affected disk can bulge out of place or the material that is contained inside the disk may bulge out (herniated disk). This places pressure on a nerve root giving you symptoms including back or buttock pain, hip pain, or radiating pain down the back of the thigh or the outside of the calf. You can also experience numbness or tingling down your thigh and leg and even into your foot. The nerve root that is irritated will dictate which part of your thigh, leg, or foot is affected. In severe cases, you can even experience weakness of the muscles involved (such as a foot drop, a situation in which you can't elevate your foot well and consequently trip when you walk), or your doctor may find that your reflexes are unequal between your two limbs. If you have any of these symptoms, you should definitely see your physician before going back to your running regimen.

Piriformis syndrome is a common cause of sciatica in runners. The piriformis is a small muscle in the buttock that externally rotates the hip to the outside. The large sciatic nerve travels deep to this muscle and if the muscle becomes inflamed or grows in size, the sciatic nerve can suffer undue pressure. This will cause irritation and/or inflammation to the nerve and the symptoms can be similar to those of a herniated disk. The treatment for piriformis syndrome is almost always nonoperative with aggressive stretching therapy and anti-inflammatory medication.

SACROILIAC JOINT PAIN

The sacroiliac joint is the joint formed between the sacrum (below the last lumbar vertebra) and the ilium (pelvic bone). The sacrum fits like a wedge between the two iliac bones and is designed to support the weight of your trunk. The ligaments that attach the sacrum to the two hipbones are some of the strongest ligaments in the entire body. The joint is not primarily constructed for movement—it is reinforced by a number of very strong ligaments—though it is capable of some gliding and hinge-type movement. Normally, very little movement should occur at these joints. If the mechanics of your pelvis, feet, and hips are not synchronized, there will be stresses and strains on your sacroiliac joints.

Sacroiliac joint pain can be difficult to treat. A precise diagnosis is essential. You should consult a sports medicine physician/orthopedist for this. I start by examining the patient to identify any muscular or skeletal imbalances. Some patients have a leg-length discrepancy (one leg is shorter than the other) or pronated (flat) feet. These can cause a skeletal imbalance, which in turn can lead to abnormal stresses to the sacroiliac joint causing compensatory muscle spasms. There may also be an overuse injury caused by ill-constructed footwear, poor running surfaces, or overtraining that can inflame the joints and cause the muscle pain as well. X-rays are rarely useful in this situation. Once the diagnosis is made, intensive treatment in the form of physical therapy, anti-inflammatory medication, and often footwear modifications (for leg-length discrepancy or pronated feet) can begin. The physical therapist will focus on dynamic stretching as well as muscle strengthening for balance.

Sometimes, a cortisone injection directly into the inflamed joint will help the athlete turn the corner toward recovery, but physical therapy and appropriate shoe modification will still be necessary.

RUNNER'S KNEES

It is safe to say that the knee is the joint runners injure most often. Females, as I have pointed out numerous times in this book, have particularly vulnerable knees. Knees are not simple joints. Attempting to balance one stick lengthwise upon another and then move it not only forward and backward, but also through a few degrees of rotation, requires a complex structure of soft tissues such as cartilage, ligaments, tendons, and muscles. Distance runners often have knees that creak and crunch (and hurt). There is often pain behind or around the kneecap (patella). It is most often caused by abnormal tracking of the kneecap. Pain between the kneecap and underlying bone in the front of your knee (femur or thighbone), known as patellofemoral pain, or runner's knee, is a problem for many distance runners. (See Chapter 22.)

In running, where G-forces are magnified 3 to 10.5 times with every step, problems manifest rather quickly. This is fortunate because *pain* is then the first symptom and not slowly degenerative and irreversible joint disease, as might be the case in a sedentary person.

To understand why particular parts of the body suffer at any one time you need only understand the complex series of movements during the running cycle and the forces to which the body is subjected.

All forces entering the body come via the feet. Whatever your feet do determines what your legs do; what your legs do determines what your pelvis does; and so on—right up to your neck and head. Your foot is a miraculous structure ideally suited to its differing functions. It has 26 bones, 33 joints, a great number of muscles, tendons, ligaments, nerves, lymphatics, and blood vessels, all functioning together to allow you to walk or run over all sorts of surfaces. If the terrain causes you a foot problem, shoe inserts or special shoes may help provide you with a comfortable running and walking surface.

RUNNER'S/WALKER'S FEET

At some point we have all experienced pain in the arches of our feet—usually when we have been standing too long, walking too much, or running too far—but when the pain seems to come on gradually, without any incident of trauma, and then turns intense, a common cause is plantar fasciitis. People with fallen arches (flat or pronated feet) are at higher risk for plantar fasciitis, which is a medical term for inflammation of the tough fascia at the bottom of the foot that attaches the heel to the toes. Plantar fasciitis is a very common cause of heel pain in runners. It can generally be treated without surgery through exercises and shoe modification or orthotics. (See Chapter 22.)

Heel Spur Syndrome

When we walk or run the heel is the part of our bodies that first contacts the ground. It dissipates the shock and force of a virtually unyielding surface. When you run fast, the force going through each heel can be more than 10 times your body weight. Nevertheless your heel (in cooperation with other shock-absorbing mechanisms of your body) is usually very efficient.

Why, then, is heel pain so common? There are a number of reasons. Heel spur syndrome, for example, is a frequent and disabling heel problem. The pain is typically worse when you walk or run immediately after a period of rest because inflammatory fluid has a chance to build up in the area. The fluid is pressed away when you walk around but builds up again when you rest your feet. Pain occurs in the area of attachment of the plantar fascia (the broad ligament in the sole of the foot that acts as a tie-beam connecting the heel with the forefoot) into the bump on your heel bone. The white fibers of the fascia are composed of collagen, a connective tissue that is not able to stretch very much. If you have flat feet, your arches flatten abnormally and great stress is then exerted on the plantar fascia. This can cause some of the fibers around your heel bone to tear. A little bleeding may occur. Calcium salts invade the blood clot along the fascia and eventually new bone is laid down, beginning at the heel bone's bump and extending forward as a flat shelf of bone. On x-ray it appears as a spur or spike of bone, but it is actually a thin shelf. Every step potentially damages it, which causes the condition to become chronic. The inflammation that results from this trauma causes pain in a very localized area. If it is present at all, the spur of bone is not the cause of the pain but rather one of the signs of this pathological process.

Achilles' Heel

For many runners the most vulnerable part of their anatomy is quite literally their Achilles' heel—or at least the tendon attached to it. In some ways it is surprising that this area is not injured more often. With every takeoff it has to withstand forces transmitted through it from the muscles of the calf. This is in addition to the normal up and down movement of the heel bone, which contributes to twisting and untwisting within the tendon. The twisting might cause small partial ruptures to the tendon. Often they occur where the back of the running shoe impinges on the tendon when the toe is pointed. You may feel pain and stiffness when you touch your heel or when you first get out of bed in the morning. This happens because of a normal tendency to sleep with the toes and ankle pointed in a position known as plantar flexion and a small amount of bleeding from the previously injured tendon forming itself into inelastic scar tissue, which then is torn painfully apart as your heels first hit the deck the following morning.

Achilles' heel is sometimes just a nuisance but it *can* be crippling. The injuries that affect it are those of complete or partial rupture, inflammation of the tendon, or death of some of the central tissue as a result of poor blood supply. Pain is most common a little above the top of the heel bone (calcaneus), though it can also manifest at the insertion of the tendon into the back of the heel or at the junction of the calf muscle and its tendon. A complete rupture is a dramatic affair, often accompanied by a pain similar to a gunshot as the tendon snaps across its length, and the elasticity of the calf muscles pulls the upper end into the lower calf, leaving a space that rapidly fills with blood and fibrous scar tissue. (See Chapter 22.)

Choosing the Right Running Shoe

The most significant equipment for a runner is shoes. Shoes are the protective barrier between the runner and the road. Here are some tips for finding the right shoes (reprinted with permission from the American Academy of Orthopaedic Surgeons):

- Do not retrieve old shoes from the closet for your new program. New, carefully fitted shoes reduce impact shock and chance of injury.
- When selecting a running shoe, look for good shock absorption and construction that will provide stability and cushioning. Make sure that there is a thumbnail's width between the end of your longest part of your foot and the toe end of the shoe.
- Try on shoes at the end of the day when your foot is at its largest.
- When the shoe is on your foot, you should be able to wiggle all your toes.
- When trying on shoes, wear the same type of sock that you will wear when running.
- Always relace the shoes you are trying on. Begin at the farthest eyelets and apply even pressure as you crisscross the laces to the top of the shoe.
- The shoe should grip your heel firmly. Your heel should not slip as you walk or run.
- New shoes should be comfortable as soon as you try them on. There should be no need to break them in.
- Keep your shoes dry. Midsummer runs can soak shoes with sweat. A wet shoe may not control the foot as well as a dry shoe.
- If you run up to 10 miles per week, you should consider replacing your shoes every 9 to 12 months. Sixty percent of a shoe's shock absorption is lost after 250 to 500 miles of use.

If you participate in a sport three or more times a week, you need a sport-specific shoe. Athletic shoes are grouped into basic categories: running, cross training, walking, jogging, hiking, and race walking.

A good walking shoe has a comfortable soft upper, good shock absorption, smooth tread, and a rocker sole design that encourages the natural roll of the foot. Features you should look for in a jogging shoe include cushioning, flexibility, control and stability in the heel counter area, lightness, and good traction.

Athletic shoe companies produce running and walking shoes for various foot types, gait patterns, and training styles. It is always best to ask your coach about the best shoe for your sport.

For more information about running shoes, check out the following resources:

ROAD RUNNERS CLUB OF AMERICA
RRCA National Office
510 North Washington Street
Alexandria, VA 22314
Telephone: 703 836-0558
E-mail: office@rrca.org
rrca.org
The Road Runners Club of America is the national association of not-for-profit running clubs dedicated to promoting long-distance running as both competitive sport and healthful exercise. RRCA's mission is to represent and promote the common interest of its member clubs and individual runners through education, leadership programs, and other services.

INTERNATIONAL FEDERATION OF POPULAR SPORTS/INTERNATIONAL
    VOLKSPORTS FEDERATION (IVV)
AVA.org/ivvwr.htm
The IVV is the worldwide association of walking clubs. It is the largest walking organization in the world.

NORTH AMERICAN RACEWALKING FOUNDATION (NARF)
Elaine Ward, NARF President
P.O. Box 50312
Pasadena, CA 91115-0312
Telephone: (626) 441-5459
Fax: (626) 799-5106
E-mail: NARWF@aol.com
Since 1986, NARF has been promoting the development of race walking.

AMERICAN RUNNING ASSOCIATION
Telephone: (800) 776-2732
E-mail: run@americanrunning.org
americanrunning.org

The American Running Association, founded in 1968 as the National Jogging Association, provides comprehensive information for people interested in running.

U.S.A. Track & Field (USATF)
One RCA Dome, Suite 140
Indianapolis, IN 46225
Telephone: (317) 261-0500
usatf.com
The USATF is the national governing body for track and field, long-distance running, and race walking in the United States.

WALKING.ABOUT.COM
This site offers information about walking and running sites as well as about equipment.

14

GOLF

In the Swing of Things

THERE ARE FIVE MILLION WOMEN golfers in the United States, and 40 percent of new golfers are women. Females annually spend an estimated $6 billion on golf merchandise and playing fees. Golf is a sport that women can play alone, with other women, or with men. Although they may not be as strong as their male counterparts, women golfers often develop winning skills.

The golf swing is a complex, coordinated movement of the hands, wrists, arms, trunk, and legs. It can be broken into four basic movements.

- **Backswing.** In this phase you rotate your trunk, raise your arms, and cock your wrists while pulling the club head away from the ball in a smooth and coordinated motion toward your "trailing" side. (Your "leading" side is toward the target and your trailing side is away.) Eventually the club head is positioned above and behind your head, which is the point from which your downswing begins.

- **Downswing.** You swing the club toward the ball by using your shoulder and wrist levers. In a smooth motion, your body turns toward the target, your arms swing down, and your wrists start to uncock. This phase ends when the shaft is about 30 to 45 degrees from the ground.

• **Acceleration and ball strike.** This is the quickest part of the swing. Your arm and trunk motions continue, and your wrists and forearms are rapidly uncocked. The leading wrist turns inward and the trailing wrist turns outward to maximize the speed of the club head as it connects with the ball.

• **Follow-through.** After you strike the ball, the natural momentum of your swing continues. The club head ends above or even behind you.

The motion of a correctly executed golf swing can lead to problems in many parts of your body. The swing causes you to make a large trunk rotation and requires you to move both shoulders through a wide range of motions at very high speeds. You may not be conditioned to make these motions.

Although you may sprain an ankle or get conked by a golf ball, most golf injuries stem from overuse, misuse, and/or disuse, usually because of faulty form. Golf is usually considered a low-level activity, but golfers often suffer bodily harm. More than 50 percent of touring professionals have had to stop playing at some point due to injuries. The following are common golf injuries, many of which can be prevented with good conditioning, a safe environment, and proper equipment. For more detailed information on each body part's injury and therapy, refer to Chapters 21 through 23.

BACKACHES

The back is the Achilles' heel of golfers. Constant bending over causes extreme stress on the muscles and joints of the lower back. Swinging a golf club requires good trunk rotation. If you don't perform proper rotation, you will have inadequate movement of your shoulders, which results in excessive use of your hand and arm muscles, as well as poor balance on your feet. You may shift your pelvis too much to the side to compensate for the lack of chest rotation. This can lead to a severe form of chronic low back pain that is sometimes called poor lumbo-pelvic rhythm or "the tail that wags the dog." Additional problem areas may include your upper spine and even your neck bones. All these conditions may result in nerve irritation. Some golfers believe that muscle-strengthening exercises, particularly weightlifting, will hurt their golf game. Wrong! The stronger and more flexible your body is, the easier it will be to keep your scores low. Furthermore, poor flexibility and low muscle strength can cause minor strains in the back that can easily become severe injuries.

If you are an amateur, you will most likely put more strain on your back than a professional does. Amateurs have been found to reach 90 percent of their peak muscle activity during a golf swing, while professionals reach only about 80 percent. Amateurs' greater spinal loading and muscle activity during the swing are caused by poor swing mechanics. These players only increase the loads as they swing harder—instead of more skillfully—to hit the ball farther. The resulting increased loads may predispose amateur golfers to muscle strains, herniated disks, and damage to the facets, which are small joints in the spine that connect the vertebrae in the back. Facet arthropathy—which means damage to these joints—may result in inflammation, bone spurs, and pinching (impingement) on the nerve roots. You may reduce the strain on your back by adjusting your golf swing.

A backswing that minimizes the difference between shoulder rotation and hip rotation will also help reduce the amount of rotation and resulting back strain. A follow-through during which your spine is perpendicular to the ground is much gentler on your back than the reverse-C finish—in which extreme overextension puts a large load on your spine. As you hyperextend your spine, the facet joints are stressed and may cause irritation, inflammation, and, ultimately, degeneration or acceleration of underlying arthritis in these joints.

Spinal fractures may occur in golfers who have osteoporosis (fragile bones), an important factor considering how many postmenopausal women play golf. During your golf swing the lower back (lumbar spine) undergoes a compressive load about eight times that of your body weight, which may be enough to cause spinal compression fractures if you have osteoporosis. Many women have the disease and don't know it. So check with your physician if you are postmenopausal, have had a hysterectomy, or if you are an endurance athlete who experienced amenorrhea (cessation of menstrual periods) for an extended period of time.

Golfers can also suffer upper back pain from stress fractures of the ribs. Weakness in the group of muscles overlying the front of the ribs (the serratus anterior) is believed to cause muscle fatigue that eventually may lead to a stress fracture. The leading rib muscles are almost constantly active throughout the golf swing and thus may become fatigued. Diagnosis is relatively straightforward with x-rays or a comprehensive bone scan. Treatment is similar to that of other stress fractures, including relative rest, nonsteroidal anti-inflammatory drugs (NSAIDs), and muscle strengthening.

Most back problems, however, are simply muscle or ligament strains, which usually get better in a few weeks with rest, NSAIDs, and some simple strengthening exercises. Changing technique and equipment can help you if you have chronic back pain and still want to play, although it's important to remember that pain is a symptom that something is wrong. You would be wise to undergo examination by an orthopedist.

Check out the newer, longer golf clubs. They may allow your body to remain closer to an upright position and help relieve stress on your back.

GOLFER'S ELBOW

The elbow is the second most commonly injured area in golf. If you experience pain on the inside of your elbow, it may be due to excessively tight grip and/or poor backswing and follow-through. You've probably heard of tennis elbow (lateral epicondylitis), an inflammation of the tendons that connect some of your forearm muscles to your elbow. These tendons actually extend or cock upward your wrist extensors. Golfer's elbow (medial epicondylitis) is an inflammation of the forearm muscles that flex down the wrist (wrist flexors). The incidence increases with age and frequency of play. More than two to three rounds per week can lead to golfer's elbow. The disorder is most often associated with overuse and excessive grip tension. Proper grip tension optimizes the function of your forearm muscles, allowing smooth, rapid rotation and reduced stress on the wrist tendons at the elbow.

Your doctor will probably suggest that you take stress off your forearm and elbow while playing. You may be able to do this by changing your swing. For example, if you are right-handed, swing with your left elbow bent. If you are left-handed, bend your right elbow when you swing. This classic swing technique puts less stress on your elbow. Particularly important is correct swing plane—the plane that the club shaft describes during the backswing and downswing. If it is too steep (too close to perpendicular to the ground), the hands and wrists overcompensate to position the head for ball impact, increasing the risk of hitting it fat, which means striking the ground a bit behind the ball so that the velocity of the club head is significantly slowed by the time it actually makes contact with the ball. The ball does propel away from where you are standing—but it doesn't go very far. A fat shot usually results from dipping your head during the downswing. But it can also result from overly stiffening the left elbow just before contact. When you hit the ground instead of the ball, you can send a bad force into your upper body, which can cause many types of injuries, including acute golfer's elbow and inflamed tendons in the shoulder. I have even treated golfers with rotator cuff tears that resulted from fat shots.

Changing equipment may help. Flexible golf shafts are made of materials that absorb shock that would otherwise travel through your upper extremities. Using cavity-backed irons that have larger heads and sweet spots will dampen the vibrations transmitted to the wrists and forearms from off-center hits. Graphite shafts are more flexible than steel shafts and will reduce vibrations from hitting fat shots. A professional golf shop can help you select club heads and shafts based on your swing.

Two common therapies for golfer's elbow are larger club grips and wearing a brace. Many authorities believe the braces do not help. The effectiveness of larger club grips is still unclear; they do not change muscle activity or relieve symptoms. Neither therapy will change your swing mechanics, which may be what's causing your elbow problems. The forearm braces may reduce the stress that reaches the elbow, but there is no firm evidence to prove it. In my opinion, the best therapies are prevention—flexibility and strength of the forearm muscles as well as a good swing technique and good equipment—and aggressive stretching of the forearm muscles if you do develop golfer's elbow. (See Chapter 21.)

SHOULDER PAIN

If you have shoulder pain, it is usually caused by overuse rather than any specific component of your swing. During your golf swing, your leading shoulder is subject to an extreme range of motion, from internal rotation and adduction across your body at the top of your backswing to abduction and external rotation at the end of your follow-through. This range increases the risk of injury, particularly to the acromioclavicular (AC) joint at the top of the shoulder. In contrast to an acute tear of the ligaments surrounding the AC joint (as when you crash on your mountain bike), the AC joint is subject to degenerative changes or arthritis after enough repetitive stress across it. The stresses in golf are greatest at the top of the backswing and at the end of the follow-through.

Just where and when your shoulder hurts can offer your doctor diagnostic clues. Impingement of the rotator cuff or bursitis (inflammation of the bursa) generally produces pain in the front (anterior) or side (lateral) area of the shoulder and may be painful at night as well as during a game. Pain in the back of your shoulder may be caused by shoulder capsule tightness—scarring in the back capsule (ligaments) of your shoulder that limits internal rotation.

One way to reduce the stress on the AC joint of the leading shoulder without sacrificing club head speed is to shorten the swing by ending the backswing with the club head at a one or two o'clock instead of a three o'clock position. Conditioning the rotator cuff and scapular muscles with light weights or other resistance training may also help. With the help of a golf pro to ensure proper mechanics, developing a grooved swing can also be useful. To generate power, you should strengthen the chest and back muscles. The back muscles (latissimus dorsi) are very large muscles and they bring your arms toward your body.

WRIST AND HAND INJURIES

Your wrist position changes rapidly during the golf swing. At the moment of impact, the leading wrist is turned and contributes to your club's speed.

Wrist injuries are among the most common mishaps in golf. Weakness in your forearms, wrists, and hands will prevent you from having adequate wrist control during your swing. Whether excessive wrist motion is a cause or a result of injury remains unclear. Nevertheless, strengthening the forearm muscles to help reduce undue wrist motion during the swing could bring relief or prevent problems altogether.

Holding a golf club requires a relaxed grip and wrist rotation as well as repetitive use of your thumb. In golf, turning your lead wrist may stress its tendons as you hit the ball. In addition, you may prematurely uncock your wrist at the beginning of the downswing rather than during the acceleration and ball-strike phase. This can trap your leading thumb between your trailing hand and shaft and stress your wrist tendons. This faulty maneuver may also lead to carpal tunnel syndrome. (See Chapter 21.)

Trigger Finger (Stenosing Tenosynovitis)

This problem may occur in your leading hand because of excessive grip tension that can irritate the tendons of your index finger. A larger, softer grip may help prevent too tight a grasp and reduce flexion of your index finger. If this measure fails, using a neutral grip rather than a strong grip may change the placement of the club in your palm and reduce the irritation of the finger's tendon.

Golfer's Wrist

Hamate fractures account for about 2 percent of all sports-related wrist fractures—but 33 percent of these fractures are golf related. The hamate is a hooked bone in the wrist on the same side as the pinky finger. (See Figure 21.3.) This injury is usually caused by a fat shot, especially one in which the club head strikes a relatively heavy or immovable object, such as a rock or root. The butt of the club is forced against the lower inside of the palm of the leading hand, breaking the hamate's hook. This injury causes the golfer pain when she flexes her ring and little finger to grip the club. Golfers usually do not seek immediate attention because symptoms are often vague. This common fracture, which causes chronic hand and wrist pain, often goes undiagnosed for several weeks to months. Persistent pain, especially with range of motion and grasping, may send them to a doctor.

To prevent a hamate fracture you'll need clubs of the proper length with correctly sized grips. The butt of the club should extend slightly beyond the palm of the leading hand rather than dig into the soft bump of your palm on the same side of your hand as your pinky finger.

PLAYING WELL

As with any sport, it pays to warm up. Stretch beforehand focusing on the neck, shoulders, arms, and back. You can also swing your club back and forth to loosen your upper body. The best way for golfers to stretch their muscles and avoid injury is sometimes considered old-fashioned. Before your round of golf, engage in some simple stretching exercises. Then get a bucket of balls and hit a few on the driving range. It not only will help your game, it will make you healthier in the long run. Touring professionals, whose muscles are conditioned to play golf, often hit a few balls before a game to loosen up. The average weekend golfer typically starts out with the hardest swing of the day—the drive off the first tee.

STRENGTH TRAINING FOR GOLF

Strength training is exercise that uses resistance—for example, free weights—to strengthen and condition your muscles and bones, thereby improving muscular strength, power, and endurance. The benefits of golf-specific strength training are improved power for more club-head speed, stronger muscles and tendons, decreased risk of injury, corrected muscular imbalances, improved stability for more consistency, better quality practice and play, and much more.

FLEXIBILITY FOR GOLF

Flexibility training will help you make bigger backswings and hit more consistent shots. When you are flexible, your joints can move through a full range of motion. The benefits of a stretching program for golf include improved range of motion in backswing and improved technique. The muscles and joints will suffer fewer strains while in optimal golf positions. Flexible golfers also have better muscle coordination, posture, and golf performance as well as decreased risk of injury, muscle soreness, and low back pain.

HEARTBEATS FOR GOLF

The benefits of cardiovascular exercise for golf include reduced fatigue and improved performance, muscle soreness prevention, improved concentration, decreased body fat, and weight management. Because golf is not an aerobic activity, it has always been considered as a leisure game. However, golf often involves walking four to five miles. A round of golf can take more than four hours to complete. If you do not participate in cardiovascular training off the course, your game will suffer. Are you able to play 18 or even 9 holes without becoming too fatigued? Aerobic capacity is your body's ability to use oxygen for longer periods of time. Aerobic exercises will help not only your heart, but also your game. You will be less fatigued, improve your performance, and reduce muscle soreness if you train aerobically.

The older you are, the more likely it is that you have lost some cardiovascular efficiency. The direct result is a decrease in coordination due to mental fatigue. Bringing more oxygen to your brain through aerobic exercise will enable you to concentrate better, as well as lose body fat and reduce your weight. Doing two to three aerobic sessions each week will improve your golf performance. Most pros on tour do four to five aerobic workout sessions each week—and that's while playing in a tournament.

WHY GOLF IS GOOD FOR YOU

While golf is not played for fitness, it does benefit your body. You will help yourself get fit if you walk the course instead of using a golf cart. The five-plus miles you walk will allow you to expend a moderate number of calories and improve your cardiovascular health. Carrying your clubs will help you build your upper body strength. Golf also improves your hand-eye coordination.

The game can be socially and emotionally fulfilling—and sometimes incredibly frustrating, especially for beginners. However, one good swing or shot always keeps a golfer coming back for another day. Between walking 18 holes and waiting for everyone to finish each hole, you have plenty of time to chat with your companions. You can also play by yourself and concentrate on your own game while enjoying the outdoors.

SOME MISCELLANEOUS HINTS

It's easy to understand why millions of females have become enthusiastic golfers. You can play this sport in beautiful surroundings with as many people as you like for as long as you like—even at a very advanced age. To add to your enjoyment and safety:

- Choose appropriate attire: skirts, shorts or slacks, hats, visors, or sunglasses.
- Always wear sunscreen.
- Select clubs that are the correct length and grip size for you.
- Choose golf bags, tees, and golf balls that are the right weight and size for you.

As pointed out throughout this chapter, most golf injuries are related to the golfer's technique and equipment. If you have an ideal swing, you will have a successful performance while producing little stress to your body. Professionals usually do not have as many injuries as amateur golfers because they play with better form. A few lessons from your local golf pro may help you improve your swing and avoid injury. However, beware of trying to swing exactly as the pros do. They have conditioned their bodies to tolerate a swing that may be very wrong for you. If you have some injuries that hamper your golf game, seek professional help so you can continue playing this great (and often addictive) sport.

For further information check out these resources:

GOLF.COM
This website offers complete coverage, results, and feature stories, about women golfers.

PROFESSIONAL GOLF ASSOCIATION OF AMERICA (PGA)
PGA.com/women
Founded in 1916, the PGA annually conducts four premier golf events. It is the largest sports organization in the world, comprised of more than 27,000 men and women promoting the game of golf.

LADIES PROFESSIONAL GOLF ASSOCIATION (LPGA)
lpga.com
This website provides news, features, tournament-by-tournament coverage, and schedules.

WOMEN'S GOLF TODAY (WGT)
16629 Lescot Terrace
Rockville, MD 20853
Telephone: (301) 570-7979
This organization is designed for women interested in golf and associated activities.

15

WEIGHT TRAINING

Gaining Strength

WEIGHT TRAINING IS A HIGHLY EFFECTIVE way to improve your abilities within your sport and to prevent sports injuries. It also helps you in your daily life when you have to lift toddlers or heavy bags. In 2001, women outnumbered men in health clubs and fitness centers across the United States, according to a report from the International Health, Racquet and Sports Club Association. Women's membership in this group has grown 81 percent since 1987, while men's has grown 71 percent. Women outnumber men in barbell-based group strength-training classes.

Weight training uses resistance exercises with weights to increase strength and muscle mass. When I used to train hard I worked out five to six days a week. I alternated body parts so that each muscle group would have at least 48 hours to recover. For instance I would work my back, biceps, and hamstrings one day and my chest, triceps, and quadriceps the next. Visible results will be different for each female, but most see some positive results of weight training after about three weeks. Weight training is a great way to burn fat too. More muscle mass increases your metabolism, which means you can burn more fat throughout the day with normal activities. Weightlifting is a weight-bearing exercise and is also important to build strong bones and decrease the risk of osteoporosis.

You don't have to develop into an Arnold Schwarzenegger. It's never too late to start. Daylle Deanna Schwartz, a New Yorker and author of *All Men*

Are Jerks Until Proven Otherwise (Adams Media, 1999), is a recent convert to weight training.

"I read that as women get older, they're so concerned with their skin and bones, they ignore their muscles, which can contribute to their overall well-being," Daylle says. "I'm very health conscious and wanted to get into better shape. I saw a TV show about slow motion weight training and found a gym that does it.

"It's like concentrated weight training done once a week with a trainer. I began with fairly heavy weights. The technique is to lift *very* slowly and smoothly. I call it yoga–weight training because I use breathing and concentration to keep the weights going. There's no momentum allowed. No rest. Doing the weight machines in slow motion is *very* hard and painful. My trainer pushes me when I can't do any more, and I do another. The slow motion puts the most strain on muscles in the least amount of time. I've read it's the fastest way to build muscle. Now that I've built up my body, I'm working out on my own in a regular gym."

Daylle says that weight training has helped her lose weight, stay fit, and relieve stress. Has she injured herself weight training? "No, but I'm careful. I often hurt for a few days after but that's normal," she says.

If possible, you should have a qualified person to help you learn the techniques of safe weight training, as Daylle did, because lifting weights improperly can lead to muscle and tendon tears, joint pain, and shoulder and knee injuries.

BENEFITS OF WEIGHT TRAINING

Over the last decade, researchers have begun emphasizing the benefits of weight training for women including those over 50. Research studies have demonstrated that even moderate weight training can increase a woman's strength by 30 to 50 percent and that women can develop their strength at the same rate as men. Another benefit that may intrigue you is how weight training can slim you down. Wayne Westcott, Ph.D., of the South Shore YMCA in Quincy, Massachusetts, found that the average woman who strength trains two to three times a week for two months will gain nearly two pounds of muscle and will lose 3.5 pounds of fat. As your lean muscle increases so does your resting metabolism, and you burn more calories all day long. Generally speaking, for each pound of muscle you gain, you burn 35 to 50 more calories each day.

Many women fear that they will bulk up and look like Mr. America but such fears are for the most part unfounded. Women don't have as much of the hormone that causes big muscles as males do. Unfortunately, there are some females who unwisely take steroids and other supplements to increase their muscles—this is a dangerous and potentially lethal practice. You can gain strength and muscle naturally without jeopardizing your health.

Research has also found that weight training can increase spinal bone mineral density (and enhance bone modeling) by 13 percent in six months. This, coupled with an adequate amount of dietary calcium, can help prevent bone fragility (osteoporosis).

Softball or tennis players will be able to smack the ball harder with weight training. Golfers can significantly increase their driving power. In fact, whatever sport you play, weight training can improve your performance as well as decrease the risk of injury. Strength training builds not only stronger muscles, but also stronger connective tissue, which acts as reinforcement to increase joint stability. This helps prevent injury. If done carefully, weight training can ease the pain of osteoarthritis.

PRECAUTIONS

Weight training is not without risk, especially for unsupervised beginners. Weight training may be dangerous if performed improperly or without supervision. It is important first to ask your doctor if a weight-training program is right for you. There are medical problems that could keep you out of the weight room. If you have a history of back problems, herniated disks, high blood pressure, or hernias, you must talk to your physician at length before engaging in a weight-training program.

There are many injuries common in weightlifting. You can injure any body part if you are not warmed up and flexible before your lifts or if you overdo it. The "no pain no gain" attitude can get you into a lot of trouble.

The most common complaint I see coming out of the gym is shoulder pain. Shoulder impingement and bursitis are common overuse injuries (see Chapter 21) in women who perform a lot of upper body weightlifting. Power lifters who push tremendous amounts of weight can injure the AC joint, developing distal clavicle osteolysis, which can lead to arthritis in this small shoulder joint. The treatment is usually nonoperative but I have seen a couple of cases where surgery was necessary. Back injuries are common, especially if your form is poor or if your abdominal muscles are weak. Any muscle that you are working can become strained if you overdo it. Be cautious and wise. The best preventative measures include the following.

- Get instruction so that you will learn good form.
- Start light on all lifts and gradually increase them as your strength increases.
- Warm up aerobically for 15 to 20 minutes (e.g., using a treadmill or taking an aerobics class).
- Stretch all of your major muscle groups.
- Wear a weight belt.
- Strengthen your abdominals at the end of your workout.

As with any exercise, always warm up before you start lifting weights. I recommend warming up on an exercise bike first to warm up the muscles and tendons to make stretching more effective. Then stretch for at least 10 minutes before you start lifting. Don't use weights that are too heavy for your training stage and don't overdo your sessions. Your body has to adapt to the increased stresses. Lift and lower your weights slowly. Exhale as you lift the weight and inhale as you lower the weight. Use a comfortable range of motion throughout the movement. Keep good posture in your spine during lifting whether you are standing, sitting, or lying down.

COMPETITIVE WEIGHTLIFTING

Some women athletes are into competitive weightlifting. In fact, weightlifting became an Olympic event for women for the first time in 2000. You can snatch, clean and jerk, and dead lift barbells if you wish. You must have proper supervision at all times. Be wary of muscle pulls, ruptured disks, knee problems, and shoulder and neck injuries. Stretch fatigued muscles immediately following a weightlifting session. This not only helps to increase flexibility, but also enhances muscular development, and will actually help decrease the level of postexercise soreness. (See Chapter 23.)

FINDING A FACILITY

You can work out at home or in a gym or health club. At home, unless you are financially well off, you probably won't have the advantage of weight machines, but you can use free weights. A word of warning: It can be very dangerous to lift free weights without a spotter, especially when bench pressing or heavy squatting. When you lift, do it with a buddy.

If you opt for a gym, figure out your schedule and pinpoint the time of day when you will be able to work out consistently. Choose a gym that has a comfortable atmosphere. Make sure it is clean and properly equipped. Most gyms now will have weightlifting machines, but the quality will vary. There should be some qualified instructors around willing to give you advice.

For more information, check out these resources:

NATIONAL STRENGTH AND CONDITIONING ASSOCIATION
1955 North Union Blvd.
Colorado Springs, CO 80905
Telephone: (719) 632-NSCA
E-mail: ncsa@nsca-lift.org
nsca-lift.org/menu.htm
Membership in this organization is comprised of strength and conditioning coaches, personal trainers, exercise physiologists, athletic trainers, researchers, educators, sport coaches, physical therapists, business owners, exercise instructors, fitness directors, and students training to enter the field. It offers the only two nationally accredited certification programs in this area.

USA WEIGHTLIFTING (USAW)
One Olympic Plaza
Colorado Springs, CO 80909-5764
Telephone: (719) 866-4508
usaweightlifting.org
USAW is the national governing body for Olympic weightlifting in the United States and is a member of the International Weightlifting Federation (IWF). It conducts a variety of programs to develop Olympic, World Championship, and Pan American Games winners on the junior and senior levels.

16

GYMNASTICS AND CHEERLEADING

Twist, Tumble, and Shout

IN THE UNITED STATES TODAY more than 600,000 children take part in school-sponsored and club-level gymnastics competitions. Some gymnasts start training as early as four or five years old, and they practice for several hours each day. The average age of champions and Olympic gold medal winners has gone down significantly over the past 20 years. And with this trend of greater and earlier gymnastics participation has come an increased level of training.

Cheerleading has also changed dramatically over the past 20 or so years. Females not only cheer a team on, they take part in a competitive sport that includes nearly 1.5 million participants. Cheerleading routines may include gymnastic elements, tumbling runs, partner stunts, pyramid formations, and dance routines. There are regional and national competitions, and training is a year-round activity.

Both gymnastics and cheerleading can help participants build skills, coordination, strength, and self-esteem. These sports can often cause injuries, however, so it's a good idea to look at the risks as well as the benefits.

GYMNASTICS

The junior elite female gymnast—10 to 14 years old—trains, on average, 5.04 hours per day, 5.36 days per week. Unfortunately, mounting evidence suggests that the processes of growth, particularly those associated with periods of rapid development, render the young female gymnast more susceptible to injury than the postpubescent.

Injuries and Gymnastics

In a study of high school athletes, gymnastics was the fourth leading cause of injury, with a rate of 56 percent. Club gymnastics programs had a rate of injury as high as 22 percent. Gymnastics activities on bars and beams appear to present the greatest risks.

The majority of gymnastics-related injuries are mild to moderate. The most common are sprains, strains, and stress fractures. Ankles and knees are the usual sites of injury, typically resulting from faulty dismounts and landings. Injuries to the lower back are also common. Although acute injuries are rarely severe, as many as half of all injuries lead to chronic pain and bone fractures, which may in turn cause long-term physical problems.

Floor exercises are the most frequent source of injury because of the number of bends, twists, and landings required in those routines. Trying moves that are too complicated for one's skill level, failing to use safety harnesses or spotters, getting overtired, and spending long hours practicing contribute to the high rates of injury. The Consumer Product Safety Commission (CPSC) encourages schools to consider alternative program options to replace high-risk activities.

Further research is needed as to whether a young gymnast's growth is stunted by the tough exercise and diet restrictions required to be the best in gymnastics. Certainly it is a point of controversy. Some researchers say growth is not affected but others maintain that many young gymnasts will never reach their full height potential.

Gymnasts' ankle injuries are extremely common in my practice. The stress on the ankle joint with dismounts and tumbling can be significant, and if there is any error in a landing, ligament injuries or even fractures can occur. When I do preparticipation physicals for junior high, high school, and even college students, I am very likely to find some degree of ankle instability from multiple ankle injuries in the past. These repetitive injuries may be mild, but they can also be cumulative over the years. The gymnast may not necessarily seek medical treatment or advice. I recommend intensive physical therapy and bracing/taping for these girls to help prevent further injury. Sometimes surgery is necessary to stabilize the ankle. (See Chapter 22.)

Low back injuries frequently occur in gymnasts because of the excessive bending that occurs with multiple maneuvers that involve the uneven bars, floor routines, and the balance beam. An orthpedist should be consulted for lower back pain that lasts for more than a couple of weeks. Overuse injuries can actually be stress fractures in the spine and these can be serious if left untreated. Most of these injuries can be treated without surgery if the diagnosis is made early. In addition to low back pain, symptoms include tight hamstrings; pain radiating into the legs; numbness or tingling radiating into the legs; pain at night or after activities; and stiffness or pain in the back, especially with bending. If you have some of the above signs, do not try to treat this yourself or with your coach, see a specialist for a diagnosis and an appropriate treatment plan.

Tips for Preventing Gymnastics Injuries

To help girls avoid gymnastics injuries, here are some safety tips from the American Academy of Pediatrics, the American Academy of Orthopaedic Surgeons, the National Safe Kids Campaign, and other sports and health organizations.

Before a girl starts a gymnastics training program, she should have a physical exam including muscle and bone screening and maturity assessment. She should wear all the required safety gear every time she competes or practices. Gymnasts may need handgrips; wrist, ankle, or torso belts; knee, elbow, or heel pads; braces (ankle, knee, elbow, wrist); and sweat bands, socks, or tights. Depending on the activity, the performing surface, and the experience of the gymnast, a variety of footwear options are available, including bare feet, cotton socks, special gymnastic shoes, and athletic shoes. A gymnast may need certain apparel and equipment for each event.

Coaches should emphasize safety and understand the special injury risks that young gymnasts face. A teacher who is unfamiliar with any gymnastics equipment should seek assistance from appropriate support staff and refrain from using the equipment until he or she receives the proper guidance.

Equipment should be in good condition and spaced far enough apart to avoid the accidental collision of gymnasts with equipment or other athletes during workouts. The training facility should have appropriate floor padding to help reduce the force from a landing. Mats should be secured under every apparatus. Safety harnesses should be used when a child does new or difficult moves.

Skills are best taught in a progression from simple to complex. Mat work precedes use of equipment. Landings should be performed with control on the floor before working from an elevated surface. Students who demonstrate control of basic movement patterns can then go on to more complicated skills.

Spotting is manual assistance provided for gymnasts while they are performing skills on the floor or on equipment. Some feel that if a student needs spotting, it could be an indication she lacks the physical or motor skills to perform the exercise. Rather than have the student attempt the skill with a spotter, more activities that lead up to the skill might be provided. This approach prevents gymnasts from becoming dependent on a spotter. Spotting is not, in general, recommended for grammar school gymnasts. On the other hand, if a child is a serious competitive gymnast, she may certainly need a spotter when learning new skills or performing difficult moves.

Don't force girls to perform skills beyond their level of ability. When a girl displays hesitation, discuss her reason(s). After the discussion, if the coach or teacher believes that a potential hesitancy during performance of the skill could put the student at risk, the student can be directed toward a more basic skill.

A girl should be taught how to fall and land safely in a variety of situations. Many injuries that occur in gymnastics—and in other physical activities—are the result of landing incorrectly.

A girl should *not* perform through pain. Watching girl gymnasts in the Olympics struggling to complete their routines with injuries such as a badly sprained ankle, can give the wrong message—not only for this sport, but also for all competitive athletics. Peer pressure and the economic and social pressures to win may lead coaches to decisions that are not in the best interests of a girl's health, growth, and development. When injury does occur, a girl must follow her doctor's orders for recovery before she returns to the sport.

Reduce training loads for gymnasts experiencing a growth spurt, as indicated by height charts and/or maturity assessment information. When height measures and periodic checkups show that the temporary physiologic imbalance has abated, the gymnast can resume normal training levels.

Special Concern

Improper diet and eating disorders, such as anorexia nervosa and bulimia, present special concerns among female gymnasts as well as the participants of any sport that emphasizes being slim. (See "The Female Athlete Triad" in the Introduction.)

CHEERLEADING

High school and college cheerleaders account for almost one-half of the catastrophic injuries to female athletes.

How Dangerous Is Cheerleading?

A controversy exists over just how dangerous cheerleading really is. The CPSC reported an estimated 4,954 hospital emergency room visits in 1980. By 1994, that number had grown to more than 16,000—although it should also be stated that the number of cheerleading participants has increased dramatically.

Mark R. Hutchinson, M.D., is director of the sports medicine service in the department of orthopedics at the University of Illinois at Chicago (UIC). He serves as team physician for the UIC Flames and the USA Rhythmic Gymnastics national team. He caused quite a stir when he wrote about the risk of cheerleading injuries in *The Physician and Sportsmedicine*, in September 1997. He noted that compared with other sports, cheerleading carries a relatively low risk of injury, but the injuries that do occur tend to be comparatively severe in terms of time lost. He noted that a part of "time lost" may be because cheerleading requires the use of all the extremities, and that, unlike a football player, a cheerleader cannot simply tape up a sprain or participate while in a wrist cast.

Dr. Hutchinson points out that cheerleading differs from many other sports because it is a year-round activity—cheerleaders are asked to perform through three seasons, and then peak for national competitions in the spring. This constant in-season state does not allow appropriate time for recuperation or conditioning, which magnifies the risk of overuse injuries.

When Injuries Occur

The sport of cheerleading also requires the athlete to participate in a variety of activities, including dances, chants and yells, gymnastic tumbling runs, and partner stunts. Partner stunts include human pyramids, lifts and catches, and human tosses (basket tosses). Most injuries in cheerleading occur during gymnastics maneuvers and partner stunts.

The dance component of cheerleading is associated with injuries common in modern dance and ballet. These include overuse injuries of the legs such as tendonitis, ligament sprains of the foot and ankle, stress fractures, knee problems, and hip strains. (See Chapter 22.)

Injuries in the gymnastics component of cheerleading mimic injury patterns for gymnasts. Common overuse injuries include those of the shoulders, wrists, and elbows because the arms are used for weight bearing. Ankle and knee ligament injuries can occur in the landing and impact phase of tumbling runs during cheerleading routines. Low back injuries may occur because of repeated back bending.

Athletes at the base of pyramids or partner lifts require significant upper body strength. Muscle and bone failure or injury can occur in any part of the body during these stunts, but it seems to be more frequent in the arm and shoulder. In athletes who serve as bases in partner stunts, the greater incidence of arm injuries in girls compared with boys may be associated with girls' lesser upper body strength. Because of the risk of falls from mounts, athletes at the tops of pyramids and lifts run the greatest risk of catastrophic injury, fractures, and dislocations.

The National Center for Catastrophic Sports Injury Research collected cheerleading catastrophic injury data between 1982 and 2000 and found, for example, that in 1986 a college female cheerleader died from multiple skull fractures and massive brain damage after falling from the top of a pyramid stunt and striking her head on the gym floor. A middle school cheerleader was injured in October 1991 and died the next week; she fell from a double-level cheerleading stance during practice and hit her head on the gym floor. A college cheerleader was paralyzed in April 1995 after being injured while performing a double flip during a basket toss; she is now a quadriplegic. A high school cheerleader suffered a 15-foot fall in 1997 and is now paralyzed. These types of injuries, while not common, serve as a sober reminder of the dangers of the sport.

How Cheerleading Injuries Can Be Prevented

Cheerleading injuries have been attributed to lack of experience, inadequate conditioning, insufficient supervision, difficult stunts, inappropriate surfaces and equipment, poor nutrition, and poor shoes.

Because cheerleading is a relatively new sport, prevention measures are only now being put into regulations, and certification of coaches is in progress. A number of schools, both high schools and colleges, have now limited the types of stunts that can be attempted by their cheerleaders. After the death of a cheerleader in a pyramid stunt, the North Dakota and Minnesota legislatures, for example, banned pyramids at the high school and college levels. Illinois banned the use of basket tosses at the high school level after a similar catastrophic event. The Illinois State High School Association rules state, "Cheerleaders cannot toss another squad member into the air during any part of a cheer, performance, routine, or other activity." Illinois has also banned pyramid formations higher than two levels. Safety guidelines for cheerleaders vary tremendously from state to state, school to school, and organization to organization.

Decisions to abolish certain stunts, however, have been controversial. Many cheerleaders and school personnel believe it is unfair to participants in the affected areas: Without experience in certain stunts, the argument goes, athletes cannot compete for college scholarships or expect to win national events.

Fourteen states consider cheerleading a sport and organize state championship competitions. Nine other states organize cheerleading championships as a school activity. More than 74,000 girls currently participate in competitions.

The following precautions that reduce the risk of cheerleading injuries evolved from information published by Dr. Hutchinson, the CPSC experts, coaches, and the American Academy of Orthopaedic Surgeons.

- Cheerleaders should be trained by a qualified coach with training in gymnastics and partner stunting. This person should also be knowledgeable about proper methods for spotting and other safety factors.
- Cheerleading coaches should have some type of safety certification. The American Association of Cheerleading Coaches and Advisors (aacca.com) offers this certification.
- Cheerleaders should be exposed to appropriate conditioning programs and trained in good spotting techniques.
- Progression to difficult skills should be gradual and cheerleaders should receive adequate training before attempting gymnastic-type stunts and should not attempt stunts they are not capable of completing. A qualification system demonstrating mastery of stunts is recommended.
- Coaches should supervise all practice sessions in a safe facility.
- Mini-trampolines and flips or falls off of pyramids and shoulders should be prohibited.
- Pyramids over two levels high should not be performed. Two-level pyramids should not be performed without mats and other safety precautions.

When a cheerleader has experienced or shown signs of head trauma (loss of consciousness, visual disturbances, headache, inability to walk correctly, obvious disorientation, memory loss), she should receive immediate medical attention and not be allowed to practice or cheer without permission from the proper medical authorities.

For more information, see these resources:

U.S.A. Gymnastics
usa-gymnatics.org

The national governing body for gymnastics in the United States, it sets the rules and policies governing this sport. It selects and trains the U.S. gymnastics teams for the Olympics and World Championships.

AMERICAN GYMNASTICS ASSOCIATION
tumble.org
This group is dedicated to the development of artistic gymnastics for girls.

VARSITY.COM
The National Federation of State High School Associations and the Varsity Spirit Corporation (the United States' largest cheerleading organization) have teamed up to develop educational programs for the nation's school spirit leaders and their coaches.

AMERICAN ASSOCIATION OF CHEERLEADING COACHES AND ADVISORS (AACCA)
6745 Lenox Center Court, Suite 318
Memphis, TN 38115
Telephone: (800) 533-6583
aacca.org
This is a nonprofit educational association for the more than fifty thousand cheerleading coaches across the United States. Founded in 1988, it is dedicated to the safe and responsible practice of student cheerleading.

ATHLETICS FOR LIFE

17

GIRLS ON THE GO

GIRLS ARE NOT LITTLE WOMEN. There are marked differences between the two in terms of coordination, strength, and stamina. In girls, bone-tendon-muscle units, growth areas within bones, and ligaments experience uneven growth patterns, which leaves them susceptible to injury. What might be a bruise or sprain in a woman can be a potentially serious growth-plate injury for a girl, as this chapter will show.

ALL GIRLS ARE NOT ALIKE

Girls are different from women, but they are also different from each other. Girls of the same age can differ greatly in size and physical maturity. Increases in body size may be due to fat and not muscle; this can cause marked differences in strength. Therefore, there is always the possibility that a girl who is physically less mature than her peers may attempt to perform a sport at a level for which she is not ready. Parents and athletic coaches, therefore, should try to group youngsters according to skill level and size, not chronological age, particularly during contact sports.

Today more girls enjoy sports than ever before. Twenty-five percent of girls between the ages of eight and sixteen compete in an organized sports program sometime during the year. Beyond organized sports programs, millions of girls compete and participate in physical education classes, church and community intramural programs, and other recreational athletic activities. Athletics offers a fun way for girls to get physically fit, avoid obesity, socialize, keep out of trouble, and feel good about themselves. That said, a girl should not be pushed into a sport if she is not ready or doesn't want to participate.

In general a girl should be at least seven or eight years old before enrolling in organized team sports. A lot depends on the child, but many team sports involve contact, and most girls under age seven are not ready for rough play. They are not only vulnerable to physical injuries, but emotionally they may not be able to handle winning or losing. Girls under seven might instead be encouraged to participate in hopscotch, Frisbee, or jump rope. Swimming is an asset a young girl will use for the rest of her life—and it will make her safer in the water. Tag, karate, kickball, dancing, skiing, ice skating, and gymnastics are also good sports for under-sevens.

Most experts agree that a good time to introduce competitive sports for girls is between the ages of eight and twelve. Appropriate sports are softball, biking, basketball, field hockey/ice hockey, soccer, tennis, lacrosse, ice skating, and hiking. Distance running should be postponed until the teenage years. Even then, track programs for middle school–age children—sixth to eighth grade—usually limit running distances to a half to three-quarters of a mile at a time.

Young female athletes have special needs. Because their bodies are growing, they often require different coaching, conditioning, and medical care than more mature athletes. One of the most important differences between girls and women has to do with growth plates. The growth plate (physis) regulates and helps determine the length and shape of the mature bone. The long bones of the body do not grow from the center outward. Instead, growth occurs at each end of the bone around the growth plate, an area of developing tissue. The growth plate is the last portion of the bone to harden, which means it is extremely vulnerable to fracture. Because muscles and bones develop at different speeds, a child's bones may be weaker than the surrounding connective tissues. When a woman twists her knee, she most likely will injure a ligament (tissue connecting bone to bone). A child with the same twist will more likely injure or fracture her growth plate.

Although all children who are still growing are at risk, girls between the ages of 11 and 12 are especially vulnerable. Approximately 30 percent of all growth-plate injuries occur in competitive sports, such as soccer, basketball, or gymnastics. About 20 percent of growth-plate fractures happen during recreational activities such as biking, sledding, skiing, or skateboarding. Fractures can result from a single traumatic event—a fall or crash into another player—or from chronic stress and overuse. Many growth-plate fractures occur in the long bones of the fingers and the larger bone (radius) of the forearm. They are also common in the lower bones of the leg—especially in skiing and hockey.

I treated 12-year-old Julie who toppled while in-line skating. She was not wearing wrist guards, and she tried to use her hand to break her fall. She fractured her growth plate instead. Julie had significant pain, swelling within one hour of her accident, and difficulty moving her wrist. She did not have any prior history of wrist injury. Upon examination, her wrist was tender and swollen. Her x-rays were negative for a fracture but I did diagnose her with a broken growth plate because this type of injury cannot be seen on x-ray unless it extends into the bone. Certainly, Julie may have just had a bad bruise, but with the swelling and tenderness at the area of the growth plate, I had to assume it was broken. In cases like this, it's better to be safe than sorry.

Julie wore a cast for four weeks and healed well. She regained full range of motion, strength, and function quickly and without formal physical therapy and returned to in-line skating (with wrist guards).

Every bone in the body matures at a different rate. Some growth plates are still open in the late teens where other bones close in the early teens. Crushing of the growth plate is a more severe type of fracture, which almost always causes growth disturbances. If there is only a little growth left in that particular bone (in a 13-year-old for example), then the disturbance may go unnoticed because the bone is about to stop growing anyway. If injury occurs in a seven-year-old who still has a lot of growing to do, it can be devastating and lead to a shortened or severely angled bone. Any girl who experiences an injury that results in visible deformity, persistent or severe pain, or an inability to move or put pressure on a limb should be examined by a doctor.

Children's bones heal faster than adults'; therefore, a girl should be treated as quickly as possible before her bone begins to heal. Ideally, this means seeing an orthopedic specialist within five to seven days of the injury, especially if manipulation to align the bone is required. Otherwise, a girl with a growth-plate fracture could grow up with limbs that are crooked or unequal in length. Treatment depends upon the degree of damage to the growth plate. If the bone remains aligned, usually no surgery is required. Such fractures usually heal well. I do cast ankles and wrists but it's hard to generalize about casting a growth-plate injury, since there are so many variables, including type of bone, age of child, and severity of fracture. The period of immobilization required for healing, however, will not be as long as for a woman.

In addition to fractures, overuse injuries to the growth plates can occur from improper training, muscle imbalance, or just overdoing it. These inflammatory conditions of the growth plates are also known as apophysitis and can occur in different parts of the body. They all have fancy names. For example, Osgood-Schlatter disease is apophysitis at the upper front leg where the kneecap tendon attaches; Sinding-Larsen-Johansson syndrome is apophysitis at the lower end of the kneecap; Severs disease occurs at the heel where the Achilles tendon attaches; and Panner's disease occurs at the back of the elbow.

The most common location of growth-plate inflammation is Osgood-Schlatter disease of the knee. This is not technically a disease; it is an overuse syndrome. Repetitive pulling on the kneecap tendon will cause inflammation where it is attached to the bone and may even pull tiny pieces of the bone off. The pain will come and go based on your child's activity. If she rests, the pain will generally go away. This is most common in 10- to 13-year-olds during their growth spurts.

The earlier treatment begins, the better. Sometimes bracing and physical therapy can speed up recovery. Once a girl heals, the pain may recur on and off until her growth is complete. Many children who suffer with these overuse injuries may become more vulnerable to overuse injuries in adulthood.

Sports are never without risks. That said, the older the girl, the more at risk for injury she is. When grade-schoolers collide or fall, the forces upon their muscles and bones are usually not strong enough to cause them injury.

On the other hand, high school female athletes are bigger, faster, stronger, and capable of delivering tremendous forces in contact sports.

Coaches bear a prime responsibility in developing their young athletes and watching for early signs of physical problems (such as pain or limp). A coach can easily recognize a severe injury because the athlete is in pain and can't continue playing. The coach may have more difficulty spotting less severe injuries. Athletes often ignore low-grade pain. Repeated minor injuries, however, may turn into overuse conditions, which can put an athlete on the sidelines for the rest of the season.

TYPES OF INJURIES

Fortunately serious sports injuries are rare in young girls. About 95 percent are due to minor trauma involving soft tissues—bruises, muscle pulls, sprains (ligaments), strains (muscles and tendons), and cuts or abrasions. Sports injuries occur more frequently in physical education classes and free-play sports than in organized team sports. Injuries among athletic girls fall into two basic categories: overuse and acute.

Overuse Injuries

In the immature body, repetitive motions can cause a series of small injuries that may result in minor or long-term problems. *Little League elbow*, for instance, is the term used to describe a group of common overuse injuries in young throwers involved in many sports, not just baseball. Overtraining can overload the bone and cause stress fractures. A girl should gradually increase her training and not suddenly skip over steps to achieve a new level, such as running two miles a day and suddenly increasing to five.

Acute Injuries

These are caused by a sudden trauma such as a single, sudden twist, fall, or collision. Common acute injuries among girls include bruises, sprains (a partial or complete tear of a ligament), strains (a partial or complete tear of a muscle or tendon) and fractures. Girl athletes should have a calcium-enriched diet, especially during early adolescence when their bones are growing longitudinally and bone density may not keep pace with that growth. Peak longitudinal growth occurs at about 11.5 years. At that point, there will be a year or so when girls have relatively less dense bones and are therefore more susceptible to fractures, including stress fractures.

Teenage female athletes who take part in sports that involve a lot of running often have pain in their kneecaps. As explained many times in this book, female knees are especially vulnerable to injury. This is a particular problem with girls as they develop into womanhood. Their hips widen, causing the thigh and leg to form a slight angle at the knee instead of going straight up and down. (See Figure 1 in the Introduction.) Strength and balance are important to prevent joint injuries. (See Chapters 22 and 23.)

If a young female athlete develops a symptom that persists, is severe, or affects her athletic performance, she should be examined by an orthopedic surgeon whether her injury is acute or due to overuse. She should never be permitted to work through the pain. Prompt treatment can often prevent a minor injury from becoming a major one that causes permanent damage. Successful treatment requires cooperation and open communication among the girl, her parents, her coaches, and her doctors. Most injuries to girl athletes can be prevented with proper coaching, equipment, and knowledge—and cooperation by the athlete herself.

SPECIFIC SPORTS INJURIES

Millions of girls throughout the world play basketball. It is the most popular team sport in American high schools. It is also the leading cause of sports-related injury in the United States. Acute basketball injuries most often involve the extremities, especially the hands, wrists, ankles, and knees.

Researchers from the department of emergency medicine, Alfred I. DuPont Hospital for Children, Wilmington, Delaware; Bambi Lynne Taylor, M.D., a specialist in emergency medicine; and Magdt W. Attia, M.D., a pediatrician, did a retrospective study of sports-related injuries (SRIs) in children. The mean age of the females was 12.4 years. In addition to basketball, they studied softball, soccer, in-line skating, and hockey injuries.

In the younger group—5- to 11-year-olds—fractures were common. In the older group—12- to 18-year-olds—sprains occurred often. The most frequent injury location was wrist/hand (28 percent), followed by head/face (22 percent) and ankle/foot (18 percent). Contact with a person or object was involved in less than 50 percent of the sports-related injuries.

Female athletes should concentrate on what they love to do. If swimming is not for you, maybe skating or basketball is. Be open to new activities. If you are a girl and join a team, you have an obligation to practice and stick with it unless circumstances prevent you from participating, such as an injury or an inability to get a ride to the facility. If you are a parent, you should attend your girl's games as much as possible to provide encouragement and support. When possible, participate in fitness activities with her.

Girls' sports should always be fun. The win-at-all-costs attitude of many parents, coaches, and peers can lead to injuries. A young girl athlete striving to meet the unrealistic expectations of others may ignore the warning signs of injury and continue to play with pain. Coaches and parents can prevent injuries by fostering an atmosphere of healthy competition that emphasizes self-reliance, confidence, cooperation, and a positive self-image, rather than just winning. Exposure to competitive and noncompetitive sports builds a girl's level of fitness, motor skills, social skills, and lifelong appreciation for sports.

18

PREGNANT ATHLETES

Baby on Board

As I WRITE THIS, I AM six and a half months pregnant. I am maintaining a full schedule at my orthopedic surgical practice, and I have never felt better. I am able to work out, although I've had to back off on the intensity to feel good and take care of my developing baby.

If you are an athlete who is pregnant or considering becoming pregnant in the future, you may have some questions about exercising during this special time. Some of the answers are detailed in this chapter; however, every woman is different and you are therefore advised to check with your personal physician.

SPORTS AND PREGNANCY

Whether you are a competitive athlete or a couch potato who all of a sudden believes you should start exercising, you can go ahead—if your doctor OKs it.

As a pregnant woman, however, you must educate yourself about how your body and the baby you are carrying react to exertion during the various stages of your pregnancy. The information you will read in this chapter is *not* a substitute for the advice of your physician. It is based upon medical professionals' studies of pregnant athletes and the personal experiences of expectant female athletes.

Recommendations for exercise during pregnancy have changed and will continue to change. In the 1950s, for example, expectant mothers were advised to walk one mile per day, preferably broken up into several sessions. In 1985, the American College of Obstetrics and Gynecology (ACOG) endorsed the safety of most aerobic exercise but specified a 15-minute limit and a heart rate of 140 beats per minute. Some 10 years later, the organization issued new recommendations based on studies of women with uncomplicated pregnancies. In essence, these new recommendations said that pregnant women can exercise safely as long as they use the same safeguards they used when they were not pregnant.

The most important element is common sense. Do not overexert yourself. If you are pushing too hard, breathing too hard, or feeling light-headed, your baby is potentially being deprived of oxygen and being stressed.

Exercise will help you feel better about yourself as your body changes. It will also reduce leg cramps, constipation, bloating, and swelling. It will improve your mood, control your weight gain, and help you avoid hemorrhoids. It will also improve your posture; ease lower back pain; promote muscle tone, strength, and endurance; and help you sleep better. It will help regulate your blood sugar levels (which may reduce the risk of diabetes during pregnancy); improve your ability to cope during labor; and get you back in shape faster after giving birth.

However, you have to take precautions and make adaptations during various stages of your pregnancy, especially if you are an endurance or strength athlete or if you participate in a competitive sport. You must have meticulous medical supervision if you have a history of miscarriages or if you are carrying more than one baby. A doctor's supervision is also required if you have or develop any of the following conditions during your pregnancy: heart disease, lung problems, high blood pressure, a seizure disorder, obesity, underweight, a womb defect, or vaginal bleeding.

Even if you are in good physical condition without any of the aforementioned conditions, you still must take precautions and adjust your exercise to having a baby on board. It's not just that your belly is getting bigger. The changes that occur during pregnancy affect almost all your bodily systems.

• Your metabolism gets faster during pregnancy. Because exercise also increases your metabolism, it is possible to develop low blood sugar during exercise. Your baby also demands sugar (glucose), which can lower your blood sugar. To help avoid low blood sugar, consume adequate calories and limit your workout sessions to less than 45 minutes.

• Your body temperature increases when you exercise. Becoming over-heated is dangerous during pregnancy. This may cause a loss of fluids and dehydration. Overheating—a maternal core temperature of 102.6°F (39.2°C)—in the first eight weeks of pregnancy may contribute to the devel-opment of certain birth defects. Adaptive changes associated with pregnancy, however, such as increased breathing and skin blood flow; help to offset some-what the potential overheating effects of exercise. Nevertheless, avoid exer-cising in hot, humid conditions and make sure you drink plenty of fluids.

• Your respiratory rate (breathing) increases during pregnancy to naturally ensure your baby will get adequate oxygen. This can reduce the amount of oxygen available to you during exercise and can result in decreased endurance and shortness of breath. If you cannot talk easily during exercise you are prob-ably breathing too hard.

• Your blood volume increases by approximately 40 percent during preg-nancy to boost delivery of oxygen to your baby. Your heart rate also increases by approximately 15 beats per minute. During your first trimester, your blood vessels relax and get larger to accommodate the increased blood volume; this occasionally can cause you to feel light-headed. Let your doctor know if you experience light-headedness because this can also be a sign of anemia (iron deficiency).

• Your changing body shape (enlarged uterus, enlarged breasts) causes your center of gravity to change. This may affect your balance and put strain on your back. In certain sports, this change in your center of gravity may put you at risk of injury.

• When you exercise, your body releases a chemical called norepinephrine. This increases contractions in smooth muscles and may cause painless uterine contractions.

• During pregnancy, your body releases relaxin. This is a hormone that relaxes the ligaments connecting your joints in the pelvis in preparation for delivery. All joints are affected, however, and therefore are more susceptible to injuries with exercise.

• Standard target heart rate formulae do not apply when you're pregnant. Your cardiovascular and blood flow rates change. There is some evidence that vigorous exercise (heart rate above 150 beats per minute) causes bursts of rapid heartbeat in the fetus, which may be an indication of stress. Therefore, it is probably best to exercise at a moderate level based on your own feelings of exertion. Standard recommended intensities are 60 to 75 percent maximum heart rate for the unfit woman and 70 to 85 percent for the fit woman. How you feel during exercise is really the more reliable indicator of workout intensity than your heart rate.

I have had several pregnant patients come to the clinic complaining of knee sprains or muscle strains caused by only moderate activities or exercise. Nina, for example, was simply standing up for a long period of time at work and was hyperextending her knees without realizing it. She soon found herself unable to exercise after work because of knee pain. I diagnosed her with a mild knee sprain. I recommended a short course of physical therapy for muscle balancing and posture training and her pain resolved quickly.

BACK PAIN

Because this is such a common complaint among pregnant women, I feel it warrants its own section. This is the most frequent reason pregnant women visit my clinic. Studies have estimated that 40 to 50 percent of pregnant women experience some form of lower back pain during pregnancy and many women develop back pain after giving birth.

Low back pain is often a result of the increased pressure on a woman's spine caused by her weight gain and changes in her center of gravity. Another type of pain is in the sacroiliac (SI) joint in the pelvis. The SI joints connect the pelvis to the spine. When the hormone relaxin is increased during pregnancy to prepare the pelvis for birth, these joints may become more mobile, unstable, and painful.

Back pain also can occur at night, a condition likely caused by increased blood volume. A lot of the extra blood pools in your legs, which may result in leg swelling during the day. When you go to bed, the blood may pool and stretch the structures in your pelvis, which can cause back pain.

If you have a prior history of back pain, especially during a previous pregnancy, you should begin an intensive strengthening program prescribed by your doctor and supervised by a physical therapist *before* you try to get pregnant. This may help stabilize the joints once the relaxin levels increase in your blood. The most important exercises for core strengthening of your lower back are abdominal strengthening exercises. After the first trimester, you must alter the way you perform your exercises because it is not recommended to lie flat on your back. This is because the enlarging uterus can put pressure on a large vein (the vena cava) delivering blood back to your heart and can ultimately reduce blood flow to your baby.

Good posture is essential in pregnancy. In addition to keeping a neutral position to your spine (avoiding swayback), the following tips may be helpful.

- Avoid high heel shoes.
- When lifting, always bend at the knees.
- Avoid heavy lifting altogether.
- Sit comfortably with your feet resting on the floor, not dangling.
- Avoid sitting in low, deep chairs that are difficult to get up from.
- If you are standing or sitting for a long period of time, rest one foot on a low stool.
- While sleeping, find the most comfortable position—a total body pillow may be helpful during this quest.
- Don't sleep flat on your back after the first trimester (it may reduce blood flow to the baby).

- An abdominal support may be helpful in the early stages of back pain. Supporting the lower abdomen relieves stress on the back muscles.

I often recommend prenatal yoga to my pregnant patients with back pain. Yoga keeps the abdominals and back muscles strong without stressing them. It also makes you take time to take care of yourself. (Be certain the yoga class is specifically geared toward pregnant participants.) If you do suffer with back pain during pregnancy, it's important to get into a physical therapy program so that after delivery, you will be able to handle the extra stress of carrying your baby, putting your baby into a car seat and in and out of the crib, and so forth.

HOW TO KEEP FIT DURING PREGNANCY

Whether you're at peak fitness level or way out of shape, there's plenty you can do to maintain or improve your health and overall well-being while you are pregnant.

If You're a Couch Potato

If you have not bothered to exercise or get in shape before your pregnancy, don't suddenly start jogging around the neighborhood or running on a treadmill. Forget about lifting weights. The best regimen for you is a non–weight-bearing activity such as swimming, stationary cycling, or moderate walking. Begin slowly with as little as 5 minutes per day and add 5 more minutes a week until you can stay active for one 20- to 30-minute session at least three times a week at a comfortable pace.

If You're an Athlete

If you don't have any medical condition that would sideline you, you can most likely continue your prepregnancy exercise and/or sports program with some exceptions and some adaptations later in the pregnancy. Studies have shown that athletes' bodies often have easier, healthier pregnancies when they continue strenuous workouts with some late-term modifications.

Tips for a Prenatal Fitness Program

Always consult your doctor before starting a new fitness program and keep him or her up to date on your response to exercise throughout your pregnancy.

- Start slowly and pay attention to your body.
- Gradually increase your activity as long as it is comfortable. A good target program is a comfortable level of exercise 20 to 30 minutes at least three times per week.
- Prevent overheating and dehydration. Drink plenty of water during and after exercise and avoid exercising in hot or humid environments. Wear loose clothing (to allow heat evaporation) and a bra that gives you good support (and an abdominal support later in your pregnancy).
- Avoid exercising flat on your back, which can reduce blood flow to your baby and make you feel light-headed. Remember that your center of gravity is altered in pregnancy, which may cause you to lose your balance.
- Be able to talk easily during exercise, avoid shortness of breath, and never exercise to the point of exhaustion.
- Avoid interval training with anaerobic bouts of intense exercise.
- Avoid deep knee bends, sit-ups, and straight-leg toe touches.
- Be sure that your workout begins with a warm-up and ends with a cool-down. Avoid hot tubs or saunas after your workouts.

Four Helpful Exercises During Pregnancy

Although most people can do these exercises without a problem, check with your doctor before trying them during pregnancy.

Squatting. Squatting can be a useful position for labor if you have the balance and strength. This will stretch your legs and open the pelvis. Place your feet shoulder-width apart while standing straight. Hold on to a partner or the back of a chair for balance. Bend your knees as far as is comfortable while keeping your heels flat on the floor. Hold this position for a count of eight.

Pelvic Tilting and Rocking. This exercise strengthens the back and abdominal muscles to help prevent back pain. It can also improve posture and relieve back pain. Stand straight with your feet a bit wider than shoulder-width apart. While breathing out, tilt your pelvis forward and upward and pull in your abdominal muscles bringing your buttocks forward. Hold this position for several seconds and then breathe in while returning to the original position.

Abdominal Curl-Ups. These strengthen the abdominal muscles that support the uterus and the back. In the first trimester: Lie on your back and bend your knees. Raise your head and shoulders approximately six to eight inches from the floor. With your hands on your belly, gently pull yourself upward. Lower your body slowly while breathing in.

In the second and third trimesters, it is not advised to exercise on your back so you must modify this exercise. While on your side, inhale so that your belly expands; as you exhale pull your belly button toward your spine. Repeat this as many times as you can tolerate it.

Pelvic Floor Exercises (Kegels). These exercises strengthen the muscles that support your internal organs, which can prevent incontinence during pregnancy and may make labor easier. Pretend that you are trying to stop yourself from urinating by tightening your muscles for three seconds and then release them gradually.

Now let's consider some of the more strenuous activities for the pregnant athlete.

Running

If you are a competitive, physically fit runner, you can continue your routine until late in pregnancy. If you're just trying to keep yourself fit, you should probably reduce your running time to less than 45 minutes. According to the experts on this subject, women can run, but most women find they get too uncomfortable 20 to 32 weeks into the pregnancy. Listen to your body when it tells you to slow down.

Weight Training

Until recently, females were seldom known to participate in weight training during pregnancy. That is slowly changing, but you should still proceed with caution. If you want to continue your established routine, you must do so with common sense and supervision. Relatively light weights and moderate repetitions will maintain flexibility and muscle tone while minimizing the risk of ligament and joint injury during pregnancy. Lifting of heavy weights is another matter. Avoid straining or holding your breath during lifts. The use of exercise machines rather than free weights is probably better in late pregnancy when normal balance is disrupted. Later in pregnancy, you may have to switch to a lower impact activity, such as swimming. As always, listen to your body.

Swimming

Water is the ideal environment to exercise during all phases of pregnancy. The buoyant water supports your extra body weight and relieves joint stress while still allowing you to get the benefits of exercise. Don't swim underwater; holding your breath may harm your baby. Water is 12 times more resistive than air and simple walking in a pool can have great aerobic and strength benefits. Water also helps rid your body of excess fluid. There are no studies to suggest that chlorine is a danger to the baby, but try not to swallow large amounts of pool water.

Stationary Cycling and Low-Impact Aerobics

The recumbent bike offers great exercise during pregnancy. It allows an aerobic workout without stress on the back and leg joints. Again, don't overdo it, don't breathe too hard, and drink plenty of water during and after exercise. You can do low-impact aerobics if you are conditioned for that type of workout. If you have never done aerobics classes, make sure you talk to your doctor first and then begin very slowly.

Tennis

Recreational tennis is not unreasonable early in your pregnancy if you played before becoming pregnant. You must monitor the level of intensity so that you do not become fatigued or overheated. The quick pivoting movements in tennis may put a lot of stress on your hips, knees, and ankles. It is not generally recommended to continue playing past your second trimester. Avoid playing in the heat or humidity.

Sports *Not* Recommended During Pregnancy

The American College of Obstetrics recommends that pregnant women not participate in downhill skiing, ice skating, or horseback riding because these sports carry a high risk of trauma from either falling or colliding with an object or another athlete.

Here are some other sports physicians recommend you avoid during pregnancy.

• **Mountain climbing.** The risk of injury and falls puts this sport in the not-recommended category. Also, at high altitudes, where the air is thinner, you and your fetus are more likely to become oxygen deprived. One Boulder, Colorado, physician recommends that for each 2,000 feet of elevation above 5,000 feet, a pregnant woman should take one or two days to acclimatize, if she insists on participating in a high-altitude sport.

• **Scuba diving.** Diving may diminish your oxygen and increase the nitrogen in your blood, which is not good for you or your baby. You are advised not to dive during your entire pregnancy.

• **Contact sports.** In sports such as soccer, softball, martial arts, hockey, lacrosse, basketball, and gymnastics, there is a great risk of falls, blows to your stomach, or contact with a projectile. In other words, these sports present a risk to your baby and to you. Some physicians might OK participation during the first trimester but not in the second.

• **Competitive team sports.** Because of the possibility of legal suits, many organizations—even health clubs—restrict pregnant women from participating.

PRECAUTIONS FOR ALL PREGNANT AND ACTIVE WOMEN

Remember that during pregnancy, you are carrying extra weight—as much as 20 to 30 pounds near term. The extra weight in the front of your body shifts your center of gravity and places stress on your joints and muscles, especially those in your pelvis and lower back. This can make you more likely to lose your balance.

In general, you should avoid activities that call for jumping, jarring motions, or quick changes in direction that may strain your joints and/or cause you to fall. As your baby grows inside you, your uterus enlarges and pushes against your diaphragm, the thin partition between your abdomen and lungs. This may lead to shortness of breath creating a shortage of the oxygen both you and your baby need to survive.

The American College of Obstetrics and Gynecology (ACOG) recommends that women avoid exercise while lying on their backs after the first trimester because this position can decrease blood flow to the baby. Prolonged motionless standing should also be avoided.

As was pointed out earlier, about 28 to 30 weeks into your pregnancy your ligaments will become looser due to your body's dispensing certain hormones that help prepare you for delivery. While this loosening process is a necessary bodily function, it can make you more susceptible to injury during sports.

Warning Signs

Stop exercising and seek immediate professional help if any of the following occur:

- Vaginal bleeding
- Excessive fatigue
- Pain, particularly in the back or pubic area
- Dizziness or shortness of breath
- Heart palpitations
- Decreased fetal movement

- Persistent contractions
- Rupture of membranes

Delivering a baby is like participating in a triathlon. You need to train to get through it without hurting yourself. So contact your doctor and plan a safe regimen. You will not only feel better, but you'll most likely have an easier pregnancy and delivery and a happier baby.

19

MATURE ATHLETES

Never Too Old to Play

IF YOU ARE GOING TO LIVE LONGER, you want to live *better*. One of the best ways to accomplish this is to participate in athletics. No matter what your age, opportunities are available for you. Take the Senior Olympics, for example, formally known as the National Senior Games. Begun as a competition for older athletes more than a dozen years ago, it started out with 2,500 competitors and now has more than 12,000. Women and men over age 50—some of them in their 90s—vie in 18 sports from archery to volleyball. A number of Senior Olympic competitors were high school and college All-Americans a generation or two ago, but many others are late bloomers. Some participate because they are fierce competitors. Others do so because they love the camaraderie and the exhilaration of sports.

You have to qualify for the Senior Olympics but another organization, Masters Games, is open to all women and men 30 years of age and older. Formed in 1970 by middle-agers who wanted to compete athletically, it has now grown to a worldwide federation of competitions for mature athletes under the umbrella of the International Masters Games Association (IMGA). Individuals compete in five-year age groups. They have a lot of fun, incidentally, and as 101-year-old Ben Levinson observed when he competed at the 1998 Nike World Masters Games in Portland, Oregon: "At my age, just being anywhere is great!"

The IMGA ratifies and registers outstanding performances by competitors. Its motto is "The Challenge Never Ends."

Mature female athletes are capable of participating in almost all sports that young people do (although, you can probably forget about gymnastics). If you are over 40, continue to exercise at whatever level you have been practicing. You should not feel that you have to cut back unless your body and/or your physician tells you to do so.

You will have to make adjustments, however. Here are some of the bodily changes you should take into consideration:

- Your handgrip strength decreases, making it more difficult to accomplish activities turning or holding on to an object.

- As your muscles age, they begin to shrink and lose mass. Your lean muscle mass can decrease up to 10 percent per decade after age 30. A sedentary lifestyle accelerates this loss. As you age, your muscles don't use sugar as well, so your ability to respond with a burst of activity declines. The simple fact is that it takes your muscles longer to respond in your 50s than it did in your 20s.

- The mineral content of your bones decreases, so that bones become less dense and more fragile.

- The chemistry of your cartilage, which provides cushioning between bones, changes. With less water content, your cartilage becomes more susceptible to stress and injury.

- Your joint motion becomes more restricted and your flexibility decreases with age because of changes in tendons and ligaments. Your tendons, the cordlike tissues that attach your muscles to your bones, lose water content. This makes your tissues stiffer and less able to tolerate stress. Your ligaments, the connective tissues between your bones, become less elastic and contribute to reduced flexibility.

• Your heart muscle becomes less able to propel large quantities of blood quickly to your body. Consequently, you may tire more easily and take longer to recover.

• Your heart, lungs, and blood vessels deliver oxygen less efficiently to your muscles during physical activity. In most people, aerobic capacity peaks at about age 20 and decreases by about 1 percent per year thereafter. By the time you are 80, your aerobic capacity may be about half of what it was when you were 20.

• Your metabolic rate (how quickly your body converts food to energy) slows down. This can lead to obesity and an increase in LDL ("bad") cholesterol.

• If you injure yourself you may take longer to heal, so you have to be careful to rehabilitate yourself fully, and slowly, before returning to activity.

As you age, your body will be more inclined to injury, so take longer to warm up and cool down. The warm-up and cool-down periods should be almost as long as the exercise session itself. Take 10 to 20 minutes to warm up, then exercise for 20 to 30 minutes, and take another 10 to 20 minutes to cool down.

Don't put away your sports equipment and head for the couch after reading the changes described above. Almost all of them, fortunately, can be ameliorated by your participation in athletics. Many of the alterations in muscles and bones result more from disuse rather than from aging. You don't have to be a competitive athlete. Your activity doesn't have to be strenuous. If you walk for 30 minutes, for example, you gain the same benefits as if you jogged for 15 minutes.

Even though you may think your tissues are not as good as they used to be and you may not heal as fast, there are definitely exceptions. Lillian, for example, was a two-time Olympian in two sports and in the Volleyball Hall of Fame. She was 60 years old when I first treated her. She had a rotator cuff tear in her shoulder. It was a large tear and it required surgery. She was concerned about her rehabilitation potential because of her age. She was the club champion in golf and a very competitive tennis player; naturally, she wanted to get back to all of her sports. Because she was in such great shape throughout her entire life and was such an avid athlete, it turns out that she did as well as the 30-year-olds I have treated. Her tissues were strong and healthy. She recovered and was in full swing with her tennis and golf games four months after surgery.

Three basic types of exercise will help your mature female body overcome some of the signs of aging.

AEROBIC EXERCISES

Athletics that raise your pulse and get you breathing harder benefit your heart, bones, and general fitness and help you lose weight. Doing such activities for 20 to 60 minutes three to five days a week will produce significant results. If you have difficulty taking the time to exercise, do several shorter sessions each day to reach your goal. Certainly, if you have not been exercising and feel out of shape (see cautions that follow), start slowly. Begin by walking 5 to 15 minutes at a comfortable pace three times a week, and then gradually increase your distance and pace. Among aerobic exercises you may wish to try are hiking, jogging, bicycling, swimming, rowing, walking on a treadmill, stair climbing, aerobic dancing, and cross-country skiing.

If you are overweight, you may want to choose an exercise routine that is minimally stressful to your joints to reduce injury or overuse syndromes. Once you've lost some weight, become more flexible, and increased your aerobic capacity, then you can move on to a different exercise. For example, you should start with swimming or bicycling and then advance to stair climbing or jogging once you are in better condition. I have treated numerous patients who come to my office after they have decided to get into shape only to develop painful knees, hips, backs, and so on. I encourage them not to forgo their goal of getting into shape, but I counsel them to pick a different exercise for the time being, including a conditioning program to get them ready for the exercise they want to do.

RESISTANCE TRAINING

Using free weights or exercise machines to strengthen individual muscles will not only increase your muscle and bone strength, but it can help control joint swelling and pain associated with arthritis and reduce the risk of fractures. A series of exercises that focus on your arms, shoulders, and torso two to three times a week will produce results. Use small dumbbells, for example, and do one to three sets of 10 repetitions each of arm curls, upright rowing strokes, and lateral raises. To increase strength, gradually increase the number of repetitions. When you have done that, you can gradually increase the weight of the dumbbell. Similar exercises to strengthen your hips, thighs, and calves are also important. It is never too late to start. Some people have begun working out at 96 years, even with a chronic disease. As with other forms of exercise, ask your doctor before beginning resistance training.

STRETCHING

This type of exercise helps to decrease injury and improve your balance so you are less likely to fall. Flexibility exercises should be done at least three to five times each week. They are most effective if the stretch is done slowly and held for 20 to 30 seconds. If you have osteoporosis of the spine, you should avoid back flexion and extension exercises (bending forward or back from the waist). You can also increase your flexibility with dancing, water aerobics, and yoga.

KEEP YOUR BALANCE

Interest in tai chi and yoga is on the rise—and with good reason. Each has many health benefits, one of which is a marked improvement in balance. As we age, our ability to balance ourselves may decline significantly, even if we have been consistently athletic.

Tai Chi

The exact origins of Chinese tai chi are obscure and surrounded by mythology. Supposedly, the originators of tai chi studied the natural environment, and especially the movement of animals, to create tai chi postures useful in self-defense.

A study reported in the *Journal of the American Geriatric Society* found that older adults who underwent 10 weeks of tai chi exercise had fewer falls than control subjects who did not exercise. In other studies, tai chi was found to strengthen bones and increase flexibility in women 47 to 65 who'd practiced tai chi five days per week for 45 minutes per session over the course of 12 months. Of particular interest was a low dropout rate.

Yoga

Yoga is believed to be about 6,000 years old and to have originated in India. Some claim it is even older. The most popular form of yoga practiced in the west is hatha yoga, which is concerned with body control and consists of a series of positions (asanas). Medical studies, mostly from Indian researchers, have concluded that yoga practice is beneficial not only for the prevention of disease, but also for therapeutic properties that can help improve health problems such as asthma and arthritis. One theory in yoga is that the central nervous system is nourished by the spine and the condition of the spine is largely responsible for our physical and emotional well-being. In yoga, therefore, the spine is the most exercised part of the body. Yoga postures are also said to help stimulate the lymphatic system (lymph nodes act as filter traps for bacteria), thus enhancing the removal of toxins from the body, which, if allowed to accumulate, cause pain and stiffness in the muscles and joints. Yoga is also thought to aid in gland function to correct and balance the system. Correct breathing is an important part of yoga practice; this is one reason why it is being studied by western physicians as an asthma treatment. Most of us use only a fraction of our lung capacity. The benefits of proper breathing are improved circulation, reduced tension, increased oxygen supply to all body cells, and extra vitality. Yoga has also been reported by physicians to increase muscle strength and improve balance.

Yoga only requires about 15 to 20 minutes a day. Although people of almost any age and physical ability can practice yoga, it is advisable to check with your doctor before beginning a program. It is also very important to find a qualified teacher in your area who will be able to give you yoga exercises for your physical condition.

EXERCISE AND YOUR MIND

The beneficial effects of exercise on our physical and mental health have been studied extensively. Researchers have found that exercise can decrease depression, stress, and anxiety and generally improve mental health. Some studies suggest that physical exercise and activity can increase mental alertness and cognitive function; for example, women who walk regularly are less likely to experience memory loss and other declines in mental function that can come with aging. Examples of moderate activities that would reduce risk of decline would be playing tennis twice a week, walking a mile per day, or playing golf once a week.

WHAT IF YOU HAVE A CHRONIC CONDITION?

Most of us develop some wear and tear on our bodies as the years pass. The question is whether we can still participate in athletics and exercise routines.

The information in this chapter is not intended as a substitute for your doctor's supervision. It provides suggestions gathered from recent studies and my own experience.

Chronic diseases can't be cured but most can be controlled with medications and other treatments. Traditionally, exercise has been discouraged, but recently researchers have found that exercise can actually improve some chronic conditions in most older people, as long as it's done when the condition is under control. If you have a flare-up of your condition or have worsening symptoms, you may have to forgo exercise for a while. Check with your doctor.

You can't use the excuse that you are too old or too frail because, as you have read, exercise can be beneficial providing you do sports or exercises within your capacity.

If You Have Back Pain

You should *not* exercise during an acute attack but you should move around. For acute back pain I recommend walking rather than bed rest. Bed rest will cause more muscle atrophy and, ultimately, a worse prognosis for your recovery. Once the acute attack is over, if you strengthen the muscles of your stomach, hips, and thighs, you may relieve your chronic back pain and prevent your condition from worsening. Flexibility is also of vital importance for back health. A balanced fitness program of regular physical activity and specific strengthening exercises is ideal. Many YMCAs and YWCAs have special back programs.

If You Have Osteoarthritis

While there are many types of arthritis, the most common form is osteoarthritis (OA). It is the leading cause of disability in people over the age of 55, particularly women. The pain is caused by the deterioration of the cartilage and underlying bone in the joints. Normal joints in individuals of all ages appear to tolerate exercise without adverse consequences or accelerated development of OA. However, sports such as jogging or weightlifting, which subject the joints to intermittent high or violent impact loads, may increase the risk of OA. Sports injuries such as repeated sprains or fractures or naturally misaligned bones or joints may also put you at risk.

Even with creaking, painful joints, however, you still need to exercise to strengthen the surrounding muscles. Again, exercise can relieve joint stiffness and reduce pain. If one type of exercise causes pain, try a different type. You might try swimming or walking in a pool until your muscles are strong enough to try walking on a firm surface. Start with short, frequent sessions of physical activity. A number of studies have documented improved function, decreased use of medication, and psychological benefits from exercise programs for osteoarthritis.

If You Have Osteoporosis

Osteoporosis is a major cause of bone fractures in older people, particularly postmenopausal women. As pointed out at the beginning of this chapter, weight-bearing exercises such as walking, jogging, and weightlifting can stimulate bone growth and make your bones healthier. Regular exercise also will help you maintain good balance making you less likely to fall and suffer a disabling bone fracture. Stimulating bone growth and preventing bone loss through exercise should be part of your lifestyle because once you stop, the benefits begin to diminish within two weeks and disappear in two to eight months. Your doctor can help with a total plan for the treatment and prevention of osteoporosis. If you have a test that indicates low bone density for your age, certainly have this discussion with your doctor to see if you are a candidate for medications that help strengthen bones.

If You Have Had a Total Joint Replacement

If the damage to your knee, hip, or shoulder is too severe and you have limited function and severe pain, you may have to undergo joint replacement. Still, you don't necessarily have to give up exercise and sports. While you are recovering, of course, you have to follow the graduated walking program and specific exercises prescribed by your orthopedic surgeon and physical therapist to restore movement and strengthen the muscles and ligaments surrounding the new joint.

Normal, healthy levels of activity will not damage your joint replacement. In fact, to take full advantage of the surgery, you must stay active for the rest of your life. If you aren't active, your muscles will weaken, which will increase your risk of falling. Falls are a leading cause of repeat surgeries. Talk to your physician, however, before engaging in activities such as jogging, skiing, or tennis.

I have several patients who still enjoy skiing after having had a new knee or hip joint placed. The important thing is that they modify their skiing techniques and choice of terrain. For instance, 53-year-old Sandra was an avid skier her entire life. She loved the bumps (mogel runs), which, after many injuries, helped wear out one of her knees. I treated her with conservative measures for four years including activity modification, physical therapy, medication, and even injections. The pain ultimately became so severe that she couldn't enjoy life anymore. She received a total knee replacement and worked very hard at her rehabilitation. One year later, she was back on the slopes but careful to avoid the bumpy terrain. I told her that if she skis the bumps, her new knee would wear out a lot faster than if she stays on the groomed slopes. She still enjoys the exhilaration of being out on the slopes and has accepted the fact that modification will increase the life expectancy of her knee.

If You Have a Heart Problem

If you have had a heart attack recently, your doctor or cardiac rehabilitation therapist should have given you specific exercises to do. Research has shown that exercises done as part of a cardiac rehabilitation program can improve fitness and even reduce your risk of dying from heart-related ailments. For some heart conditions, however, vigorous exercise is dangerous and should be avoided, even in the absence of symptoms. Be sure to check with your physician.

If you have congestive heart failure (CHF) (inability to pump efficiently), it probably doesn't mean you can't exercise. But it does mean that keeping in touch with your doctor is important if you do exercise. For example, some studies suggest that endurance exercises, such as brisk walking, may improve how well the heart and lungs work in people with CHF, but only in people who are in a stable phase of the disease.

If You Have Diabetes

Diabetes is another chronic condition common among older people. Too much sugar in the blood is a hallmark of diabetes. It can cause damage throughout the body. Exercise can help your body use up some of the damaging sugar. The most common form of diabetes is linked to physical inactivity. In other words, if you stay physically active, you are less likely to develop diabetes in the first place.

If you do have diabetes and it has caused changes in your body—cardiovascular disease, eye disease, or changes in your nervous system, for example—check with your doctor to find out which exercises may help you and whether you should avoid certain activities. If you take insulin or other medication to lower your blood sugar, your doctor might need to adjust your dose. If you are in the earlier stages of diabetes or if your condition is stable, your doctor might find that you don't have to modify your exercises at all.

EXERCISING WELL

A number of recent studies have concluded that women who have remained physically active throughout their lives can perform the activities of daily living better than their sedentary counterparts. They can lift their heavy grocery bags, open jars, dress themselves, and do their own house- and yard work. They can also dance and shop for hours at the mall. This doesn't mean that in your 40s or 80s you are suddenly going to compete with 20-year-old sprinters. You have to listen to your body and make adjustments as pointed out at the beginning of this chapter.

You should *never* begin exercising without first checking with your physician if you have:

- Irregular, rapid, or fluttery heartbeat
- Severe shortness of breath
- Significant, ongoing, undiagnosed weight loss
- Infections, such as pneumonia, accompanied by fever
- Fever, which can cause dehydration and rapid heartbeat
- Chest pain
- Acute deep-vein thrombosis (blood clot)
- A hernia that is causing symptoms
- Foot or ankle sores that won't heal
- Joint swelling
- Persistent pain or a problem walking after you have fallen
- Certain eye conditions, such as bleeding or detached retina. After undergoing a cataract or lens implant, or after laser treatment or other eye surgery, check with your physician before you resume exercise.

Stop exercising immediately if you:

- Have pain or pressure in the left or midchest area—or left neck, shoulder, arm, or jaw
- Feel dizzy or sick
- Break out in a cold sweat
- Feel unexpected shortness of breath

- Feel pain in your joints, feet, ankles, or legs
- Have muscle cramps

The key to maintaining your exercise is doing something you enjoy. You might even enjoy your housework if you sweep, vacuum, or rake to upbeat music. The key is to find something that you enjoy doing and do it regularly. To keep things interesting, you may want to alternate your activities or join a friend or a group to keep you going.

If you are a competitive, mature athlete, you can obtain information about the Masters Games and the Senior Olympics through these resources.

THE INTERNATIONAL MASTERS GAMES ASSOCIATION
    (IMGA)
Thomas Jordan, Executive Vice President/Secretary
2110 Fairmont Blvd.
Eugene, OR 97403
E-mail: tjordan@nwevent.com

NATIONAL SENIOR GAMES ASSOCIATION
P.O. Box 82059
Baton Rouge, LA 70884-2059
Telephone: (225) 766-6800

CDC NATIONAL CENTER FOR CHRONIC DISEASE PREVENTION AND
    HEALTH PROMOTION
Division of Nutrition and Physical Activity
MS K-46
4770 Buford Highway, N.E.
Atlanta, GA 30341-3724
Telephone: (888) CDC-4NRG or (888) 232-4674
cdc.gov

AMERICAN COLLEGE OF SPORTS MEDICINE
P.O. Box 1440
Indianapolis, IN 46206
acsm.org

AMERICAN PHYSICAL THERAPY ASSOCIATION
111 North Fairfax Street
Alexandria, VA 22314-1488
Telephone: (800) 999-2782
apta.org

50-PLUS FITNESS ASSOCIATION
P.O. Box D
Stanford, CA 94309
Telephone: (650) 323-6160
50plus.org

THE PRESIDENT'S COUNCIL ON PHYSICAL FITNESS AND SPORTS
DHHS/OS/OPHS
200 Independence Avenue, S.W.
HHH Building
Washington, DC 20201
Telephone: (202) 690-9000
fitness.gov

20

NUTRITION FOR THE FEMALE ATHLETE

How MUCH DOES WHAT YOU EAT and drink affect your athletic performance?

Everyone agrees that food is fuel for your body, but there is a lot of controversy over what and when you should eat. In general, athletes use at least 20 times more energy when they are engaged in a sport than when they are not. Several factors, however, influence the amount of energy each individual will need to train and compete successfully. These factors include the type, intensity, and frequency of training as well as size, age, and gender.

Your muscles work by means of electrochemical signals sent between your nerves. How do you keep your muscles fired up for an athletic pursuit? And how do you restore their strength when they are exhausted? Most experts agree the answer is muscle glycogen—a sugar. Where do you get glycogen in your diet? Your body stores limited amounts of carbohydrates—starches and sugars—as glycogen in your muscles and in your liver. The theory is that pre-exercise carbohydrates stimulate muscle glycogen storage and may help your body delay fatigue. Carbohydrates consumed during exercise that lasts more than 60 minutes help your body maintain blood sugar availability late in exercise. Postexercise carbohydrates help improve muscle glycogen storage, especially within 30 minutes after the activity.

Carbohydrate metabolism during exercise is different for women than it is for men. Just how and why it differs is not well understood. Studies have shown utilization of muscle glycogen is lower in females compared to males during the same type and intensity of exercise. Carbohydrate metabolism in the postexercise recovery period also appears to be altered in women.

Mark Tarnopolsky, Ph.D., of the Department of Kinesiology, McMaster University Medical Center (Hamilton, Ontario, Canada), and associates have reported that muscle glycogen stores are not increased in trained women in response to a standard carbohydrate-loading regimen. This reduced capacity to make more glycogen also appears to depend on menstrual cycle phase. Dr. Tarnopolsky, in *Gender Differences in Metabolism: Practical and Nutritional Implications* (Modern Nutrition, 1998), says he wrote the book to encourage future investigators to consider gender differences in metabolism. Most studies of carbohydrate loading have used male subjects only.

Dr. Tarnopolsky writes that he became intrigued with the metabolic differences in genders; he wondered why females are generally smaller than males and have greater amounts of fat and whether this had to do with evolution. One theory is, he notes, that because women have more fat they were able to withstand a period of starvation and still remain fertile. This may be the reason, in part, why female athletes have enhanced energy conservation.

While the issue of female athletes and carbohydrate intake remains something of a puzzle, millions of female athletes are practicing carbohydrate loading before an athletic event.

CARBOHYDRATE LOADING

Carb loading, or glycogen loading, is a dietary means of building up glycogen stores for the muscles. When muscles are first depleted of glycogen and then replenished by means of a high carbohydrate diet, the glycogen content of muscle is about twice that achieved with a normal balanced diet.

The original carbohydrate loading involved draining glycogen stores by exhaustive exercising and a diet low in starch—during the first half of the week before an event. The athlete would then get a rebound effect during the second half of the week by eating a diet very high in carbohydrates and not exercising at all. This regimen can severely stress the body and cause heart and kidney problems. It is *not* recommended!

A modified adaptation has better results. This modified carbohydrate loading allows athletes to eat their normal high-carbohydrate training diet.

In the final three days prior to competition, athletes push daily carbohydrate intake to between 525 and 550 grams of carbohydrate or 65 percent of calories from carbohydrate, whichever is greater. This final push of carbohydrate will enhance glycogen storage within the body. Intakes *above* 500 to 600 grams of carbohydrate per day do not contribute significantly to muscle glycogen storage or athletic performance. (The method does not benefit athletes who are involved in training or competition for less than 90 continuous minutes.)

If you want to try carb loading, give starchy foods particular emphasis during the days right before the event by building your main meal around a high-starch entree such as spaghetti and meatballs. Make sure the other food groups are also represented. Decrease your physical activity the day before and the day of the event. Practices directed by your coach are enough. Rest up!

Many of today's athletes are convinced a candy bar, a sports drink, or a bowl of pasta will power them to greater athletic feats. There is no magic carb. Whether you are a competitive or recreational athlete, carbohydrate-containing foods should take up about two-thirds of the plate at each meal and before, during, and after exercise.

APPROXIMATE CARBOHYDRATE VALUES
1 slice of bread = 15 grams
¾ cup of cereal = 15 grams
½ cup rice = 15 grams
½ cup of pasta = 15 grams
½ cup dried beans or peas = 15 grams
½ cup starchy vegetable serving = 15 grams
½ cup fruit or 1 small whole fruit = 10–15 grams
½ cup green or yellow vegetable serving = 5 grams
1 cup milk = 12 grams
1 glass sports drinks = 10–15 grams

It's important to eat a variety. Besides providing energy, carbohydrate-rich foods such as grain and cereal products, fruits, vegetables, and legumes are excellent sources of fiber, vitamins, and minerals.

Examples of Carbohydrate Amounts for Athletics

- *Pre-exercise:* 50 to 100 grams of carbohydrate 30 to 60 minutes before exercise (for example, a bagel, two granola bars, or a concentrated carbohydrate sports drink)
- *During exercise:* 30 to 75 grams of carbohydrate per hour (sources may include gels or sports drinks)
- *Postexercise:* 75 grams of carbohydrate within 30 minutes (include sucrose- or glucose-containing foods, such as cereal with fruit, crackers, or a health bar)

PROTEIN POWER

If carbohydrates fuel endurance, then proteins fuel strength. Protein is necessary for muscle growth, strength, and repair. Many power athletes maintain high-protein diets, which lead to increased muscle mass and strength gains. Just as with carbohydrates, however, there is no magic protein. Low protein intakes, however, can be detrimental. An athlete does need slightly more protein (0.5 to 0.9 grams of protein per pound of body weight) than the nonathlete (0.4 grams of protein per pound of body weight). When an athlete consumes adequate calories to meet the energy demands of her sport, chooses high-quality foods to supply those calories, and follows a well-balanced diet, she is virtually assured of getting enough protein. Many of the foods (breads, pasta, cereals, etc.) that contribute to meeting that high percentage of carbohydrates also contribute to the day's protein pool.

Proteins are the chief nitrogen provider, an essential constituent of every living cell. We lose nitrogen when sweating but studies have shown that 100 grams of protein per day is adequate to cover all needs of athletes perspiring profusely. Some athletes tend to overdo on protein intake. A high-protein diet or one with supplemental protein increases risk of certain cancers, amplifies calcium excretion, and may lead to osteoporosis (fragile bones). High-protein diets also lead to a reduced intake of vitamins, minerals, fiber, and plant nutrients. On the other hand, some athletes barely meet their protein needs. The primary functions of protein are growth, maintenance, and repair of body tissue. Using protein supplements for energy is inefficient. Food is the easiest, safest, most effective, and least costly way to meet protein needs. Among good proteins sources are poultry, vegetables, fish or shellfish, eggs, grains, cheese, dry beans, soy products, milk or yogurt, and nuts or seeds.

CREATINE CONTROVERSIES

Amino acids are building blocks of proteins and neurotransmitters (the electrochemicals that send messages between cells). There are 22 amino acids, nine of which are called essential meaning the body cannot make them and they must be obtained from food. Creatine is naturally processed by the liver, pancreas, and kidneys from the precursor amino acids arginine, glycine, and methionine. Dietary creatine is also available in meats and fish, but creatine content is depleted rapidly when foods are cooked. There is approximately 2 grams of creatine per pound of raw red meat. Of the creatine we make in our bodies and obtain from food, we usually store about 60 to 80 percent, according to some reports. Advocates say supplementing with creatine, therefore, improves high-power performance of short duration; increases muscle mass; and delays fatigue. According to its advocates, creatine supposedly does for the sprinter what carbohydrate loading does for the long-distance runner.

Currently there are no dosage amounts agreed upon. Creatine absorption is quickened when taken with a high-sugar drink such as grape juice. Ingesting creatine with a meal will also provide the same effect due to increased insulin production. Some studies have also shown that exercised muscle will absorb about 12 percent more creatine than a nonexercised muscle. It follows that taking creatine directly after a workout may be more helpful, although not necessary to achieve benefits.

Athletes have been using creatine since the mid-1960s, but now widespread use has put it at the top of the sports-supplement list. Synthetic creatine production began in the early 1960s, mainly in countries of the former Soviet Union. Several British Olympic athletes were reportedly supplementing with creatine before the 1992 Olympic games in Barcelona. The Olympic Games in Atlanta were jokingly referred to as the Creatine Games, as a number of athletes supplementing with creatine were awarded gold medals. Keep in mind that the FDA does not regulate creatine. What you buy may or may not contain exactly what the label says, so check out the manufacturer carefully. Some producers have put out creatine especially for female athletes and claim it doesn't cause the bloating and water retention—common side effects of the supplement. There have been some reports of creatine increasing muscle cramping, strains, and pulls as well as kidney damage and heat illness. So if you swallow it, increase your fluid intake and be aware that its long-term effects are unknown.

THE BONE-DIET CONNECTION

Although growing children and pregnant and lactating women have the highest calcium needs, all of us need calcium in our diets throughout our lives. Bone tissue is constantly breaking down and being reformed. About 30 percent of your bone mass is influenced by outside factors including exercise and nutrition. If your body does not get enough calcium from your food, it steals the mineral from your bones. Your bones will then grow thin and weak, with a greater risk of fracture or other injury. You need sufficient vitamin D (400 IU per day) to be able to process calcium and phosphate to make strong bones. Small amounts of calcium help to regulate other body processes, such as the normal behavior of nerves, muscle tone, and blood clotting. Foods rich in calcium include dairy products, green-leafed vegetables such as broccoli, as well as salmon and some shellfish, and calcium-fortified products such as bread.

You also need protein. The Framingham group followed the four-year change in the bones of 391 women. The results indicated that lower protein intake was associated with greater bone loss. There is also growing support for the importance of alkali-forming fruits and vegetables in achieving better bone health.

Manganese is another element needed for normal tendon and bone structure. It is an important part of many enzyme reactions. It occurs in minerals and in minute quantities in animals, plants, and water. Manganese is abundant in many foods, especially raisins, tea, nuts, peas, and beans.

FATS FOR FUEL

Fat is another important fuel source, particularly for female athletes. It has more than twice as many calories as an equal weight of carbohydrate. When you are working out or competing, carbohydrate initially furnishes about 90 percent of the energy, and fat about 10 percent. As you continue to compete in a sport, you derive less of your energy from carbohydrate and more from free fatty acids. At the end of a competition, most of your energy is derived from fat. Aerobic training increases your body's ability to use fat as an energy source so that the glycogen in your muscles can be spared. However, fats cannot be used exclusively as fuel. Some carbohydrates must always be available as a fuel source even in the best-trained athlete.

Body fat storage will vary from athlete to athlete. Even if you are fairly lean, you will find you have a good energy source from stored fat. A diet high in animal fats is not the goal; however, the "good fats" such as nuts, olive oil, and fatty fish (i.e., salmon or tuna), may benefit your health and help prevent injury.

Although some researchers are investigating fat loading prior to exercise, the current advice is to eat a mixed meal of carbohydrate, protein, and some fat. Fat sources include butter, margarine, oil, nuts or nut butters, cream, steak, cheese, and fatty fish.

IRON AND EXERCISE

Iron is an important part of hemoglobin, the protein in red blood cells necessary for transporting and making use of oxygen. Iron is also needed for muscle function.

The only way a significant amount of iron can leave the body is through a loss of blood. Because women have menses, we lose blood every month. Women can lose large amounts of iron during pregnancy or while breast-feeding. Female athletes who exercise 50 minutes three times a week may also have a considerable loss of iron in their blood. Therefore, you may develop an iron deficiency and need to take an iron supplement. Do so only under medical supervision because an overload of iron can cause serious health problems.

Iron-rich foods include all varieties of beans. A citrus juice drink taken along with iron supplements or iron-rich food may aid replenishment of iron. The vitamin C in the citrus juice helps the body absorb iron. Do not drink tea, however, when you're eating iron-rich foods because tannins in tea inhibit iron absorption.

ELECTROLYTES

Electrolytes are any compound that, in solution, conducts current in electricity and is decomposed by it. Sodium and potassium are electrolytes in your body that are vital during exercise.

You lose sodium when you sweat. Your body has a mechanism to conserve sodium. However, if your sodium drops too low, it can cause your blood pressure to drop to shock levels. This is rare, but it does happen. Too much sodium raises blood pressure and causes water retention. Not everyone is equally susceptible to water retention, but just before their periods, most women are. Unfortunately, many convenience foods for athletes are very high in sodium. Drinking more water is effective in reducing sodium levels. The average American diet today contains far more salt than your body needs; but if you're working out in hot weather, don't completely eliminate salty foods. Some extra salt may be necessary to compensate for salt lost through sweat.

The healthy body contains about nine grams of potassium. Most of this potassium is inside body cells. Potassium plays an important role in maintaining the body's water and acid balance. It is vital to the transmission of messages between your nerves and from your nerves to your muscles. It also acts as a catalyst in carbohydrate and protein metabolism. Potassium is important for the maintenance of normal kidney function. It has a major effect on the heart and all the muscles of the body.

Some diuretics (water pills) commonly used to treat high blood pressure, are also employed by some athletes to reduce their weight. This is *not* recommended! Diuretics cause potassium loss.

Potassium replacement has to be done very carefully and only under the supervision of a physician. It can have serious side effects. Rather than take a potassium supplement, eat foods that are high in potassium such as bananas, oranges, melons, skim milk, and dried peas. These foods are also great sources of carbohydrates and proteins as well as vitamins and minerals.

Low potassium can cause muscle cramping. If you experience this, increase your intake of bananas. If the problem does not resolve, consult your physician.

KNOW WHAT TO DRINK AND WHEN

When I cover athletic events as a physician, dehydration is a common problem that I see and treat. Remember that by the time you actually feel thirsty you are most likely already dehydrated. Water is one of the most important factors in sports nutrition. It makes up about 60 percent of your body's weight and is involved in almost every one of your bodily processes. During heavy exercise, respiratory water loss may exceed 130 milliliters per hour, as compared with a normal loss of 15 milliliters per hour. Thirty minutes of exercising in the heat can bring about dehydration. A 3 percent weight loss leads to impaired performance; a 5 percent loss can result in some signs of heat exhaustion; a 7 percent loss may produce hallucination and put the athlete in physical danger. A 10 percent loss can lead to heat stroke and circulatory collapse.

Fluids taken before and during the event will not fully replace fluid loss, but partial replacement reduces the risk of overheating, according to the American Dietetic Association. After the event, you should continue to drink water at frequent intervals. You can make up the loss of potassium and sodium at meals later.

Cool water is the best fluid to keep you hydrated during workouts or events lasting an hour or less. As far as sports drinks, I recommend them to my endurance athletes in a 50 percent diluted formula. I agree that the better-tasting drinks encourage drinking and the electrolytes are a bonus. Sports drinks (i.e., 6 to 10 percent carbohydrates) are useful for longer events. Most of these drinks should be diluted approximately 50 percent with water. Drink even if you are not thirsty. Thirst is not a reliable way to tell if you need hydration. You won't start feeling thirsty until you have already lost about 2 percent of body weight—enough to hurt your performance. And if you stop drinking water once your thirst is satisfied, you will get only about half the amount you need.

An easy monitoring technique to determine fluid loss is to examine your urine. If it is too yellow, it indicates a lack of fluids. Drink enough fluids until your urine becomes clear or straw colored. Another good way to determine your need for fluid replacement is to weigh yourself before exercising and immediately after. Replace each pound lost with two to three cups of water. Make sure your body weight is back to normal before the next workout.

Unless you have an allergy to milk (lactose intolerance), there is no reason to avoid 1 percent or skim milk. Either is an excellent source of both carbohydrate and protein with very little or no fat. Having eight ounces of skim or 1 percent milk or yogurt up to two hours before a competitive event can even help boost blood sugar for the early minutes of the competition. The protein will kick in with additional fuel a little later.

Many athletes use caffeine, especially those athletes who perform high-intensity sports such as sprinting or weightlifting. Keep in mind that caffeine is on the banned-substance list for athletes in international competition. Those in favor of caffeine claim it improves athletic performance, increases energy, delays fatigue, improves fat burning, spares muscle glycogen, and enhances body fat loss. Research shows that it does act as a central nervous system stimulant, raises the levels of epinephrine (a stimulant), increases alertness, delays fatigue, and may slightly spare muscle glycogen. It doesn't help you lose fat. It has also been reported that 3 to 6 mg/kg of caffeine one hour prior to exercise improves overall endurance. If you don't mind the potential side effects—nausea, muscle tremor, heart palpitations, and headache—you may decide to try it.

One cup of coffee contains between 50 and 150 milligrams of caffeine. Other sources of caffeine include soft drinks and some over-the-counter medications, including analgesics, appetite suppressants, and stimulants. Incidentally, caffeine potentiates the stimulant, ephedrine. You should not take ephedrine at all! It has been linked to some deaths of athletes. At this writing, the FDA is trying to ban products with "natural" ephedrine—substances such as ephedra and ma huang, which athletes may take believing them to be harmless. Many of the supplements or diet substitutes I've seen my athletic patients take are not approved by the FDA. So not only do you not know what the purity may be, you cannot be certain that it is what the label says it is. Be especially cautious about buying some of these supplements on the Internet. These can hurt your wallet, but they definitely can hurt your health as well.

VITAMIN E AND ENDURANCE

Athletes may do well to swallow a vitamin E supplement before exercising. Research has shown that vitamin E can minimize muscle damage and reduce inflammation and soreness. More research is necessary. While 400 milligrams of vitamin E may help prevent muscle damage, there is no guarantee.

THE WIN-WIN DIET

You aspire to be in top shape as a female athlete. You may want to challenge your competition and there are many products and techniques out there that will try to convince you that they create miracles. The truth is that to support training, performance, and health you need a balanced diet. How do you get a balanced diet? For breakfast, choose one item from each of the following categories: bread, cereal, and grains; fruits and juices; and skim or 1 percent milk or other low-fat dairy products. For lunch and dinner, choose one item each of bread, cereal, and grains; fruits and juice; milk; vegetables; fish, poultry, and lean meat; and fats and oils. For seconds and snacks, if you're still hungry or you're trying to bulk up, choose from vegetables; fruits and juices; bread, cereal, and grains; or skim milk. As an athlete, you may want a specialized diet for a particular exercise challenge. For a limited period of time you may want to emphasize high carbohydrates and not a balanced meal or a high-protein diet. Here are some examples of choices for a high-carbohydrate diet.

BREAKFAST
Pears
Pineapple juice
Oat cereal
English muffin and jam
Pancakes with syrup or bran muffin

LUNCH
Spaghetti
Fresh green beans
Rye bread
Potato pancakes
Whole-wheat toast and tomatoes
Cranberry or other fruit juice

DINNER
Fettuccini
Baked potato stuffed with vegetables
Barley
Eggplant
Vegetable casserole
Apricots or cherries

You can use snacks as another opportunity to power up with starch—and don't forget that snack at bedtime. Cold cereal with milk is a great quick snack at any time.

If you want to be as sharp as possible and use your memory, or if you are going to participate in a strenuous athletic competition, you may want to eat a high-protein diet for a while. Here are some examples of choices for this type of eating plan.

BREAKFAST
Eggs
Cottage cheese

Yogurt
Fish or meat
Milk

LUNCH
Egg salad
Sliced turkey
Cheese
Sliced chicken
Soybean products, such as tofu
Chili
Tuna

DINNER
Steak
Lamb chops
Veal chops
Pork chops
Halibut
Blue fish
Chef's salad
Salmon steaks
Cheese soufflé or cheese pizza
Milk

Pregame Meal

According to the American Orthopaedic Society for Sports Medicine and other experts, what you eat several days before endurance activities affects performance. Your food the morning of a sports competition can ward off hunger, keep blood sugar levels adequate, and aid hydration. Avoid high-protein or high-fat foods on the day of an event, as these can stress the kidneys and take a long time to digest. You want your upper bowel to be empty by competition time. Here are some general guidelines to ensure this.

- Eat a meal high in carbohydrates.
- If you eat a big meal (about 1,200 calories) before a game or competition, make sure you finish at least three to four hours before your activity. If you opt for a light meal (about 600 calories) finish eating two hours before a game or competition. If you have only a snack, you only need to wait an hour or less before you play or compete.
- Choose easily digestible foods (i.e., not fried).
- Avoid sugary foods/drinks within one hour of an event.
- Drink enough fluids to ensure hydration (i.e., 20 ounces of water one to two hours before exercise, and an additional 10 to 15 ounces within 15 to 30 minutes of an event).

Replenishing fluids lost to sweat is the primary concern during an athletic event. Drink three to six ounces of water or diluted sports drink every 10 to 20 minutes throughout a competition.

Get Proper Rest

Your training program should include at least one, if not two, rest days per week. Otherwise, you'll feel chronically fatigued and you'll be at risk for injuries. If you fear that rest means fitness loss and fat gain, relax. Your eager appetite may scare you into thinking you'll gain weight, but actually your muscles are very busy refueling on your rest days. The carbohydrates you eat will be used to replace glycogen. With each ounce of glycogen you store in your muscles, you'll also store about three ounces of water. As a result, the scale will go up, but this reflects a gain of water, not fat.

Get What You Need

To estimate how many calories you need, first multiply your weight in pounds by 15. This is how many calories you need for your moderate daily activities. If you are very active throughout the day (apart from any workouts you do), add 10 to 20 percent. If you are inactive, subtract 10 to 20 percent. If you exercise routinely, add about 200 to 300 calories per 30 minutes of moderately hard exercise (such as running, step aerobics, or bicycling). This number represents the total daily calories you need. If you need to lose weight, subtract about 20 percent from the total calories.

These menu options represent a balanced diet for an athlete.

Breakfast
OPTION ONE
Plain fat-free yogurt with low-fat granola and mixed fresh berries
½ cup orange juice

OPTION TWO
2-egg omelet made with low-fat cheese and chopped veggies
1 low-fat ham or turkey slice
Whole-grain toast topped with fruit spread
½ cup grapefruit juice

OPTION THREE
Shredded wheat cereal with skim milk and sliced banana
1 slice whole-wheat toast with peanut butter
½ cup tomato juice

Lunch
OPTION ONE
Hearty vegetable lentil soup
1 slice whole-wheat bread topped with low-fat cream cheese
½ grapefruit
1 cup skim milk

OPTION TWO
Turkey sandwich on whole-grain bread
1 cup dark greens (kale or spinach) with low-fat dressing
1 medium tangerine
1 cup skim milk

OPTION THREE
Grilled chicken sandwich on whole-grain bread
½ cup sliced tomatoes
1 large orange
1 cup skim milk

Dinner

OPTION ONE
3 ounces fillet of sole
Baked potato topped with low-fat sour cream or plain yogurt
½ cup steamed broccoli
sliced peaches
1 cup skim milk

OPTION TWO
3 ounces grilled flank steak
½ cup vegetable pasta salad
½ cup steamed spinach
Sliced pears
1 cup skim milk

OPTION THREE
3 ounces baked chicken and ½ cup cooked rice
1 cup tossed dark greens with low-fat dressing
2 small plums
1 cup skim milk

Snacks

Remember to eat every three to four hours throughout the day to keep energy levels high. Eat one of these snacks at midmorning, midafternoon, and in the evening if you're still hungry and active.

½ cup dried fruit mixed with ¼ cup nuts
Apple or banana with 1 tablespoon peanut butter
Orange slices and 1 ounce low-fat cheese
1 cup high-fiber cereal with skim milk
½ turkey or ham sandwich on whole-grain bread
½ cup chickpeas, chopped tomatoes, and cucumbers with 2 tablespoons
    low-fat Italian dressing
½ whole-grain English muffin with 1 ounce melted cheese

½ whole-grain bagel with 2 tablespoons hummus
1 boiled egg with 1 slice whole-wheat bread
1 cup plain yogurt with ¼ cup low-fat granola
½ cup water-packed tuna with 6 low-fat crackers

For more information, refer to these websites:

FEDERAL CITIZEN INFORMATION CENTER at pueblo.gsa.gov. This site offers booklets on sports nutrition.

WHAT YOU NEED TO KNOW ABOUT at nutrition.about.com/cs/sports nutrition. This site features nutritional information for sports, endurance athletes, weight lifters, and active adults. It covers everything from supplementation and ergogenic aids to hydration and energy.

AMERICAN DIETETIC ASSOCIATION at eatright.org. This site offers lots of helpful information on sports nutrition.

INJURY PREVENTION AND TREATMENT

UPPER BODY INJURY AND THERAPY

Neck, Shoulder, Elbow, Wrist, and Hand Injuries

YOUR UPPER BODY IS A COMPLEX STRUCTURE. This chapter will focus on one area at a time and discuss injuries and treatments.

NECK

The neck is one of the most vulnerable areas of any athlete's body. Looking up to throw into the basket or falling down and sustaining a whiplash can cause ligament sprains and muscle strains in your neck. This might be mild and temporary or it might be incapacitating or, rarely, even fatal. One of the problems with an injured neck is that symptoms often do not appear until hours later. Sometimes a neck injury will not cause obvious neck pain. The most common neck injury I see in female basketball players is a trapezius muscle strain. The trapezius is a large triangular muscle that goes from your neck to your shoulder and down your upper back. A trapezius injury may cause neck, shoulder, or back pain. A significant trapezius strain can also cause you to suffer headaches. The pain can become progressively worse over a couple of days following the injury and can often cause significant pain and loss of motion in your neck and/or your shoulder. Neck injuries can cause shoulder pain and shoulder injuries can cause neck pain. If your pain does not improve over two or three days, see your physician. If you develop any pain, weakness, numbness, or tingling in your arm or hand, you must see your doctor without delay—you could have a pinched nerve in your neck. If this is the case, your doctor may be concerned about nerve impingement and therefore may order an MRI scan.

To avoid this type of injury and others, you must strengthen your neck muscles with exercise.

SHOULDER

The shoulder is susceptible to many types of injury. Proper coaching and equipment can help you avoid unnecessary injuries. This section will discuss some of the most common shoulder injuries.

Shoulder Impingement/Bursitis

If you play racquet sports, golf, basketball, volleyball, softball (pitchers), gymnastics, swimming, or any activity that requires you to perform overhead or repetitive shoulder movements, you may develop shoulder pain. Your shoulder (see Figure 21.1) is made up of a series of four muscles and tendons (tissues that connect muscle to bone) that cover the head of your upper arm bone (humerus). These tendons rotate and elevate your shoulder. They also give your shoulder some dynamic stability. The tendons are collectively called the rotator cuff. This complex of tendons lies under a bony ceiling called the acromion bone. The acromion is an extension of your shoulder blade (scapula) and can be a source of pinching (impingement) on your rotator cuff. If your rotator cuff rubs on your acromion, it can get inflamed and very painful. This is called tendonitis.

A soft sac (subacromial bursa) lies between your shoulder's acromion bone and the rotator cuff tendons. The bursa is normally filled with a small amount of lubricating fluid that minimizes friction. Bursas are usually found near joints either between the skin and underlying bones or between tendons and bones. In your shoulder, if a bursa is irritated by pressure or injury to the nearby joint, the little sac may become inflamed and swollen. This is called bursitis.

Inflamed tendons and bursa are often considered overuse injuries, commonly caused by overtraining or playing your sport without proper condi-

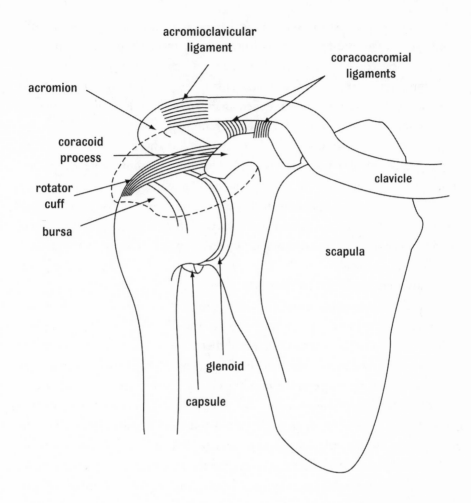

acromioclavicular
ligament

coracoacromial
ligaments

acromion

coracoid
process

clavicle

rotator
cuff

bursa

scapula

glenoid

capsule

Figure 21.1

tioning. The typical patient that I see with either tendonitis or bursitis complains of progressively worsening shoulder pain over a period of weeks or
months without a known precipitating injury. They cannot pinpoint when it
started or what caused the pain. They say it hurts to raise their arms over their
heads, to the point where they have difficulty washing their hair. Night pain
is common, especially when they accidentally roll over onto the affected

shoulder. Shoulder stiffness often occurs over time, and after a while anti-inflammatory medications such as aspirin or ibuprofen cease to have an effect.

Physical examination generally reveals moderate to severe pain with overhead motion, weakness of the rotator cuff muscles, and pain when the bursa or rotator cuff are purposely pinched against the acromion (this is a maneuver your doctor may perform to check for impingement).

Your doctor may take x-rays to determine if there are any bone spurs attached to the acromion that could be pinching the bursa or rotator cuff. Bone spurs are outgrowths of bone that develop when cartilage at the end of the bone is worn away, or when there is chronic tendonitis. If the pain is chronic or if there is suspicion of a rotator cuff tear, your doctor may recommend an MRI scan, a technique that uses a magnet instead of radiation to show soft tissue and bone. MRIs are able to reveal around 90 percent of rotator cuff tears.

Initial treatment of shoulder impingement and bursitis is nonoperative. Rest and icing should be started as soon as the diagnosis is suggested. Once the acute pain is under control, physical therapy is essential to strengthen the rotator cuff muscles to reduce the impingement. Most of the therapy can be done at home if you are motivated but you need to learn how to do it correctly. If there is too much inflammation and pain, the exercises you learn in therapy may be too excruciating. If the inflammation is really severe, and over-the-counter or prescription nonsteroidal anti-inflammatory drugs (NSAIDs) are not helpful, your orthopedic surgeon may recommend a cortisone injection. Cortisone is a type of steroid that acts as a very powerful anti-inflammatory medication. If the cortisone is not used wisely, it can be a very harmful. I do not recommend repeated cortisone injections into the shoulder because the medicine can potentially injure the rotator cuff and even cause degeneration of the tissue and ultimate tearing. However, if cortisone is used conservatively and judiciously, the risk is extremely low and the benefit can be huge. I do not recommend more than two cortisone injections into one shoulder in a lifetime. If you do get an injection, don't expect it to work immediately. It often takes one to three days to kick in.

If you don't seek medical help, inflamed tendons can turn into a rotator cuff tear, which may require surgery. Also earlier treatment will generally get you back to your sport sooner and with greater ease.

Rotator Cuff Tears

Rotator cuff tears are rare in people under the age of 40 but they do happen, especially in athletes who perform aggressive overhead or repetitive shoulder motions—for example, pitchers. A traumatic injury can also cause a rotator cuff tear but again this is rare in younger athletes.

Patients with rotator cuff tears frequently have the same complaints as those with shoulder impingement or bursitis, but they often experience a more sudden onset of weakness or inability to raise their arm over their head if the tear was caused by a specific injury. They may also have a sensation of catching or grinding while moving the arm around.

The physical examination for this injury is similar to that for impingement but the weakness of one or several of the rotator cuff muscles is more profound. One simple way to decide if there is a tear or just tendonitis is to inject the shoulder with a numbing medicine such as Xylocaine. This is a short-acting local anesthetic (similar to what your dentist uses) that safely numbs the inside of the shoulder. If the rotator cuff muscles are still weak even in the absence of pain, it increases my suspicion that the injury is an actual tear. However, if the strength returns once the pain is gone, then it is probably not a tear (or if there is one, it is most likely small and will have a chance to improve without surgery).

Doctors frequently take x-rays to look for bone spurs and arthritis. A bone spur develops when cartilage is worn away and will increase your chance of sustaining a rotator cuff tear. If there is a large rotator cuff tear, the head of the arm bone will be free to raise upward in the joint and could injure the cartilage in that joint, which often leads to arthritis. An MRI can be useful for the diagnosis.

If the tear is very small, your doctor may prescribe a nonoperative rehab program first. If this fails, surgery is indicated. If you have a full-thickness rotator cuff tear of significant size you will likely need surgery. If your tear is complicated by the tendon pulling away from the bony attachment, then surgery is absolutely necessary without delay; otherwise the muscle may atrophy (shrink and weaken), which can be irreversible.

If the rotator cuff tear is small, arthroscopic surgery (a small fiber-optic camera and small instruments through tiny incisions) may be possible. If it is somewhat larger, your doctor may try a mini-open surgical approach; this is a combination of arthroscopic and open techniques. A massive rotator cuff tear usually requires open surgery.

If you do require surgery, the rehabilitation time can be long and difficult. Most patients take three to six months to fully recover from the surgery and must participate in a program of extensive physical therapy after an initial immobilization period. The amount of time is based on the size of the tear, the tissue quality, and the type of repair.

Shoulder Tendonitis

Tendonitis in the shoulder is most common in the rotator cuff as discussed above. It may also involve the long head of the biceps tendon. The biceps are two muscles, the short head and the long head that bend the elbow. At the elbow, one tendon attaches both biceps to the radius bone (one of the bones of the forearm). The long head can become inflamed or irritated during overhead activities such as volleyball, tennis, or weightlifting. Once inflamed, the condition is called biceps tendonitis.

If you have it, you will feel pain in the front of your shoulder, which gets worse when you raise your arm overhead. You may hear and feel an occasional snap or pop in the front of your shoulder, which can also elicit pain.

Your orthopedist will perform several tests to localize the problem, which is often isolated in the long head of the biceps tendon. X-rays rarely help with this diagnosis but an MRI can often reveal the problem. Treatment initially should consist of rest, ice, NSAIDs, and physical therapy. Once your pain is gone and your strength has returned, it is important keep up a routine of stretching and strengthening so that your tendonitis does not return.

Shoulder Dislocation/Instability

The shoulder has the most range of motion of all of the joints in your body. Due to this incredible mobility, however, it is also at risk of becoming unstable should injuries occur. Unlike the hip joint where there is a large ball-and-socket joint, the bony anatomy of the shoulder is likened to a large golf ball (humeral head) on a relatively flat golf tee (glenoid). (See Figure 21.1.) Without fibrous tissues (glenoid labrum), ligaments, tendons, and muscles, your shoulder would dislocate constantly. Fortunately you have the labrum and ligaments (the capsule), which work together to give your shoulder stability at all times. The glenoid labrum is a soft fibrous tissue rim that deepens the socket by up to 50 percent to give the head of your arm bone some steadiness in the socket. The labrum is also an attachment for the capsule. The rotator cuff muscles and tendons give your shoulder dynamic stability while your muscles are working. If your labrum or capsule is injured, however, your shoulder may become unstable and dislocate (come out of the joint). The reason people with these injuries do not dislocate every other minute is because the trusty rotator cuff is working hard to keep the shoulder in place most of the time. However, if your rotator cuff doesn't do its job, your shoulder can come out of place over and over again; this is what we call shoulder instability.

There are different severities of shoulder instability. A partial dislocation is called a subluxation. This occurs when the head of your arm bone comes only partly out of the socket. A complete dislocation is where the head comes completely out of the socket.

Subluxation: Partial Dislocation

A subluxation is not uncommon in females with loose ligaments throughout their bodies. By the way, there is no such thing as being double jointed. If you are really flexible in certain parts of your skeleton—for example, if you have the ability to pull your fingers back toward the back of your hand or rotate your thumb so that it touches your forearm—then you have generalized ligamentous laxity, not double joints. Women with generalized ligamentous laxity are at a greater risk of developing shoulder pain with certain sports: Their shoulders may not be stable enough to withstand forces exerted while in a vulnerable position such as sustaining a block in volleyball with the arm in an elevated position. A subluxation can also occur in more normal ligament structures. The ligaments can become partially torn or stretched enough to allow the joint to come partway out of the socket.

If you sublux your shoulder, you may sense it slipping in and out of place, and you may feel it pop. It will be painful mostly in the front of the shoulder. Sometimes your shoulder will swell. If you think you may have subluxed your shoulder you should see your orthopedic surgeon. He or she will examine your shoulder and take x-rays. You will likely wear a sling for several days to several weeks depending on the severity of the injury. I recommend applying ice to the shoulder four to five times a day for 20 minutes at a time. I also suggest anti-inflammatory medications (if your doctor agrees) for pain and swelling. An MRI may be necessary to see if there are any labral or ligament tears. If the MRI shows a large tear of either or both of these structures, you may need surgery. If there are no significant tears, I recommend physical therapy to regain range of motion and strength. If you do have ligamentous laxity, you can often compensate for it with intensive muscle strengthening. If you continue to partially dislocate your shoulder despite physical therapy and strengthening, you may need surgery to stabilize the shoulder. This can often be done arthroscopically with a fiber-optic camera and very small incisions in the shoulder.

Dislocation

Shoulder dislocations often occur when the person's arm is in the throwing position. This is called an abducted and externally rotated position. It occurs in many sporting injuries—from falling while skiing with the arm in this position to getting blocked in volleyball with your arm in the throwing position. If you dislocate your shoulder you will know it. Most often the shoulder comes out toward the front of the joint and gets stuck there. This causes pain with any attempts to move the shoulder. Your arm will be most comfortable against your body being supported by your other arm; your shoulder will look squared off, and you may have numbness or tingling down your arm and hand.

You should have a physician put the shoulder back into place rather than try to do it yourself or have a friend do it. Your physician will take x-rays to make sure there are no bony fractures and then will reduce the dislocation (put it back into place). There are several ways to accomplish this. Sometimes, the shoulder goes right back into place easily. In some cases, however, you may need an IV and medications to relax your mind and your muscles. Only rarely is surgery necessary to put the shoulder back into place (open reduction). Once the shoulder is in place you will wear a sling for at least a couple of weeks. Then rehabilitation will begin.

If you dislocate again and again, surgery will be necessary to stabilize the shoulder. People under the age of 20 are more likely than others to develop recurrent shoulder dislocations. People over the age of 40, on the other hand, are more likely to tear their rotator cuff with a dislocation than younger people. Regardless of the treatment necessary, you should not return to your sport until you have full shoulder strength back and your orthopedic surgeon tells you that it is safe to return.

Labral Tears

As described earlier, the labrum is a soft fibrous rim of tissue that deepens the socket of the shoulder. The labrum surrounds the entire shoulder socket and can be pictured as a rim around a clock. The top part of the labrum would be at 12:00 and the bottom would be at 6:00. Injuries to the labrum can occur acutely with trauma or with repetitive overuse.

Traumatic injuries can occur because of sudden pulling of the shoulder such as lifting a heavy weight in the gym; aggressive reaching overhead with a pulling on the shoulder, such as when trying to stop sliding down a cliff or steep hill; and direct impact to the shoulder and elbow during a fall.

Repetitive overuse injuries can occur in rock climbers, weightlifters, throwing athletes, and kayakers.

Labral tears can occur anywhere on the socket. The most common tears I see with acute injuries are on top of the labrum, 12:00, or near the bottom and in front of the labrum, 5:00 or 7:00, depending on the right or left shoulder. The tears closer to the bottom often are associated with shoulder subluxations or dislocations. SLAP (superior labrum anterior [front] posterior [back]) lesions are tears of the labrum at around 12:00 where the biceps tendon attaches. Signs of labral tears can be similar to those of other shoulder injuries and therefore can be very difficult to diagnose. Symptoms include pain with only certain motions of the shoulder (depending on where the tear is located), most commonly overhead; intermittent clicking, catching, or locking in the shoulder as if something is in the wrong place; weakness with certain arm motions; stiffness in the shoulder; a sense of instability in the shoulder; and pain at night.

If you have some of these symptoms after an acute injury or if the symptoms just appear and do not go away after a couple of weeks, you should see an orthopedic specialist. Many primary care physicians are not familiar with these shoulder problems and the diagnosis can be missed. Your orthopedist will have a battery of physical tests to help localize the problem. Often the diagnosis can be made with the history and physical examination alone. X-rays are generally negative, as the problem is in the soft tissue, which does not show up on x-rays. MRIs to look for labrum tears often produce a false negative. If you have an MR arthrogram (where a dye is injected into your shoulder right before you have the MRI), then your doctor's chances of seeing the labrum tear are improved but there still are a lot of false negatives. I generally trust my history and physical examination for these particular injuries more than the MRIs. I nearly always try a nonoperative treatment program first, which includes rest from any aggravating activity, physical therapy for rotator cuff strengthening, and anti-inflammatory medications. If these fail, arthroscopic surgery will be necessary to both make the diagnosis and to treat the problem. If the patient actually locks the shoulder, which is a sign of a large labrum tear, then I proceed right to surgery because the labrum otherwise will be at risk of further tearing. During surgery the labrum tear will either be shaved (if a partial tear) or reattached to the bone if it is torn off of its bony attachment. After labrum repair, you will need a long rehabilitation program of physical therapy for range of motion and strengthening before you return to your sport.

AC Separations (Separated Shoulder)

The acromioclavicular (AC) joint is made up of the acromion (an extension of the shoulder blade) and the end of the clavicle (collarbone). There are several ligaments that attach this joint together, which are all at risk of injury. (See Figure 21.1.) AC joint injuries occur frequently in a variety of sports. Among the most common are those that result from striking the boards or the ice in hockey, falling off a bicycle or a horse, or crashing on a snowboard.

The injury occurs when you strike the point of your shoulder onto something hard or immovable driving your shoulder downward without fracturing your collarbone. When the shoulder is driven downward the ligaments can tear between the collar bone (clavicle) and shoulder blade (scapula) causing a separation between these two bones. There can be a partial or complete tear of one or more of the ligaments. The ligament that attaches the acromion to the collarbone is called the AC ligament (acromioclavicular ligament). There are two additional ligaments that attach the collarbone to another part of the shoulder blade called the CC ligaments (coracoclavicular ligaments).

If you land on your shoulder or strike it against something hard, you should suspect an AC separation if you have any of the following symptoms: pain at the top of your shoulder over your AC joint; a bump at the top of the shoulder that is painful to the touch; movement of the bones at the top of the shoulder where the bump is located and pain with overhead movement or when moving the arm attached to the affected shoulder across your chest.

There are many different severities of AC separations. To recommend appropriate treatment your physician will take an x-ray to determine how severe yours is.

There are six different grades of AC separations:

1. Partial sprain of the AC ligament without a bump. It does not show up on x-ray and generally heals in two to four weeks.
2. Tear of the AC ligament and partial sprain of the CC ligaments may have a small bump, may show up on x-ray, and generally heals in four to six weeks.
3. Tear of both the AC and CC ligaments will have a large bump, will show up on x-ray, and will take at least six weeks to heal. You will always have a residual bump with these but functionally you should be fine. Some surgeons will operate on grade 3 injuries, but this is a bit controversial. I only operate on grade 3 injuries in an elite overhead athlete where the subtle functional differences could present problems for competition. Treatment for all of these injuries begins with sling immobilization for a few days to a couple of weeks, ice, and anti-inflammatory medication. I recommend physical therapy once the acute pain has resolved to regain full range of motion and strength in the shoulder.
4.–6. Tears of both the AC and CC ligaments with the clavicle displaced into a position that is not replaceable without surgery. Grades 4, 5, and 6

do require surgery within seven days of the injury. If you don't have surgery, you may experience functional limitations as well as chronic pain. The surgery generally has an excellent outcome.

COLLARBONE FRACTURES

Falling off of bicycles, crashing on snowboards, or running into the boards in hockey are common causes of collarbone fracture. The injury occurs if you either fall directly onto the shoulder or land on an elbow driving the shoulder upward. The collarbone (clavicle) is part of the shoulder and plays a role in connecting the arm to the body. The collarbone is considered a long bone and it generally breaks in the middle. Fractures can occur on either end of the bone, however, and these can sometimes be more serious. If you take a fall and feel pain in the collarbone region, you should suspect a fracture. Symptoms include pain when attempting to raise the arm forward or across your chest; a grinding noise in the clavicle with movement of the arm; a sharp pointy bone fragment from the fracture that elevates the skin causing tenting; swelling within an hour or so of the injury or a bump in the middle portion of the clavicle where the fracture is located.

In the physician's office or emergency room, the physical examination usually reveals the diagnosis; however, the physician may suggest an x-ray to see the extent and exact location of the fracture.

Treatment is almost always nonoperative. I recommend a simple sling for up to six weeks. Gentle range of motion of the shoulder can begin as soon as the pain is tolerable but you should avoid overhead activity (or activities bringing the arm across your chest) for four to six weeks or until these movements are pain free. Icing and nonsteroidal anti-inflammatory medications such as ibuprofen can be used immediately for pain and swelling. By three weeks, physical therapy exercises can begin, including some strengthening exercises. Most people are healed enough by six weeks that they can increase their activities and start getting back into at least some of their sports. If the fracture was really severe (in several pieces), this may take up to 12 weeks.

Surgery is rarely necessary unless the fracture came through the skin at the time of injury (open fracture) or if the fracture does not heal after conservative treatment (non-union). Certain breaks at the ends of the clavicle may, however, require early surgery especially if ligaments are involved. Most athletes do very well after surgery.

One thing to expect after a clavicle fracture is a bump—a normal part of the healing process. Functionally you will be able to do all of the activities that you used to do. If you don't want a bump, you can have surgery, but you will be left with a scar. I personally recommend not doing surgery for the average clavicle fracture because the bumps are not usually very pronounced and it is better to avoid the risk of surgery.

ELBOW

Elbow pain and injury can stem from a number of causes. This section will cover some of the more common ones.

Tennis Elbow and Golfer's Elbow

Tennis and golfer's elbow is a painful inflammatory overuse condition. I most often see this condition in patients who don't play racquet sports or golf at all. Many activities can cause the discomfort.

The bony prominence on the outside of your elbow is called the lateral epicondyle and the one on the inside of the elbow is called the medial epicondyle (see Figure 21.2). Tennis elbow is an inflammation of those outside tendons and thus is called lateral epicondylitis. The pain can radiate down your forearm and can increase with extension of your wrist (cocking the wrist

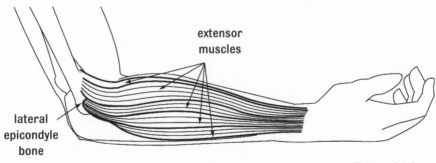

extensor muscles

lateral epicondyle bone

Figure 21.2

backward with resistance). Golfer's elbow is an inflammation of the flexor tendons that originate from the inside of the elbow and is called medial epicondylitis. The pain can radiate down the forearm and can increase with
flexion of the wrist (bending the wrist forward with resistance).

These inflammatory conditions generally occur from overuse rather than
specific trauma. Tiny tears occur in the tendons near the elbow bones. If you
do not treat this condition early, the pain will worsen because the inflammation increases; simple tasks such as picking up a tennis racquet or pouring a
glass of milk can become intensely painful. You may have pain at rest and have
difficulty sleeping. The diagnosis is easy with just examining the elbow and
finding out you have a history of repetitive elbow activity. The first step in
treatment is to stop performing the painful activity. If it is tennis or golf, you
must stop playing. Rest will give the tiny tears a chance to heal. For the acute
inflammation, I recommend ice massage five times a day for 20 minutes at a
time. You freeze water in a small paper cup and tear the top of the cup off
once it's frozen. Flip the cup over and you have a nice handle to hold the ice.
Then rub the ice gently over the painful area in a circular motion. Nonsteroidal anti-inflammatory medications can also be useful.

Stretching is one of the most important elements to successful treatment.
For tennis elbow, you want to flex the hand and wrist downward (with the
elbow straight) to stretch these extensor tendons. (See Figure 23.16.) For
golfer's elbow you want to extend the hand and wrist backward to stretch these
flexor tendons. (See Figure 23.17.) Stretching is very important because it can
increase the blood supply into these areas and help break up scar tissue that
may have formed. You really can't stretch enough. Every time you think about
it you should stretch for several minutes.

If you are unable to resolve the pain on your own in two to three weeks,
you should see your doctor. He or she may recommend a course of physical
therapy and/or a cortisone injection to knock out the inflammation. Stretching is still important after the injection. If it doesn't cure your pain, then you
can bet that there is a significant amount of scar tissue in the tendon; in this
case, surgery may be necessary to remove scar tissue. Before surgery however, talk to your doctor about acupuncture. I have found that acupuncture
can be a powerful tool for certain inflammatory or scar conditions such as
tennis elbow. Ever since I began recommending acupuncture for these cases

a few years ago, I have not had to perform surgery on a single case of tennis elbow. I know that a lot of my orthopedic colleagues would roll their eyes at this but it is hard to argue with results.

Once you are ready to return to your sport, you may want to examine your technique to prevent a recurrence of the problem. You can also wear a forearm brace, which will help absorb the stress of the activity before it strikes your elbow.

The best treatment is still prevention, so if you want to engage in sports with repetitive forearm motions, get into a good stretching program and have a professional help you with your equipment and your technique.

Elbow Bursitis

Bursitis of the elbow is a very common condition. It can occur suddenly with a blow to the elbow or it can come on gradually from chronic rubbing of the elbow on an ill-fitting elbow pad. The bursa in the elbow is a sac of tissue between the skin and the olecranon bone. The olecranon is the bony prominence on the back of your elbow, which is pointed when you bend your elbow fully. The bursa is normally flat. However, when you develop bursitis, the bursa fills with fluid and forms a large lump that can be quite painful. Treatment for the most common type of olecranon bursitis is to avoid the activity that caused it or any painful activity; ice the bursa for 20 minutes at a time four or five times a day; wrap the elbow with an Ace bandage or a neoprene sleeve (available at drug stores) in between icing sessions; and elevate the elbow above your heart whenever possible.

If there is significant pain in the elbow after a blow to it, you should have a physician evaluate you, as you may have an injury in addition to the bursitis. If you are unable to alleviate the bursitis with the measures described above, then your physician may recommend draining the fluid from the bursa, placing a compressive dressing on it for several days, and then treating you with an anti-inflammatory medication such as ibuprofen. If this fails and you continue to get fluid in the bursa, your physician can inject the site with cortisone. The last resort is surgical removal of the bursa.

Occasionally you can get an infected bursitis. This can be extremely painful and typically manifests as a hot red bursa, a fever, and pain with elbow movement. A physician must evaluate this promptly.

Elbow Tendonitis

The most common forms of tendonitis in the elbow were discussed above with tennis and golfer's elbow. However you can also develop inflammation of two other tendons that cross the elbow—the biceps and triceps. The biceps bends the elbow whereas the triceps straightens out the elbow. Overuse injuries in sports can affect either of these tendons with tiny tendon tears leading to inflammation and pain.

Treatment is the same as for elbow bursitis. If the pain persists for more than two to three weeks with treatment, you should see your doctor for a definitive diagnosis and physical therapy. Sometimes you can sustain a traumatic injury to these tendons where they tear completely or tear away from the bone. These injuries require immediate attention by an orthopedic surgeon for reattachment. I recently took care of an elite rock climber who had fallen off a rock ledge. When she tried to stop her fall with her hand, the severe pulling on the elbow caused her triceps tendon to pull right off her bone. She required surgical reattachment of the tendon to the bone and went on to heal beautifully, although she was out of rock climbing for six months.

Funny Bone Pain: Ulnar Neuritis

At some time in your life you surely have struck your funny bone. It actually isn't a bone at all. It's your ulnar nerve. This very important nerve travels through a little groove on the inside of your elbow called the cubital tunnel. The nerve is extremely close to the skin in this region before it dives into some muscles and disappears into your forearm on its way to your hand. Striking the nerve suddenly can cause severe electric type pain, which can zap all the way into your ring and pinky fingers. The pain can last for seconds, minutes, days, or even weeks depending on the amount of force that was applied to the nerve. Some of the small muscles in your hand, which get their signals from the ulnar nerve, can become weak if the nerve is injured. A more severe injury to the elbow, such as a fracture or a dislocation, can also be associated with an ulnar nerve injury. If there is significant swelling in the cubital tunnel, the ulnar nerve doesn't have enough room and the nerve's protective covering can be damaged. This can affect long-term nerve function. In more chronic cases, where ulnar nerve function is impaired for a very long time, the effects may not be reversible.

Ulnar nerve symptoms that should send you to a physician include:

- Numbness or tingling in your ring and pinky fingers when your elbow is flexed or bent
- Pain or tingling in your hand while driving or at night in bed
- Weakness in your hand with fine motor movements such as typing or playing piano
- Weakness of grip or pinching motions
- Sensitivity or pain on the inside of your elbow

Your doctor will diagnose the problem through a thorough history of your symptoms, a physical examination, and, sometimes, diagnostic tests. If the condition was instigated by a fall or a direct blow to your elbow, then x-rays may be necessary to rule out a fracture. Sometimes an EMG (electromyelogram) is necessary to make the diagnosis of a nerve entrapment or nerve injury.

Treatment is generally nonoperative. If the elbow is fractured, the treatment will begin with the appropriate recommendations for the fracture. If there is no fracture, then rest from any pain-inducing activities is mandatory. Keeping your elbow extended will take pressure off the nerve and help to give it more room in the tunnel until the inflammation decreases. Avoid crossing your arms over your chest and excessive bending of the elbow such as holding a telephone to your ear for a long time. A night splint to keep the elbow straight can be very helpful especially in the early phases of treatment. If you do return to your sport, be sure to wear well-fitting elbow guards to avoid further accidental bumps or bruises to the nerve.

Surgery is rarely necessary. However, if your muscles continue to weaken (atrophy) or if you have intractable pain, your nerve must be moved to a new area. The surgery is called an ulnar nerve transposition. Your surgeon will move the nerve out of the tight cubital tunnel to the front of the elbow where there is much more room.

Elbow Fracture

One of the most common elbow fractures that occurs during sports is the olecranon fracture. The olecranon is the large pointy part of the elbow that is visible when you bend your elbow fully. There are no muscles covering its tip—just skin and a bursa (thin sac of tissue); therefore, it is at risk of injury if you strike your bent elbow against a hard surface. Signs of a fracture include severe pain immediately after the injury and early swelling and tenderness at the point of the elbow. If the fracture is displaced (moved out of position) or associated with a dislocation of the joint your elbow may appear deformed. You may also have numbness in your hand and severe pain with any movement of the joint.

It is important that you see a physician for evaluation and x-ray examination to determine whether or not you have a fracture. There are several types of breaks and your doctor will recommend the appropriate treatment depending on the fracture pattern. Treatments range from a temporary splint and sling to immediate surgery. The problem with the elbow joint is that if you immobilize it too long, the joint will get stiff and normal range of motion may never return. Therefore, if the fracture is in good position and is stable (meaning it doesn't move out of place with gentle range of motion) then your physician will recommend a splint, ice, and rest for about a week. You will have another set of x-rays, and if the fracture is in good position, you will begin gentle range-of-motion wrist and hand exercises.

If your fracture has displaced bone fragments or if the fracture is unstable (the pieces move in and out of place with motion), then surgery is necessary. The surgery involves placing metal wires and screws or a plate with screws to hold your fracture in place. This will allow you to move your elbow as early as a couple of days after surgery to prevent stiffness in the joint. The bone generally takes 6 to 12 weeks to heal. As the bone is healing and becoming stronger, more advanced physical therapy exercises will be introduced to help you regain strength so you can return to your sport.

Occasionally, the triceps tendon may have pulled off a piece of bone at the very tip of the elbow bone. This is called an avulsion fracture of the olecranon and may require surgery to remove the small piece of bone and reattach the tendon to the olecranon.

There are other bones in the elbow that can fracture, for instance, the distal humerus (bottom of the arm bone) and the radial head (top of one of the forearm bones). I have treated my share of bottom of the arm bone fractures in snowboarders. I call them a "bag of bones" because they are often in so many pieces they can be a real challenge to put back together. If you have significant elbow pain or swelling after a crash, you should be examined by a physician right away.

Elbow Dislocations

The elbow is the most commonly dislocated joint in children and the second most common dislocated joint in adults. Dislocation occurs when you fall onto an outstretched hand and the bones in your elbow come out of place. I write from experience when I describe the severe pain involved with this injury. When I was 13 and a gymnast, I was practicing my backhand springs and I landed badly on my outstretched arm. My entire body weight (even though it wasn't much) torqued my elbow right out of position and I fell onto the ground. The pain was so intense I can remember it to this day. My elbow didn't look like an elbow anymore and I couldn't bend or straighten the joint at all. The ride to the emergency room is also something I'll never forget; I can still map out every pothole and bump in the road. Once at the emergency room and after a painful x-ray, the doctor diagnosed me with a dislocated elbow and called for the orthopedic surgeon (my first of many encounters with such a person). As soon as he put the elbow back into place, my pain was essentially gone. Unfortunately for me, back then doctors didn't realize that long immobilization periods were bad for elbow joints. They put me in a long arm cast for six weeks and it took me 18 months of very painful rehabilitation and physical therapy to regain my range of motion. I did get it all back, but I was one of the lucky ones.

When I treat elbow dislocations I look for associated fractures on x-rays. I immediately reduce the dislocation (put it back in place), with the help of intravenous (IV) pain medication if necessary. Sometimes I can slip the elbow back into place quickly and easily without starting an IV. If the elbow has been out of place for several hours, I prefer to give the patient some IV medicine to relax the muscles and make the reduction easier on the patient (and me). If the patient cannot tolerate the procedure even with IV medicines then general anesthesia is necessary. Once the dislocation is reduced, I test the elbow through a full range of motion to ensure that it is stable and will not dislocate again. I do another round of x-rays to see if any fractures are present or have been displaced with the reduction maneuver. The patient will be in a splint and a sling for 7 to 10 days. I recommend ice and encourage the patient to elevate the elbow as much as possible.

After the short immobilization period, intensive physical therapy begins. This is important to regain range of motion. Some people can take several months to fully recover from this injury if physical therapy is started early. Otherwise, as in my case, it could take years.

The good news is that my elbow injury sparked my interest in orthopedics.

WRIST

Wrist pain can stem from a number of causes. This section discusses the more common ones.

Wrist Sprains

A sprain is an injury to a ligament in a joint. Ligaments are tissues made of collagen; they connect bones to bones. The wrist contains many ligaments. The wrist itself is made up of eight bones (carpal bones) and these are sandwiched in between the forearm bones (radius and ulna) and the hand bones (metacarpals). If you fall onto your hand and bend your wrist forward or backward, you can stretch or tear these ligaments. The more damage there is to the ligament, the more severe the sprain will be. A mild sprain is just a stretch, and you can expect a relatively quick recovery. However, a severe sprain is one in which there is a complete tear of the ligament or a tear of the ligament away from the bone. The ligament may even pull a tiny piece of bone off with it; this is called an avulsion fracture. These more severe injuries may require surgery and a long recovery time.

Symptoms of a wrist sprain include:

- Pain immediately after the injury, which may progress over several hours
- Swelling in the joint

- Bruising over several hours or days
- Pain with motion of the wrist
- Tenderness when you touch certain areas of the wrist
- Warm skin sensation in the affected area
- Clicking or popping inside the wrist with certain motions

If you have some of these symptoms, you should see a doctor. Without an x-ray it can be difficult to distinguish between a sprain and a fracture. Your doctor must determine whether your sprain is severe enough to require surgery or other treatments. If you have only mild swelling and pain the best way to treat a sprained wrist is rest and immobilization of the joint. Ice the wrist for 20 minutes at a time four or five times a day. Between icing sessions wrap the wrist with an Ace wrap or a neoprene sleeve. Elevate the wrist above your heart whenever possible. You may wish to take a nonsteroidal anti-inflammatory medication such as ibuprofen.

If your pain persists, you should see a doctor. Once a diagnosis is made and you begin treatment, it may take anywhere from two weeks to three months to recover from the sprain.

Prevention is the best medicine. For sports such as in-line skating, snowboarding, and skateboarding—the most common causes of wrist injury I see in my practice—wrist guards decrease the possibility of wrist injuries significantly.

Wrist Fractures

Wrist fractures are extremely common in many sports such as snowboarding, in-line skating, ice skating, skateboarding, mountain biking, and horseback riding. Just about any sport where you can fall forward or backward and land on an outstretched hand can cause a wrist fracture. Putting your hands out to break a fall is a natural instinct to protect the rest of your body. There are many bones in the wrist that can fracture with this type of fall (see Figure 21.3). Here are the most common types I see in my practice.

Colles Fracture. This fracture is located at the lower end of the radius (one of two bones in the forearm) just above the wrist. Colles fractures are

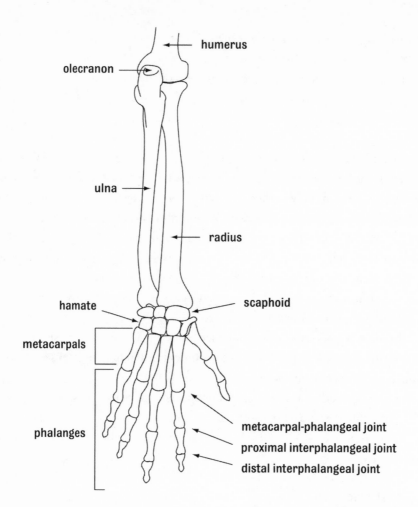

olecranon

humerus

ulna

radius

hamate

scaphoid

metacarpals

phalanges

metacarpal-phalangeal joint

proximal interphalangeal joint

distal interphalangeal joint

Figure 21.3

more common in middle-aged or older women but they can occur in any age group. Symptoms of a Colles fracture include:

- Immediate pain
- Swelling
- Deformity at the wrist that can look like a dinner fork

- Inability to move the wrist because of pain
- Crackling in the bones (crepitus)
- Numbness and tingling in the fingers (acute carpal tunnel syndrome) from swelling at the fracture site (Carpal tunnel syndrome is described in a later section.)

If you suspect you may have a wrist fracture, you must have an x-ray. If there is simply a crack in the bone, a doctor will put a cast on your wrist for four to six weeks. Then you'll need physical therapy to regain your joint motion, strength, and overall function. If there is a deformity in the bone, your doctor will most likely try to fix the fracture by pulling on it, putting it back into place, and then applying a splint or cast. This is called a closed reduction; it can usually be done in the clinic or emergency room with some mild form of local anesthesia or IV medication.

If the fracture is really severe, surgery will be necessary to put the bones into place and hold them there with plates and screws, pins, or an external fixator, a device that holds the fracture in place from the outside.

No matter how good a job your doctor does fixing your fracture, some of the more severe fractures can damage the joint cartilage to the point where it is not repairable. This can lead to posttraumatic arthritis—with stiffness and chronic pain—over time.

Scaphoid Fracture. The scaphoid bone, also known as the navicular bone, is one of the eight bones (carpals) that make up the wrist. It is shaped like a cashew and is located on the thumb side of the wrist where the forearm attaches. The blood supply to this small bone is poor in that it only gets blood from one end of the bone. If there is a fracture at the mid-portion of the bone and treatment is delayed, the other end may not get enough blood. This can lead to bone death (avascular necrosis), which in turn can cause severe arthritis and collapse of the affected area of the wrist.

With this type of fracture there is often little swelling. There is no deformity, and the pain can be minimal. You may think you have a mild sprain, which makes this type of fracture easy to miss. Scaphoid fractures generally occur in people between the ages of 20 and 40 and are rare in children and older adults. A fall on an outstretched hand with the wrist in at least a 90° extension is the mechanism of injury. Symptoms of a scaphoid fracture include pain and tenderness on the thumb side of the wrist, minimal swelling of the thumb side of the wrist, and pain and weakness with grip.

If you have any of these symptoms see a doctor. You will probably need an x-ray, but be aware that scaphoid fractures often do not show up on the initial x-ray. If your doctor's examination reveals evidence of a fracture, you will need treatment.

If there is tenderness at a very specific location of the wrist (called the anatomic snuffbox), I place the patient in a short arm-thumb spica cast (even if the x-ray is negative), which goes across the wrist and includes the thumb. Ten days after the injury I obtain another x-ray. If the x-ray is still negative, then the diagnosis is a sprain and I treat the patient accordingly. If the x-ray reveals a fracture, the patient will remain casted—usually for about three months.

If the fracture is displaced, the patient will need surgery to align the bone. If the diagnosis is delayed, the bone may not heal, which means surgery with a screw and bone graft will be necessary. Only 75 percent of patients will heal after this type of surgery and there is a higher chance of bone death because of the delayed treatment.

Hamate Fracture. The hamate bone is one of eight carpal bones in the wrist. It is on the same side of the wrist as the pinky finger (see Figure 21.3). The bone has a hook that protrudes toward the palm (you can feel it on the base of your hand). Pain in this location may be a sign of a fracture. In tennis, it is often an overuse injury from repetitive stress from the racquet on the hook of the bone.

If you have pain in this area, you should see an orthopedist. Often routine x-rays of the hand and wrist miss hamate fractures. You really need the expertise of a specialist for this diagnosis. Sometimes computerized tomography (CT scan) is necessary. A CT scan is a special type of image that shows the cross section of a bone; it enables your doctor to see a lot more detail of the bones. If there is a fracture and it is diagnosed early, a cast will allow healing. However, if the fracture is missed and does not heal, surgery will be necessary to remove the hook of the bone. If your evaluation with your orthopedist does not reveal a fracture, you probably have a bruise. Treat it with rest; and get your racquet grip resized. If your bone doesn't heal—the hook may be separated from the rest of the bone by scar tissue—you may require surgery to remove the hook.

Wrist Ligament Tears

There is a complex of ligaments and cartilage on one side of the wrist called the triangular fibrocartilage complex (TFCC). It is on the same side of the wrist as the pinky finger (ulnar wrist). Injuries to this region can be quite painful. Overuse injuries to this small complex are common, especially in tennis. You can also get tendonitis of the extensor carpi ulnaris tendon (ECU), which is a neighbor of the TFCC. The proximity of these two can make the diagnosis difficult.

Signs of injury to the TFCC or ECU include:

- Tenderness over the ulnar wrist
- Occasional popping or catching in the ulnar wrist
- Sensation of the wrist locking up at times
- Noises (crepitation) in the ulnar wrist joint
- Pain in palm-up position (supination) or bending toward the ulnar side (ulnar deviation)
- Swelling over the ulnar wrist
- Pain with forced bending of the wrist

This type of injury can be difficult to diagnose. I recommend a specialist. Your orthopedist will examine you, and will most likely be able to differentiate between a TFCC tear and ECU tendonitis. X-rays will not be able to diagnose either of these problems but can rule other problems out such as a fracture. Initial treatment is bracing of the wrist to avoid painful ulnar deviation. Ice, anti-inflammatory medications, physical therapy, and rest are important for healing either condition. You may have to avoid the sport or activity that led to this injury for a while to allow healing. If there is a tear of the TFCC (which is rare in racquet sports but possible), then a longer period of rest, splinting, and physical therapy may be prescribed. If the tear does not heal, surgery may be necessary—especially if there are mechanical symptoms such as locking.

If initial conservative treatment fails, sometimes an MR arthrogram is helpful in diagnosing a tear of the TFCC. If a tear is present and is not responding to treatment, then a small surgery using an arthroscope (fiber-optic camera) can clean up or repair the tear.

Carpal Tunnel Syndrome

The carpal tunnel is located at the wrist on the same side as the palm. It is made up of a bony floor and a roof called the transverse carpal ligament. The tunnel contains nine flexor tendons of the fingers and thumb and a large nerve called the median. The median nerve travels through the tunnel on its way to the hand where it gives strength to several muscles and gives some of the digits sensation (thumb, index, long, and half of the ring finger). If there is pressure on the median nerve as it travels through this tunnel, then you can experience one or more of the following symptoms:

- Numbness or tingling in one or more of the associated digits
- Pain radiating into the hand or up into the forearm or even up to the shoulder
- Electric shocks into the fingers if you tap the carpal tunnel
- Pain in the wrist and hand that wakes you up at night
- Weakness in your grip
- Clumsiness with small-motor activities and perhaps atrophy (shrinkage) of some of the muscles in your hand

Causes of carpal tunnel syndrome include:

- Thickening of the transverse carpal ligament and of the tendon sheaths (coverings over the tendons)
- Arthritic changes in the wrist bones, especially rheumatoid arthritis

- Trauma to the wrist with acute swelling
- Diabetes
- Thyroid disease
- Pregnancy
- Hormonal changes associated with menopause

Carpal tunnel syndrome can also occur from overuse injuries in sports. For instance, repetitive bending or flexing of the wrist when throwing a softball can cause carpal tunnel syndrome. It is also common in computer operators and sometimes an adjustment of their workstation will cure the problem.

If you feel that you have any of the above symptoms you should consult your physician. They will be able to diagnose you with a history of your complaints and a physical examination. Sometimes a nerve test (electromyelogram) is necessary to see if the nerve is in danger and surgery should be done early. Nonoperative treatment includes bracing (especially at night), avoidance of repetitive wrist bending, physical therapy, vitamin B supplements, and anti-inflammatory medications. Other treatments may include acupuncture or a cortisone injection into the flexor tendon sheaths to reduce inflammation and increase the space in the tunnel for the median nerve.

If these measures fail, surgery will be necessary to prevent irreversible damage to the nerve and irreversible atrophy to the muscles that rely on the median nerve. The surgery is called a carpal tunnel release and is relatively simple. It is done as an outpatient procedure often under local anesthesia. You can stay awake for the procedure if you wish or you can be sedated with IV medication. A small incision is made over the carpal tunnel area and the transverse carpal ligament is divided or released to make room for the median nerve.

After surgery most of my patients experience relief of their pain immediately. Normal nerve function will return over time depending on the amount of nerve damage that had occurred. Sometimes full function will not return but most patients can resume normal activity in a matter of three to six weeks after surgery. Some may need extensive physical therapy to regain strength in the hand and fingers.

Wrist Tendonitis (DeQuervain's)

There are many tendons crossing the wrist making their way into the hand, fingers, and thumb. All these tendons are at risk of becoming inflamed from either acute injury or overuse during sports activities or daily living. There are two tendons particularly at risk of an inflammatory overuse syndrome called DeQuervain's tenosynovitis. These two tendons live in a tendon sheath and travel to the thumb. On their way there, they cross a bony prominence on the arm bone just above the wrist. Inflammation can occur in the tendon sheaths in this area on the thumb side. If there is inflammation in the sheath that houses the tendons, then any stretch involving the tendons can cause severe pain.

If you have pain in this region for a couple of weeks that doesn't respond to rest, icing, and anti-inflammatory medications, you should see your doctor. She or he will ask you how you think you developed this problem. Most patients can pinpoint repetitive thumb use as the cause. If the doctor moves the wrist to the side away from the thumb tendons with your thumb hiding inside a grip of your fingers, you may feel severe pain. This simple maneuver, called a Finklestein test, will help your doctor diagnose DeQuervain's, although you may also need x-rays to rule out other possible sources of pain.

Treatment of DeQuervain's includes rest, bracing of the wrist and thumb, icing, nonsteroidal anti-inflammatory medications, and physical therapy.

If these fail, you can try acupuncture or your doctor can give you a cortisone injection. I have not had to operate on a case of DeQuervain's in more than seven years. However, if you procrastinate about going to your doctor and delay treatment, your prognosis worsens. If you wait too long, you may need surgery.

HAND

Think about how much you use your hands. Now think about how your life would be affected if injury or overuse caused a limitation of your hands' ability to function. Most of us take our hands for granted, although we notice quickly enough when we injure them. Here are some of the more common sports-related hand injuries.

Skier's Thumb

You don't have to be a skier to sustain this injury. Many sports that may involve falling (such as mountain biking) can cause it. It is most common in skiing, however, for one simple reason: ski poles. To break a fall, you naturally put your hands out. If you fall with a ski pole strapped to your hand this can force the thumb into a very unnatural position and cause this injury.

The ulnar collateral ligament is located at the base of the thumb, which is at risk of injury if you fall onto your hand and your thumb gets pulled in a direction away from the other fingers. The ligament can tear partially (mild sprain) or completely (severe sprain).

Signs of ulnar collateral ligament injury include pain and swelling on the inside base of the thumb, weakness in pinching objects, skin discoloration, and pain when moving the thumb.

If you think you may have injured the ligament, see an orthopedist. Your doctor will move your thumb to test its stability and determine the severity of the sprain. X-rays will reveal whether or not there is an associated fracture. Sometimes the torn ligament will pull a piece of bone off with it. This is an important consideration to determine appropriate treatment.

There are three types of ulnar collateral ligament injuries:

- **Grade I:** A mild sprain that can be treated in a small splint that holds the thumb stable for two to three weeks. Ice and anti-inflammatory medications are helpful in the early stages.

- **Grade II:** A moderate sprain that is still treatable without surgery with a splint or a cast for approximately four to six weeks. Physical therapy may be needed after the immobilization period to regain full range of motion, strength, and hand function.

- **Grade III:** A severe sprain. If you sustain this injury, you probably will need surgery. The ligament pulls away from its bony attachment and is caught behind another structure and cannot find its way back. As a result, the ligament is unable to heal back to its original location. If it is left untreated, chronic instability, weakness, and even arthritis will occur at the joint. Surgery is usually done on an outpatient basis by anesthetizing only the hand and returning the ligament to its original position. A cast is necessary after surgery for approximately four weeks followed by a splint and physical therapy for an additional four to eight weeks. The success rate of this surgery is excellent if it is performed within seven to ten days of the injury.

There is no sure way to prevent this injury. However, when skiing, if you don't use the straps on your poles, you have a chance of ditching your poles as you fall, which can decrease your risk.

Baseball Finger

Baseball finger can occur in softball too. It is an injury to the tip of a finger when the ball strikes it and bends it downward forcefully. This is also called a mallet finger. Normally your joint near the fingertip (distal interphalangeal joint, or DIP) can only flex toward the palm about 40 degrees. When the force of the striking ball pushes the finger down more than 40 degrees something has to fail. Normally the extensor tendon (which straightens the DIP joint) will tear or it will pull a piece of bone off with it. When the tendon or bone fails, the DIP joint will not be able to actively straighten out and the tip of the finger will simply hang down like a limp fish. You will most likely have decent grip strength but no ability to straighten out your finger by yourself.

The finger may swell quickly and be extremely painful. Apply ice and elevate your hand above your heart. You may need an x-ray to see if you have sustained a fracture or a dislocation. If you have a mallet finger and are treated in a splint right away for six weeks, you should heal well without surgery. Physical therapy may be required after splinting to regain full range of motion.

If there is a fracture and the piece of bone is not sitting where it belongs, surgery will be necessary to either pin the piece of bone back into place or to remove a small bone fragment and reattach the tendon correctly. If you wait weeks before seeing a doctor, splinting may not work. In this case you can either live with the deformity or have surgery. The results of a late surgery are never as good as they would have been with early splint treatment.

The message here is that if a ball strikes your finger and you suddenly can't straighten it without assistance, see a doctor right away.

Finger Fracture/Dislocation

Finger injuries are very common in sports such as basketball and volleyball. There are many bones and ligaments that make up each of our fingers and thumbs. There are three bones (phalanges) and three joints in each finger, and two bones and two joints in each thumb. Multiple ligaments connect these bones and help keep them in good alignment so that we can use our hands for fine motor skills and manipulation as well as for activities that require strength.

If you jam or tweak your finger and have pain, deformity, swelling, or an inability to move your finger, see a doctor immediately. Don't ask your teammate or coach to try to fix it. They could miss a serious injury. If you have a team doctor present, he or she may try to stabilize the injury and allow you to finish the game if you are able to deal with the pain. This can be a controversial decision. After the game, go immediately for an x-ray and appropriate treatment.

Dislocated Finger

A joint doesn't dislocate without torn ligaments. The goal is to get the joint back into place and allow the ligaments to heal so you will have a stable joint and avoid future dislocations. If you have a dislocated finger, your doctor will gently pull on the finger and put it back in place. This can generally be done without surgery. If you are in severe pain, the doctor can numb the finger with local anesthesia. Sometimes the shots from the anesthesia hurt as much as putting the finger back in so your doctor will give you the choice. Once the joint is in place your doctor will tape your injured finger to a neighboring finger to act as a splint (buddy taping). This will allow early range of motion of the injured finger so there will be less stiffness. The neighboring finger will keep the injured finger from dislocating again while the ligaments are healing. Rarely, there are soft tissues in the way of putting the joint back in place. In that case, you will have to go to the operating room for an open reduction during which the surgeon will make an incision to free up the soft tissues. These tissues are then repaired to maintain stability of the joint.

Finger Fracture

There are many types of fractures that can occur in the fingers and thumb. Simple fractures, which are in good position, can be treated with buddy taping the affected finger to an adjacent finger. However, more complex fractures can occur that could lead to severe functional deficits in the hand if not treated correctly—for example, a spiral fracture of one of the finger bones can rotate the finger. The rotation can be minimal enough that with the fingers extended everything looks normal but with the fingers flexed there is a deformity. Usually such deformity causes overlap of the injured finger onto its neighboring finger. This can be a disaster if left untreated. Your doctor will decide whether to treat this deformity with a cast or splint or whether surgery is necessary to pin or wire the bone into a good position. If you have surgery, postoperative immobilization may lead to stiffness. In that case, intensive physical therapy will be necessary to regain normal range of motion, strength, and hand function.

22

LOWER BODY INJURY AND THERAPY

Hip, Knee, Leg, Ankle, and Foot Injuries

LIKE THE UPPER BODY, your lower body is vulnerable to injury. This chapter will describe the various parts of the lower body, as well as potential injuries and treatments.

RICE THERAPY

RICE (rest, ice, compression, and elevation) is a treatment that can be used for many injuries, especially those in which there is swelling. The first letter in RICE stands for rest, the toughest part for most of my patients. You can use a plastic bag filled with ice and wrapped in a cloth. Apply it directly over the skin of the involved area. Your skin will turn red, feel numb, and burn. These are all normal reactions to the cold. Don't leave the ice on for more than 20 minutes or you may suffer ice burns. After 20 minutes, remove the ice for at least an hour. You can repeat this process three to five times a day for the initial 24 to 48 hours. Apply compression in the form of an elastic wrap unless your trainer or physician rules against it because it might be wrong for your particular injury. The last part of RICE is elevation. Your affected extremity should be elevated above your chest. RICE will help minimize the swelling.

HIP

The hip joint is a large ball and socket made up of the femoral head (top of the thighbone) and the acetabulum (the socket of the pelvis). Large ligaments hold the joint together, and many muscles cross over the hip joint or attach to it. These muscles go into the abdomen and buttocks and down the thigh. The hip is vulnerable to both injury and normal wear from aging. This section highlights some of the more common hip problems.

Hip Pain

Causes of hip pain include trauma (fractures and dislocations), arthritis, bursitis, and muscle strains. You can also develop hip pain from a back problem such as a herniated disk. The most common cause of hip pain, however, is from a muscle strain, which is when a muscle stretches or tears from either an acute injury or chronic overuse.

Symptoms of a hip strain include:

- Pain when the muscle is touched
- Swelling or deformity of the muscle
- Black and blue marks several days after an injury
- Pain with use of the muscle
- Weakness of the muscle
- Difficulty walking without a limp
- Stiffness when getting up after prolonged sitting or rest

Your doctor will examine all your hip muscles to localize the injured one. An x-ray often can rule out an avulsion fracture, which may have similar signs. Treatment is nonoperative. For an acute injury, it is a good idea to perform ice massage. Freeze a paper cup of ice and tear off the top. Flip the cup over and use the bottom as a handle. Massage the strained muscle with the ice for 15 to 20 minutes at a time. Alternate this therapy with heat using heating pads or hot soaks. Wrapping the injured muscle with an elastic bandage can be helpful as well. If you find you are limping, use crutches or a cane for a couple of days. Start stretching and strengthening as soon as the pain is under control, but you should avoid aggressive training until you are pain free. For moderate to severe strains, a physical therapist can use several anti-inflammatory modalities to help speed the recovery. It is important to avoid any painful activities in the first couple of weeks after the injury. The best prevention for a muscle strain is a good stretching program to warm up your muscles before you begin your activity.

Hip Bursitis

A bursa is a small sac that lies over bony prominences throughout the body meant to cushion tendons, muscles, and skin over the bones. These sacs are generally empty, but if they fill with fluid from either injury or overuse, they can become a source of pain called bursitis. In the hip, a large bursa lies on the outside of the upper thighbone (greater trochanter of the femur). Several large muscles are anchored on the greater trochanter.

Symptoms of trochanteric bursitis include:

- Pain and swelling
- Pain radiating down the outside of the thigh to the knee
- Difficulty lying on the affected hip
- Night pain and pain with certain activities such as stair climbing, hiking downhill, and sitting

Causes of trochanteric bursitis include acute trauma, which may involve falling onto the hip or a direct blow from an object (hockey stick). Symptoms of an overuse injury include a tight iliotibial band (ITB) that snaps across the greater trochanter repetitively and can inflame the bursa. Other causes include imbalance of lower-extremity musculature or inflexibility; leg length inequality; foot abnormalities; scoliosis (curved spine); and previous hip surgery and/or lying on your hip for extended periods.

If your hip pain does not respond to rest, ice, stretching, or anti-inflammatory medication, you should see your physician. It is important to detect any misalignments in the spine and lower extremities as well as muscle imbalances. An x-ray may rule out other possible causes of pain including arthritis, fracture, or calcium deposits in a tendon (calcific tendonitis). Treatment includes:

- Rest
- Icing for 20 minutes at a time, four or five times a day
- Taking nonsteroidal anti-inflammatory medication
- Stretching and strengthening hip muscles, ITB, and back muscles
- Physical therapy for anti-inflammatory modalities such as ultrasound
- Modifying shoes for any foot abnormalities or leg-length inequalities
- Avoiding direct pressure on the upper hipbone (greater trochanter)

If these treatments fail, your physician can give you a cortisone injection, which can be safe and very effective. If this also fails, your physician may recommend an MRI scan to rule out other possible hip problems. Treatment of hip bursitis is almost always nonoperative. I have not had to operate on a patient with bursitis for more than six years.

The Shimmy Muscle: Piriformis Syndrome

The piriformis is a small muscle behind the hip that externally rotates the joint. It is located deep in the buttocks and can be a source of pain in the hip. With overuse injuries this muscle can become inflamed or tight and put pressure on the sciatic nerve. The sciatic nerve is formed from several nerve roots that exit the lower spine. This large nerve lies under the piriformis muscle and can be pinched if the muscle is inflamed.

Signs of piriformis syndrome include pain and tenderness in the back of the hip or deep in the buttocks, numbness or tingling in the lower extremity (back of the thigh or outside of the calf), weakness of the lower extremity, and pain aggravated by athletic activities or by extended periods of sitting.

If you have these symptoms for several weeks you should see an orthopedist. Physical examination often reveals piriformis syndrome. Tenderness over the piriformis muscle, pain and weakness with forced external rotation of the hip, and pain with internal rotation of the hip are common findings. A nerve examination is also necessary. If the diagnosis is suspected but not certain, an MRI scan may be necessary to determine if there is any nerve compression by the piriformis muscle. A herniated disk can cause similar symptoms.

Treatment is generally nonoperative and involves stretching, anti-inflammatory medication, physical therapy, and, in extreme cases, a cortisone injection. If these treatments fail, a surgical release of the muscle may be necessary to relieve the pressure over the sciatic nerve.

THIGH

The thigh has many muscles running through it from the hip down to the knee. The major muscle groups include the knee flexors, knee extensors, and the hip adductors. The knee flexors or hamstrings bend the knee yet also extend the hip. The knee extensors or quadriceps straighten the knee and also flex the hip. The hip adductors pull the thighs toward each other. All of these muscle groups are at risk for tearing or pulling injuries during sports either from an acute injury or from overuse repetitive injuries. When the muscle tears it is called a muscle strain. A common cause of muscle strains in the thigh is a quick burst of activity, such as running to first base or diving for a basketball.

Common signs of a thigh muscle strain include a popping or tearing sensation at the time of acute injury, swelling, and significant pain or tenderness to the touch over the injured muscle.

When muscles tear, they can bleed quite a bit and cause significant swelling. You may also have pain and weakness with use of the muscle and/or difficulty walking without a limp. If you have a large tear, you may be able to feel a divot or hole in the muscle belly. Black and blue marks may show up days later.

A muscle strain can be serious. Returning to sport when you are in pain from such an injury can be dangerous because of further damage to the muscle. Participating and compensating for the pain can put other parts of your body at risk for injury as well.

If you think you have a significant strain, you should see your physician. Examination will determine the location of the strain and the severity of the damage. There are three grades of muscle strains. Grade 1 is mild and will generally resolve in 10 to 14 days. A grade 2 strain can take several weeks to several months to resolve. A grade 3 strain is very severe and can take up to six months to fully resolve. An x-ray may be necessary to see if a piece of bone has been fractured off from the sudden pull of a tendon.

Treatment of the acute injury follows the RICE protocol. Your doctor may prescribe an anti-inflammatory medication and physical therapy to get you back to your sport sooner. Do not return until you have full flexibility and pain-free strength.

Prevention is invaluable, so get yourself on a good stretching regimen, keep all of your thigh muscle groups strong for balance, and be certain to warm up before your sport and cool down afterward.

KNEE

The knee is the largest joint in the body—it is also the most common reason for an orthopedic visit. It is made up of the lower end of the thighbone (femur) and the upper end of the shinbone (tibia). The kneecap or patella is a bone that lives inside a tendon. The kneecap glides in a groove on the thighbone and protects the knee joint from blunt trauma. The kneecap also makes the muscles and tendons that go across the front of the knee work better. There are four major ligaments, which give the knee stability, and two shock absorbers in between the femur and tibia (the meniscus). The ends of the bones within the joint are lined with cartilage. The knee joint is complex in that it doesn't just bend and straighten (flex and extend), it also allows rotation of the lower leg.

Ligament Injuries

A ligament is a tough cord of connective tissue that connects bone to bone. In the knee there are two cruciate ligaments (anterior and posterior) and two collateral ligaments (medial and lateral; see Figure 22.1). The cruciate ligaments cross one another. The anterior cruciate crosses in front of the posterior cruciate. These ligaments are important for stability in the knee. Each is at risk of tearing during sports injuries.

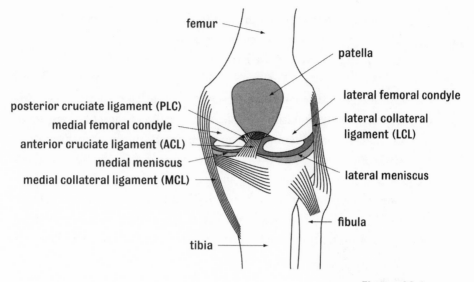

femur

patella

lateral femoral condyle

posterior cruciate ligament (PLC)

medial femoral condyle

anterior cruciate ligament (ACL)

medial meniscus

medial collateral ligament (MCL)

lateral collateral ligament (LCL)

lateral meniscus

fibula

tibia

Figure 22.1

Anterior Cruciate Ligament (ACL) Tears

The anterior cruciate ligament (ACL) is one of the most important ligaments in the knee. This tough fibrous band connects the thighbone to the shinbone and keeps the shinbone in place but allows certain rotational forces in the knee.

Injuries to the ACL can occur in any activity, but certain sports present higher risks than others. They include skiing, basketball, soccer, volleyball, softball, and tennis. Female athletes are especially prone to such injury.

One injury occurs when you hyperextend your knee with your foot planted while the rest of your body propels forward. Other common injuries come from pivoting or rapidly changing in direction, stopping suddenly, and landing poorly from a jump. Direct contact to your knee from an opponent in a contact sport (soccer) is yet another way to injure your ACL.

Some symptoms of injury include

- A pop in your knee at the time of the injury
- Nausea after the injury

- Pain in your knee (not always present until the knee swells)
- Swelling within the first hour or two after injury
- Instability when you try to walk or resume your sport

If you have any of these symptoms you should see an orthopedic surgeon before resuming other activities. Any further stresses to the knee without an intact ACL can cause significant damage to other structures in the knee (such as the cartilage).

If you came into my clinic with a suspected ACL injury, I would look for swelling and tenderness on the sides, front, and back of your knee. Then I would test for stability by gently placing your knee and leg into different positions to see if it moves as it should. Although a ligament injury will not generally show up on an x-ray, some ACL tears are associated with a tiny fracture off of the bone, which can provide an additional clue toward diagnosis. Most experienced orthopedists can diagnose an ACL tear without expensive studies such as an MRI scan. This is especially true if the patient comes in soon after the injury. For instance, when I'm covering my ski clinic at Crested Butte or Telluride and Ski Patrol brings in a patient who was injured less than an hour earlier, the exam is easy. If you wait to see your doctor until days after the injury—when you have a lot of swelling and apprehension and pain—the diagnosis may be impossible without an MRI scan. This scan is capable of diagnosing ACL tears around 90 percent of the time depending on the strength of the machine and the skill of the technicians.

Initial treatment includes RICE and physical therapy. The swelling can be significant and may take a couple of weeks to resolve. Treatment can be either operative or nonoperative. In the active young athlete, surgical reconstruction of the ACL is a must. If the athlete were to engage in sports without a stable knee, the damage to the other structures such as the meniscus and articular cartilage could lead to severe osteoarthritis and destruction of the knee joint at a relatively early age. In my patient population, I have older people who engage in aggressive pivoting sports such as skiing. For them, I recommend surgery unless they can make a choice to modify their lifestyle. These people must work to balance their lower body muscles and perhaps wear a functional brace. If they suffer instability with nonpivoting activities or activities of daily living, then they should consider surgery as well. Surgery is not indicated, however, until swelling is resolved, full range of motion has returned, and the thigh muscles are firing well. For the average patient, this can take two to four weeks. If you have the surgery too soon after the injury, complication rates can be higher.

The ACL is bathed in joint fluid and does not have the capacity to heal. It cannot be sewn together either. Once you tear your ACL it must be replaced or reconstructed with a tissue graft. The procedure is performed by an experienced surgeon with an arthroscope (fiber-optic camera) and many small instruments introduced through tiny incisions in the knee. The graft goes through bone tunnels drilled into the thighbone and shinbone. It is then secured to the bone.

Prior to surgery, you and your surgeon should discuss the graft choices that are available. The most common grafts come from your own knee. One is a strip of kneecap tendon with bony blocks off of the kneecap and shinbone. Another is called a hamstring graft, which goes around the inside of the knee to the back of the thigh. Both of these grafts have been shown to be equally effective, yet the hamstring graft may have fewer problems postoperatively. I prefer hamstring grafts for ACL reconstruction especially in skiers and in women. The bottom line is whichever graft your surgeon feels most comfortable with is the graft that he or she should use on you.

Surgery is not without risks and your surgeon should discuss these with you. The risk of arthrofibrosis—in which your body lays down tremendous amounts of scar tissue after surgery—is high when surgery is performed on a swollen, painful knee with limited range of motion soon after the injury is sustained. The risk drops dramatically if surgery is delayed for a couple of weeks and the patient participates in physical therapy during the delay. Most orthopedists agree that surgical timing is extremely important in reducing this complication.

Properly performed surgery is only a small element in the outcome of the newly reconstructed knee. I tell my patients that the surgery is responsible for 10 percent of the successful outcome and physical therapy is responsible for the other 90 percent. You must be compliant; you cannot return to pivoting or cutting sports for an average of four to six months. Some orthopedists may keep you out of sports for up to one year. If my patient has been compliant with physical therapy and has full range of motion and excellent strength and balance at four to six months, I'll let her return to sports. However, I warn her to start slowly and progress incrementally because becoming truly confident with a newly reconstructed knee often takes up to a year.

There are confusing studies in the literature regarding brace wear after successful ACL surgery. I am not really a brace advocate provided the knee has been well reconstructed. The ACL functional braces are expensive and can be cumbersome. If my patients have a stable knee, good range of motion, and excellent strength, then I don't feel that these braces will be of any use. I do recommend a small neoprene sleeve, however. These inexpensive pieces of rubber send messages to the brain to help with muscular control in a knee that has lost its normal ACL nerve fibers (this is called proprioceptive feedback). However, if your surgeon recommends bracing after surgery, please accept the option. Every patient is different; your surgeon may have good reason to recommend a brace for you.

The success rate for ACL reconstruction is about 90 percent. After surgery and rehabilitation, most athletes can return to their preinjury level of sport.

Posterior Cruciate Ligament Tears

The posterior cruciate ligament (PCL) is the ligament behind the ACL. It is important in keeping the shinbone (tibia) from being pushed backward on the thighbone (femur). Injuries to the PCL are much less common than those to the ACL. Generally, a blow to the front of the knee will stretch the PCL or actually tear it. It is a common injury in car accidents during which the knee strikes the dashboard. During sports it could happen by simply falling onto the front of a bent knee.

Signs of a PCL injury include a pop in your knee, swelling within one to two hours after the injury, pain with motion (this may not be present until there is swelling), and an occasional feeling of instability.

Most sports medicine physicians and orthopedists are able to diagnose a PCL injury easily by taking a thorough history and conducting a physical examination. If you are in too much pain for the doctor to examine you thoroughly, an MRI is sometimes necessary to determine if other structures are involved. Sometimes, a piece of bone from the tibia is pulled off by the PCL (avulsion fracture) and this can be diagnosed with a plain x-ray in the doctor's office or in the emergency room.

Treatment of a PCL injury includes RICE therapy, crutches for a short time, anti-inflammatory medications, and physical therapy. Fortunately, PCL injuries rarely cause instability that bothers the patient and are usually treated without surgery. Rehabilitation takes 8 to 12 weeks. It's important to maintain muscular strength (especially of the thigh muscles) and flexibility during the rehabilitation phase. If there is an avulsion fracture as described above, surgery is indicated and your surgeon will reattach the bone with a screw.

Collateral Ligament Tears (MCL and LCL)

The collateral ligaments include the medial collateral (MCL) on the inner side and the lateral collateral (LCL) on the outer side of the knee. (See Figure 22.1.) They both connect the tibia (shinbone) to the femur (thighbone) on their respective sides. They give stability to stresses in the side-to-side motion (varus and valgus stresses). Collateral ligament sprains can be mild (partial stretching or tearing) or severe (significant tearing). LCL injuries are relatively rare, whereas MCL injuries are among the most common knee injuries in sports.

The MCL is injured when a stress is applied to the outer portion of the knee. For instance, if a soccer player gets struck by an opponent on the outer knee and the knee is forced inward (valgus stress), the MCL can tear or stretch. Another common way to tear the MCL is to fall and twist the knee while skiing. It is the number one lower body injury in skiing. The ski acts as a long lever arm, which can torque the knee ligaments if the bindings on the skis do not release during a fall or a crash. The LCL may be injured if there is a stress to the inner knee causing the knee to buckle toward the outside (varus stress). An LCL tear can happen in combination with other injuries such as a PCL tear or a tibial plateau fracture.

Signs of a torn collateral ligament include pain with range of motion or weight bearing, swelling at the site of injury within several hours (minimal if a mild sprain), and instability. A pop rarely occurs during this injury.

If you think you may have injured your collateral ligament you should see a sports medicine physician. Most diagnoses can be made with a good physical examination. I rarely need an MRI to help me diagnose a collateral ligament injury. However, if your doctor suspects an associated injury of the cartilage in your knee (meniscus), an MRI may be necessary; an MCL injury can mask a cartilage tear. An x-ray can be helpful to see if a piece of bone was pulled off with the ligament (avulsion fracture).

Treatment of a collateral ligament includes RICE therapy and perhaps crutches until you are able to walk without a limp. Anti-inflammatory medication and bracing during the healing phase are necessary to prevent future instability. Proper physical therapy is important to maintain range of motion and strength.

Unlike the ACL and PCL, the collateral ligaments lie outside the knee joint capsule and have excellent blood supply. They nearly always heal without surgery, but it is important to wear a brace and participate in physical therapy so that the ligament will heal strong and tight, which will prevent instability in the future.

Meniscus Tears

One of the most important structures in the knee joint is the meniscus, the joint's shock absorber, which is made up of two C-shaped wedges of cartilage that sit in between your thighbone and your shinbone. The lateral meniscus is on the outer half and the medial meniscus is on the inner half of the knee. The meniscus has many functions that help the knee with stability, weight bearing, gliding, and turning. It also protects against your femur and tibia grinding on each other. You can injure this cartilage in many pivoting sports, such as skiing, soccer, basketball, racquetball, and wrestling. In older people, the cartilage may degenerate to some degree and can tear easily without any trauma. For instance, a patient of mine simply squatted down to pick up a box, turned slightly while in the squatted position, and tore her lateral meniscus.

Signs of a meniscus tear may include a popping sensation, swelling (minimal compared to a cruciate ligament tear or a fracture), stiffness, and pain at the joint line. There may also be catching or locking and pain with squatting or pivoting.

Many athletes continue to play with a meniscus tear and they don't seek medical treatment right away. The danger is that the meniscus tear can get larger if you continue pivoting sports or squatting, and a repairable tear may become irreparable if you wait too long. If you suspect that you have injured your meniscus, see a sports medicine specialist or orthopedist. The diagnosis is often difficult to make on physical examination and your doctor may recommend an MRI. This type of test is not perfect, but a good-quality scan can pick up a meniscus tear about 90 percent of the time.

Treatment initially consists of RICE therapy. Crutches will help until you can walk without a limp. Your doctor may also recommend NSAIDs. The meniscus has blood supply only in its outer third (the vascular zone). If there is only a small tear in this vascular zone then rest and physical therapy may be all you need to heal your meniscus tear. However, if there is a large tear in the vascular zone or a tear in the area without blood supply (avascular zone), then surgery is more likely necessary. If you are experiencing mechanical symptoms such as catching or locking of the knee, then surgery is more urgent. If the knee is locked and you cannot straighten it out completely—and your surgeon can't either—then surgery becomes imperative to keep you from incurring more damage to the meniscus.

Surgery is generally performed with an arthroscope (fiber-optic camera) through two or three tiny incisions. If the tear is in the vascular zone, repair is done with either sutures or some type of anchoring mechanism. If the tear is in the avascular zone, then your surgeon will clean out the torn portion and smooth the remainder of the meniscus so that the tear cannot grow larger (partial meniscectomy).

The meniscus is very valuable tissue and there is no good replacement for it. In the old days (20 to 30 years ago), a torn meniscus was often removed; many patients developed arthritis in their knees as a result. We know now how important the meniscus is. Most surgeons make every effort to preserve it.

Rehabilitation after surgery is variable and depends on the repair. If you had a partial meniscectomy, no brace is necessary and you can expect recovery in four to six weeks. If you had a meniscus repair, your doctor may recommend you wear a brace for four to six weeks with weight bearing allowed in the brace. You will probably have to undergo intensive physical therapy for three to four months. Most patients are able to return to their preinjury activity levels.

Kneecap Instability and Patellofemoral Syndrome

The kneecap (patella) is a bone, which lies inside a tendon (see Figure 22.2). The kneecap connects the quadriceps muscles via the quadriceps tendon to the shinbone (tibia) via the patellar tendon. The undersurface of the kneecap has a V shape, which matches the shape of the groove of the thigh-

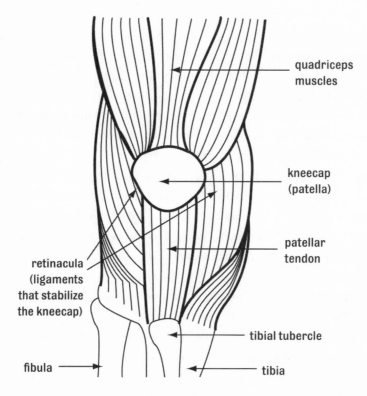

quadriceps
muscles

kneecap
(patella)

patellar
tendon

retinacula
(ligaments
that stabilize
the kneecap)

fibula

tibial tubercle

tibia

Figure 22.2

bone upon which it glides up and down with the bending and straightening of your knee. Sometimes this groove is too shallow and the kneecap may not track in the center of the groove as it should. This can lead to many types of pain, known collectively as patellofemoral syndrome. Other times, there may be a traumatic injury, which pops the patella out of place. Women are more prone to kneecap problems because of anatomic factors and because of muscle imbalances.

Patellofemoral syndrome is generally an overuse injury whereas patellar instability is an acute injury. Symptoms of patellofemoral syndrome include inflammation of the kneecap and its tendons, damage to the kneecap cartilage, and front-of-the-knee pain. You may also have night pain, pain with squatting, a popping sound when you bend your knee or climb stairs, and stiffness after sitting.

Signs of patellar instability include swelling, stiffness (especially after sitting down for a couple of hours), knee buckling, kneecap slippage to the side, pain in the front of the knee, and popping sounds when your knee bends or when you climb stairs.

If your kneecap is completely dislocated, you will see a deformity in the front of the knee, and the pain can be severe. Sometimes the kneecap goes back into place on its own, especially if you try to straighten your knee. Other times your doctor will gently reduce (put back in place) your kneecap by straightening your knee and placing gentle pressure on the outer part of the kneecap. You should have a trained professional reduce your kneecap if it does not go into place on its own. An untrained person trying to help could potentially injure the cartilage (the white cushion at the end of a bone) under the kneecap or in the femoral groove.

If you have an injury to your kneecap or if you develop chronic pain or instability without an injury you should see an orthopedist. Give your doctor a good history about your knee injuries. He or she will examine your knee to look for areas of tenderness, swelling, or muscle imbalance, and may even examine your hips and feet for misalignments. X-rays will be necessary to see if any small fractures have occurred and to determine how the patella lines up in the groove of the femur. I don't routinely recommend an MRI for this type of problem.

Treatment of patellofemoral syndrome or kneecap instability can often be accomplished without surgery. In the early stages of treatment, I generally recommend RICE and anti-inflammatory medication. I give my patients a kneecap-stabilizing brace, which allows range of motion of the knee. When they come to me after having visited the emergency room for a dislocation or partial dislocation, many athletes wear a knee immobilizer. I don't care for these devices because they can cause a lot of stiffness in the knee and are often uncomfortable for the patient. If the athlete has a history of multiple total or partial dislocations despite intensive physical therapy, then surgery may be necessary to balance the soft tissues around the kneecap. Rehabilitation for patellofemoral syndrome or unstable kneecap must focus on muscle imbalance issues. Some of these are correctable with therapy, some with surgery. Some are not correctable.

CORRECTABLE WITH PHYSICAL THERAPY/BRACING/SHOE INSERTS
Flat feet
Weak quadriceps muscles especially the VMO (vastus medialis obliquus)
Weak hip abductor muscles (brings the thigh away from the center of
    the body)
Tight hamstring muscles

CORRECTABLE WITH SURGERY
Tight ligaments on the outer part of the kneecap
Torn or loose ligaments on the inner part of the kneecap

NOT CORRECTABLE
Shallow groove in the thighbone
Large valgus angle (knocked knees)

With the right treatments, most female athletes can get back into their sport but it takes a lot of effort. The most important exercises are targeted toward quadriceps and hip abductor strengthening and hamstring flexibility. (See exercises in Chapter 23.) Bracing is a good alternative until you are able to balance the muscles.

Tendonitis

Tendonitis, inflammation of the tendons that attach muscles to the knee, can be quite painful depending upon how severe and chronic it is. In many sports it is among the most common overuse injuries—especially in women. The most common areas are the kneecap (patellar) tendon (jumper's knee) and the thigh (quadriceps) tendon. These are both located in the front of the knee and can be part of patellofemoral syndrome.

Kneecap Bursitis

The kneecap has a sac in front of it called the prepatellar bursa. If you land on the front of your knee or if you are kneeling a lot, the friction between the bursa and the ground can cause swelling. This is called prepatellar bursitis. If the swelling is significant, you can experience a lot of pain and you may become unable to kneel. The front of the knee may be warm and tender to the touch. Activities that require repetitive bending or kneeling may cause serious discomfort.

If your swelling is accompanied by a skin abrasion from a fall, there is a risk of infection in the bursa. This can become a surgical emergency, so if you have a large bursitis you should not wait to seek medical treatment. Your doctor will be able to make the diagnosis easily without any diagnostic tests. If you have sustained an acute injury, your doctor may take an x-ray to see if there is a fracture in the kneecap. Surgery is rarely necessary. Most of the time, prepatellar bursitis is treated with RICE therapy. Some cases require draining the fluid out of the bursa. Some may even need an injection of cortisone if the bursitis is chronic or recurring. If the bursa is surgically removed, recovery from the procedure generally takes three to six weeks.

Once you have successfully treated your bursitis, some methods to prevent recurrence include icing your knees after sports or workouts, stretching your knees regularly during sports, and wearing kneepads if you routinely kneel or land on your knees (as in racquetball).

Inflamed Pleats: Plicas

Your knee joints are wrapped in a tissue called synovium. Plicas are folds of synovial tissue that some people are born with that can become inflamed from overuse or acute injuries. The most common plicas are located on the inside and front of the knee next to the kneecap. Once these synovial folds become inflamed, they rub against the thighbone and can become very painful.

Signs of a plica problem include pain on the inside front of the knee, swelling on the inside front of the knee, a snapping sound with bending and straightening of the knee (which may be painful), and pain with activities such as bicycling or hiking downhill.

Many doctors are unfamiliar with plicas, so it's important to seek the advice of a sports medicine specialist or orthopedist. After a thorough physical examination, a specialist can easily make a diagnosis. X-rays are only necessary to rule out other possible sources of knee pain. I only recommend an MRI if I am suspicious as to some other cause of knee pain such as a meniscus tear, which often can be confused with a symptomatic plica.

Treatment includes RICE, physical therapy to address any muscular imbalances, quadriceps strengthening, hip abductor strengthening, and perhaps a cortisone shot to shrink the plica band. If all these fail, arthroscopic surgery may be necessary to remove the plica. Most female athletes, however, recover from this. They can prevent recurrences with the proper muscular balancing.

SHINBONE

The shin is the front part of the leg from the knee to the ankle. A shin contusion is a bruise to either the bone or the muscle beside the shinbone. When you get kicked in the shins, it is really painful because unlike other areas of your body, your shin has very little natural padding. You may feel like your leg has been hit by lightning. The natural response to this type of injury is massive bleeding under your skin. This may put pressure on nerves, which may give you tremendous discomfort. If not appropriately treated, the nerves may develop so much pressure on them they may stop doing their job. The result may be an inability to pull your foot upward—a condition called a drop foot—or your leg or foot may get numb or tingly.

If you get kicked in the shin, apply ice and elevate for 20 minutes at a time. If you feel your shinbone may be fractured, you should get yourself to a medical facility—preferably after having a trainer apply a splint or via ambulance.

Do not put any weight on your injured leg. If you have just suffered a bruise and a fracture is ruled out, you should ice your shin as soon as possible—every two hours for 20 minutes. Do not use an elastic bandage; you don't want to put any pressure on your leg at this time. Keep your leg elevated and stay off it as much as you can. If you notice that you have difficulty raising your foot, see a physician as soon as possible.

The Goose's Foot: Pes Bursitis

There are three tendons that attach to the inside front of the shinbone and are known collectively as the pes anserine, which is Latin for "goose's foot." There is a small sac (bursa) that lies between the skin and the goose's foot and can become a source of pain if it fills with fluid (bursitis). Bursitis occurs in this area from overuse or poor training techniques. Risk factors include tight hamstrings, poor training techniques with a lack of stretching, arthritis, and obesity.

The pain is located about two inches below the inside of the knee joint and there can be swelling there as well. Pain is often activity related and can be exacerbated with sports, stair climbing, and downhill walking. A specialist can easily make the diagnosis. An x-ray may be necessary if your doctor suspects a stress fracture.

Treatment includes rest from any painful activities, ice massage to the area of the pes anserine, and anti-inflammatory medication. Aggressive stretching of the three tendons attaching at the pes can be helpful, especially the hamstrings. If these treatments fail to resolve the pain and swelling, a cortisone injection may be necessary. Fortunately, surgery is rarely needed for this problem.

ANKLE

The ankle (see Figure 22.3) is one of the most frequently injured body parts. This section covers some of the most common ankle injuries.

Peroneal Tendon Dislocation

Peroneal tendon dislocations are common in skiers. Unlike ligaments that connect bone to bone, tendons connect muscles to bone. The peroneal ten-

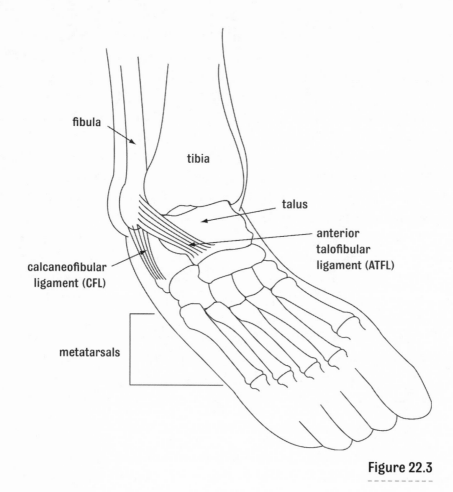

fibula

tibia

talus

anterior
talofibular
ligament (ATFL)

calcaneofibular
ligament (CFL)

metatarsals

Figure 22.3

dons are those that lie behind the anklebone (fibula) on the outside of the ankle and they live in a tunnel that is created by a ligament called the extensor reti-naculum. If the foot is turned to the outside (for instance in a ski boot) with enough force, this ligament protecting the housing of the tendons can tear, which frees the tendons to move outside of the housing and over the ankle-bone. This can cause a lot of pain and weakness in the ankle joint.

One sign of a peroneal tendon dislocation is pain on the outer side of the ankle. You may feel a pop with the injury. There may be swelling, stiffness, a painful snapping over the outer side of the ankle, and weakness in the ankle. If you have any of these signs, you should see an orthopedist as soon as possible. Delays in treatment could mean surgery. Your doctor will be able to diagnose your problem via a thorough history and physical examination. An x-ray may show a tiny fracture, which is seen with this type of injury less than 50 percent of the time. Otherwise an MRI is helpful. If a diagnosis is made early, you will need a non-weight-bearing cast for six weeks followed by physical therapy for at least another six weeks before you (gradually) return to sports. However, if diagnosis is delayed or if you develop recurrent dislocations of the peroneals, you'll need surgery to reconstruct the ligament that holds the tendons in place. Most patients can expect full recovery.

Stress Fractures

Stress or fatigue fractures are overuse injuries. They are much more common in female athletes than male athletes. In fact, female basketball players have a two to four times greater rate of stress fractures than males. Stress fractures are most common in the shinbones (tibia) and bones (metatarsals) of the foot. However, any bone can be at risk. Often the problem stems from shoes. Athletes who do not replace their shoes often enough can have this problem. After 500 miles, athletic shoes provide only 70 percent of their initial shock absorption.

Women who engage in endurance sports such as long-distance running have a greater risk of stress fractures because many of them have irregular periods (or no periods at all). Women with a history of bulimia or anorexia nervosa have an even greater risk of stress fracture. The combination of amenorrhea, eating disorders, and stress fractures is called the female athlete triad. (See the Introduction.)

Signs of a stress fracture include pain with exercise (partially relieved by rest) and possible swelling and tenderness over the fractured area. If you develop these symptoms, you should see a sports medicine specialist. You need to provide the specialist with a detailed history about your activity level and any recent changes in training. X-rays often do not reveal an acute stress fracture. Often a bone scan is necessary for diagnosis. If the bone scan is negative, then you probably have an inflammatory condition called medial tibial stress syndrome (MTSS). MTSS includes tendonitis (shin splints) or periostitis (inflammation of the layer around the bone).

Treatment for stress fractures is simply rest. Cross training such as swimming is allowed so that you can stay in shape. If you have pain while walking, use crutches until you can bear weight without a problem. Certain stress fractures of the foot require casting and no weight-bearing activity for up to six weeks. Your doctor will be able to guide you through cross training and eventual physical therapy for your injured extremity. If your doctor diagnoses you with any foot misalignments such as flat feet, then shoe inserts may help prevent a recurrent stress fracture. To heal certain chronic stress fractures, surgery with bone grafting is sometimes necessary.

Ankle Sprains

Ankle sprains are a common injury in many sports. In fact, in the United States alone, 25,000 people sprain their ankles every day. A sprain is a tear to a ligament, the strong rubber band–like structures that attach bone to bone.

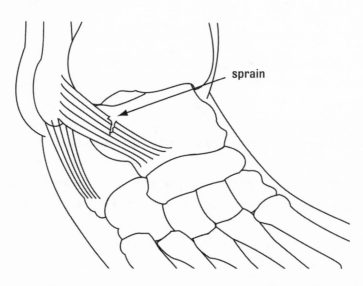

sprain

Figure 22.4

The most common ankle sprains occur when you land on an uneven surface (such as an opposing player's shoe) and your ankle turns inward. This type of force generally will tear the ligaments on the outside of your ankle. (See Figures 22.3 and 22.4.)

A common indicator of an ankle sprain is a sudden pain after twisting the ankle. You may hear or feel a pop over the outer portion of the ankle. There will probably be swelling over the ankle within an hour or two, and tenderness to the touch, as well as instability and pain with weight bearing.

If you have pain, swelling, or difficulty walking and you think you may have twisted your ankle, you should see a doctor for an evaluation and an x-ray. Your doctor will ask you if you have sprained or broken your ankle in the past. A physical examination may be limited if there is a lot of swelling and pain. X-rays will likely be necessary because a fracture and a sprain can feel and look similar in a clinical examination.

The treatment of the average ankle sprain is RICE. Use crutches if there is any pain with walking. You should also ice (20 minutes at a time, at least five times a day) until the swelling is reduced. Use compression with an elastic wrap or brace and elevate your ankle above the heart as much as possible for 48 hours. If needed, you can use anti-inflammatory medications.

You should have physical therapy for control of swelling, range of motion of the joint, and eventual strengthening and balance training. Tape or brace the ankle during sports for several months to protect it from another sprain.

If you have a severe ankle sprain with joint instability, your doctor may recommend that you wear a cast for several weeks. Surgery is rarely necessary for the acute ankle sprain. However, if you continue to sprain your ankle despite conservative therapy, then surgery can help to tighten up the ligaments. In some cases, scar tissue may develop in the joint, which puts pressure on the joint and may cause chronic pain and decreased motion. If this occurs, an arthroscopic surgery using a tiny fiber-optic camera and instruments may be necessary to clean out the scar tissue. If you do suffer from recurrent ankle sprains and do not get proper treatment, you could develop arthritis in the ankle joint. This occurs because of cartilage damage as a result of an unstable joint. If left untreated, the arthritis can result in chronic pain and stiffness and in the worst-case scenario an ankle fusion may be required to treat the chronic pain. The message here is to treat an ankle sprain early and work hard to strengthen it.

Ankle Fractures

Ankle fractures are common in sports. There are three bones that make up the ankle (see Figure 22.3), the tibia (large bone in the leg), the fibula (smaller bone in the leg), and the talus (a bone in the foot between the tibia and the heel bone (calcaneous). Falls—whether from landing on uneven ground or via a twisting injury (snowboarding or skating)—are some of the easiest ways to fracture an ankle. It is often difficult to distinguish between a fracture and a sprain of the ankle without x-rays. The symptoms of a fracture can be just like a sprain.

Treatment of an ankle fracture is dependent on the fracture location and severity. If there is just a hairline crack of one of the bones, then a splint or brace may be recommended with partial weight bearing and early physical therapy. However, if there is a larger break, then a cast or surgery may be necessary. A cast above the knee (long leg cast) may be required for the first few weeks if your orthopedist had to move the ankle and foot in a certain way to put the bones back into alignment. This can often be converted to a shorter walking cast after several weeks if an x-ray shows evidence of healing. If the fracture pieces are out of alignment or if there was also a dislocation of the joint, then surgery is necessary to hold the fracture pieces in good position. This is done with plates, screws, and/or wires. The advantage of surgery in many cases is that the patient can start physical therapy earlier than with cast treatment and will suffer less joint stiffness and muscle shrinkage. The disadvantage of surgery is simply the risk inherent in having an operation. Although that risk is small in the hands of a good surgeon, it is nonetheless present. Many athletes prefer to have surgery on their ankle fractures even if they are treatable with casting because they want to return to their sport as soon as possible. Certainly surgical treatments allow earlier physical therapy and potentially earlier return to sport but, if you have a complication, there could be permanent damage.

Whether you are treated with a cast or an operation, it is important to rehabilitate your ankle after the bone is healed to prevent reinjury to the joint.

If you do not strengthen the muscles around the ankle—or if you do not retrain balance into your ankle—then you are at risk of spraining or even refracturing the joint once you return to sports.

HEEL

Perhaps you don't pay much attention to your feet. Most people take these hardworking body parts for granted—until they experience a problem or injury, that is.

Achilles Tendon

The Achilles tendon is the largest tendon in the body. It connects the calf muscle to the heel bone. Athletes are frequently plagued with inflammation of this tendon (tendonitis). The Achilles is also the most commonly ruptured tendon in the lower body. Achilles tendonitis is an overuse injury and can occur with lack of stretching, increasing your activity level too quickly, or returning to aggressive activities too quickly after a layoff. You can also get Achilles tendonitis or a tear of the tendon with an acute injury.

The most common symptom of an Achilles tendon rupture is severe pain in the back of the leg near the heel. You may hear a pop at the time of injury. Other symptoms include pain and swelling in the back of the leg a couple of inches above the heel, weakness or inability to stand on your toes (heel raise), and inability to walk without a limp. If you have Achilles tendonitis, you may experience swelling, stiffness, pain during or after running activities, and progressively worsening pain with continued activities.

If you have signs of an Achilles tendon rupture or tendonitis, you should seek immediate treatment from an orthopedist. With a simple physical examination your doctor will easily be able to determine whether your tendon is ruptured or simply inflamed. The doctor will have you lie on your stomach with your foot hanging off the end of the table. He or she will then squeeze your calf muscle. If your foot flexes, your tendon is not ruptured. But if your foot doesn't move, there is a rupture of the Achilles tendon. X-rays can reveal if the tendon pulled off a piece of bone from the heel (avulsion fracture).

Treatment of Achilles tendonitis includes rest from any painful activities, cross training (in a pool for instance), ice, crutches if you are limping, and nonsteroidal anti-inflammatory medication. Your doctor may recommend physical therapy including ultrasound, gentle stretching, and strengthening of the leg muscles once the acute pain is decreased. A shoe insert may be helpful to relieve stress on the tendon during healing.

Surgery is rarely necessary for Achilles tendonitis; however, it is sometimes called for if fibrous scar tissue or partial tearing of the tendon prevents less invasive treatments from being successful. The goal of surgery is to remove any scar tissue from chronic inflammation of the tendon and its sheath. In addition, surgery usually repairs any tearing of the tendon.

In the case of an Achilles rupture I believe surgical repair is indicated for any athlete. Although they can be treated with a cast, surgical repair will make the tendon stronger. It will therefore have more endurance and a lower rerupture rate. After surgery, the patient is protected in a cast boot and placed in therapy. You can expect full recovery and return to sports in four to six months.

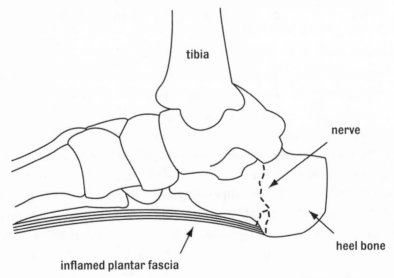

Figure 22.5

As always, prevention is the best medicine. Here are some ways to decrease the risk of developing Achilles problems:

- Warm up before running or any athletic activities.
- Stretch the calf muscles aggressively.
- Strengthen the calf muscles especially during the off season and just before the beginning of the season of your sport.
- Do not overdo your workout with a sudden increase in mileage or length of play.
- Avoid sudden bursts of sprinting if you are not accustomed to it.
- Choose your athletic shoes wisely. (Sometimes an orthotic is necessary to prevent injury.) Cool down after each workout.

Heel Pain

Heel pain is common in women athletes from overuse. The most frequent cause is called plantar fasciitis. The plantar fascia is a tough, fibrous band of tissue that travels from the bottom of your heel bone to the base of your toes (see Figure 22.5). When this fascia becomes inflamed it can cause significant pain. The pain is often most intense with your first steps out of bed in the morning. This is because when you sleep, the plantar fascia shortens as your foot relaxes. As soon as you jump out of bed, the plantar fascia is suddenly stretched. The pain also occurs after exercise rather than during exercise. Risk factors for plantar fasciitis include being female, overweight, and standing or walking on hard surfaces in poor shoes. Other factors are running with tight calf muscles, having flat feet, and having feet with high arches.

Treatment of plantar fasciitis includes rest and icing for 20 minutes at a time four or five times a day. Many people with this condition take non-steroidal anti-inflammatory medications. It is helpful to stretch the calf muscles and the plantar fascia four to five times a day, especially in the morning before your initial steps. Once you have stretched in the morning, put a pillow on the floor and walk in place on it for three minutes, then go on with your day. Sometimes, a night splint will be necessary to keep the fascia from shortening while you sleep.

If your pain does not improve you should see an orthopedist. If an x-ray is negative and a stress fracture is suspected, then your doctor may recommend a bone scan. If you have any foot misalignments (flat feet or high arches), your doctor may prescribe orthotics. If you are diagnosed with plantar fasciitis and you do not respond to the above treatments, then you may need physical therapy. If this fails after two to three months of treatment, your doctor may inject cortisone into the plantar fascia at the heel. If your pain persists, you may try a walking cast for two to three weeks. Once in a great while surgery is necessary to release the plantar fascia. This is only an option if all else fails.

TOE AND FOOT INJURIES

The foot is made up of 25 percent of all of the bones in your body. A fractured bone in your forefoot (metatarsal) or toe (phalanx) can be quite painful. Most of these injuries do not require surgery and they are rarely disabling. Forefoot stress fractures are common in overuse injuries.

Signs of a foot fracture include pain, swelling, discoloration, and pain in other parts of your body—knee, hip, or back—as a result of walking with a limp. If you have progressively worsening pain in your foot or if you have an injury in which there is a deformity in one of your toes, you should seek treatment. Your doctor will most likely recommend an x-ray. Depending on the location and severity of the fracture, you may only need buddy taping (this is a treatment in which the injured toe is taped to a normal toe next to it), or you may need casting. If you have a chronic stress fracture of a metatarsal, which is not healing despite conservative treatments, surgery and bone grafting may be indicated.

23

CONDITIONING EXERCISES

THE WAY TO ENJOY SPORTS, avoid injury, and play your best is to condition your body with appropriate exercises. You should, of course, check with your physician, physiotherapist, or trainer before beginning an exercise program—especially if you have experienced a sports injury in the past. To prepare yourself for athletics in general as well as for specific sports, there are a number of regimens from which you can choose.

WARM UP

To absorb the extra exertions and shocks of athletics, you must warm up your muscles and joints. You can do that by riding a bike slowly, swinging a bat a few times, knocking a few golf balls off a tee, jogging in place, or performing any low-intensity movements that get your heart beating a little faster and your muscles firing. This should take you about 5 to 10 minutes.

FLEXIBILITY

This is the ability to move your joints and use your muscles through their full range of motion. You should do some stretching—at least 10 to 12 minutes' worth—before you indulge in any athletic endeavor.

AEROBIC EXERCISE

You should do at least three 20-minute periods of oxygen-increasing exercises each week. Almost all the sports in this book are aerobic but you can also jump rope, take a brisk walk, or do some calisthenics and experience similar benefits.

You must know how to measure your heart rate. Heart rate is widely accepted as a good method for measuring intensity during running, swimming, cycling, and other aerobic activities. You should check with your physician if he or she has a special safe heart rate for you. Exercise that doesn't raise your heart rate to a certain level and keep it there for 20 minutes won't contribute significantly to your cardiovascular fitness. The heart rate you should maintain is called your target heart rate. There are several ways of arriving at this figure. One of the simplest is:

Maximum heart rate (220 − age) × 70 percent

Thus, the target heart rate for a 40-year-old would be 126.

To determine your resting heart rate, take your pulse after sitting quietly for five minutes. Count your pulse for 10 seconds and multiply by six to get the per-minute rate. (When checking your heart rate during a workout, take your pulse within five seconds after interrupting exercise because it starts to go down once you stop moving.) Some methods for figuring the target rate take individual differences into consideration.

STRENGTHENING EXERCISES

Researchers tell us it is only necessary to tense the muscles up to about 25 to 30 percent of their maximum capacity to get the best strengthening effect. The goal is to get your muscles to exert a force for a brief period of time and to endure muscle exertion against a force for a brief and an extended period of time. To improve muscle tone and cardiovascular performance, a good strengthening program generally requires 15 to 20 repetitions of an exercise for each major muscle group, at least four times a week for approximately 20 to 30 minutes a session. If you want to build strength, you should exercise the specific muscle group to the point of fatigue. You should not work the same muscles every day. Fatigued muscles need time to recover. If you have injured a muscle and want to rehabilitate it, your rehabilitation specialist will probably recommend that you use lighter weights and more repetitions. A rehabilitation program focuses on working the injured muscle group. An exercise professional, such as a certified athletic trainer, a sports physical therapist, an exercise physiologist, or a strength and conditioning coach, can help you design a program that is suitable for your needs.

You can buy light weights—2 to 10 pounds—at a sporting goods outlet or department store. You can also use household items, such as cans from your pantry, as weights. Lift and lower weights slowly. Don't swing the your arms or legs. Don't hold your breath. Make sure you are using a full range of motion throughout the movement. Resistance bands or tubes cost from $6 to $15 and are available in sports stores or on the Internet; they are mainly used for light strengthening.

SPORTS-INJURY PREVENTION AND REHABILITATION EXERCISES

Some activities can fulfill more than one of your basic exercise requirements. For example, in addition to increasing cardiorespiratory endurance, running builds muscular endurance in the legs. Swimming develops the arm, shoulder, and chest muscles. If you select the proper activities, it is possible to fit parts of your muscular endurance workout into your cardiorespiratory workout, which will save you time.

NECK, BACK, AND TRUNK EXERCISES

Figure 23.1
Stretching Your Neck

1. Sit tall on a step or chair, holding the side of the chair with your left hand and reaching your right hand over your head till you can touch your left ear.
2. Drop your right ear down to your right shoulder, stopping when you feel mild tension. Hold for 15 seconds.
3. Release then repeat to the left.

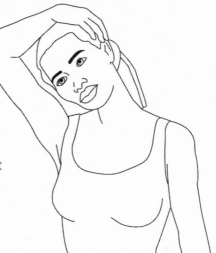

Figure 23.2
Stretch That Chest

1. Stand in a doorway holding onto either side and stepping forward out the door.
2. Relax your neck as you press against the door feeling mild tension through the chest. Hold for 15 seconds.

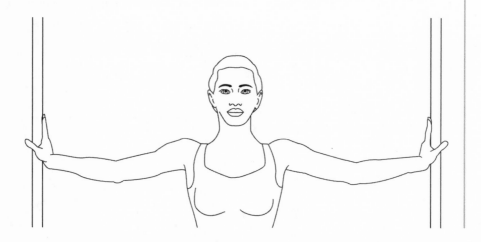

Figure 23.3
Trunk Twist

1. Lie flat on your back with your left arm straight out to your side.
2. Keep your shoulders down.
3. Bend your left leg. Try to pull it toward your chest.
4. Gently pull the bent leg over the straight leg. Hold 30 seconds.
5. Release and repeat on opposite side.

Figure 23.4
Butt and Back Strengthener

1. Lie on your back with your legs straight.
2. Bring one knee up to your chest and squeeze gently. Hold the position for 30 seconds.
3. Relax the leg down just to the point where your arm is straight.
4. Hold 15 seconds and relax with both legs resting on the mat.
5. Repeat with the other knee.
6. Do five sets. As you get stronger increase the sets and the count (unless you have any back pain).

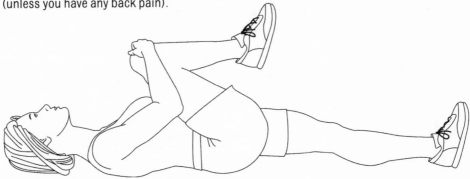

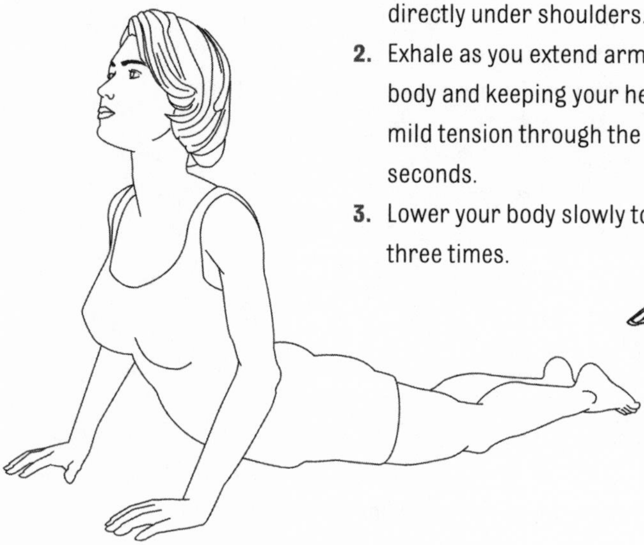

Figure 23.5
Stretch Those Abdominal Muscles

1. Lie facedown on a mat, with your palms flat on the floor directly under shoulders. Keep your toes pointed.
2. Exhale as you extend arms straight, raising your upper body and keeping your head aligned with your spine. Feel mild tension through the abdominal muscles. Hold five seconds.
3. Lower your body slowly to the starting position. Repeat three times.

Figure 23.6
Standing Torso Reach

1. Stand with feet more than shoulder width apart, toes pointing straight ahead.
2. Place your right hand on your right hip for support and reach your left arm up and overhead, bending your torso to the right. Feel mild tension up through left side of torso. Hold 15 seconds.
3. Repeat on the other side.

UPPER BODY EXERCISES

SHOULDER FLEXIBILITY

Figure 23.7
Backscratcher (Internal Rotation) Stretch

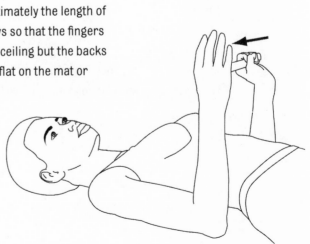

1. Standing straight, place the back of your left hand flat against your lower back.
2. With your right hand, throw one end of a towel over your right shoulder. Grab the towel's other end with the hand behind your back.
3. With your right arm, pull down gently on the towel. Pull until your left arm slides up as high as is comfortable.
4. Hold for 5 seconds, then slowly release. Repeat 5 to 10 times on each side. Build up to holding the stretch for 10 to 60 seconds and/or pulling the hand behind your back higher.

Figure 23.8
Broom (External Rotation) Stretch

1. Use a pole or stick that is approximately the length of your shoulders. Bend your elbows so that the fingers of your hands are pointed to the ceiling but the backs of your arms and shoulders are flat on the mat or floor.
2. With your left hand, grip the stick and push it into your open right hand eight times. Both hands should apply resistance. Then repeat with the hand positions reversed.

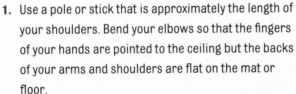

SHOULDER ROTATOR CUFF STRENGTHENERS

Figure 23.9
Supraspinatus Strengthening (Empty-Can Exercise)

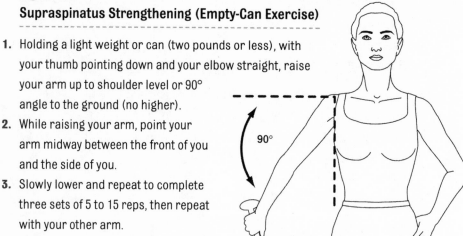

1. Holding a light weight or can (two pounds or less), with your thumb pointing down and your elbow straight, raise your arm up to shoulder level or 90° angle to the ground (no higher).

2. While raising your arm, point your arm midway between the front of you and the side of you.

3. Slowly lower and repeat to complete three sets of 5 to 15 reps, then repeat with your other arm.

Figure 23.10
External Rotator Infraspinatus Strengthening

1. On the floor or a flat bench, lie on your right side with your head resting on your right upper arm (elbow bent).

2. Bend your knees to a 45° angle with shoulders and hips perpendicular to the bench.

3. Holding a dumbbell in your left hand, bend your left elbow to a 90° angle and place it against your left hip, palm down.

4. Without changing your elbow angle, keep your left elbow resting on your side and rotate your left shoulder, raising just your forearm up as far as you can as you try to aim it straight up at the ceiling.

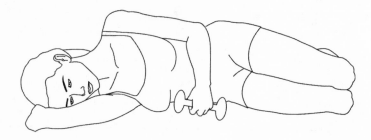

5. Slowly lower your forearm to the starting position. Repeat five times slowly for three sets. Then switch sides and repeat.

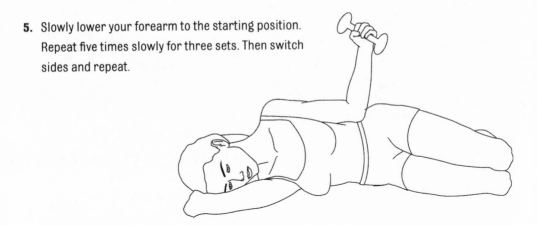

Figure 23.11
Internal Rotator (Subscapularis) Strengthening

1. Lie either on a flat bench or on the floor on your right side with your right arm at your side and your elbow bent.
2. Bend your knees to a 45° angle with shoulders and hips squared.
3. Hold a light-weight dumbbell in your right hand and without changing your elbow angle, rotate your shoulder bringing the dumbbell toward your left arm.
4. Slowly lower and repeat to complete three sets of 5 to 15 reps. Then switch sides and repeat.

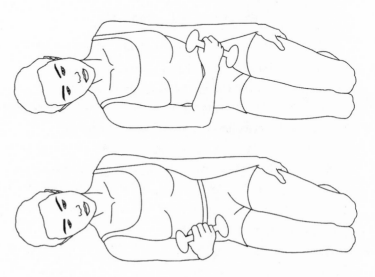

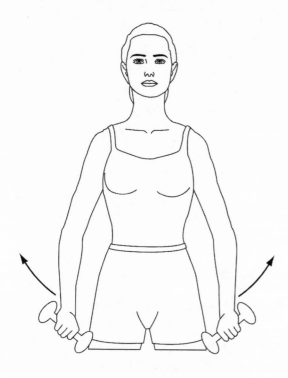

Figure 23.12
Angel Wings—Abduction Strengthening

1. With a hand weight or soup can in each hand, stand with your arms at your sides.
2. Keeping your elbows straight and your thumbs pointed toward the floor, lift your arms to waist level and slightly forward. Do not lift your wrist higher than your waist. Slowly lower your arms and repeat six times for a set. Try to do two or three sets and gradually build up after days or weeks to using heavier weights.

ELBOW AND FOREARM FLEXIBILITY

Figure 23.13
Active Elbow Flexion and Extension

This exercise is important for just about every elbow injury because there is such a high risk for stiffness after injury or surgery in the elbow.

1. Place your forearm flat against the table, your thumb pointed upward. Gently bend your elbow as far as possible. Hold 10 seconds.
2. Straighten your arm. Repeat 10 times for three sets per session.

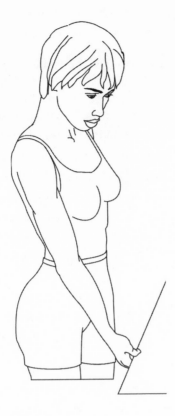

Figure 23.14
Passive Biceps Stretch

1. Grasp the undersurface of a heavy object, such as a kitchen counter, and gradually pull yourself back so that your elbow begins to straighten out.
2. Pull on the counter until you feel a strain in the muscle above the elbow, and then hold for 20 to 30 seconds. Repeat 10 times.

Figure 23.15
Passive Triceps Stretch

This is a very important stretch in many sports that use the upper extremities (e.g., racquet sports, golf, volleyball, basketball, etc).

1. Stand with your shoulders relaxed and chest up.
2. Raise your elbows above your head and with your right hand grasp your left arm above your elbow.
3. Lift your elbow up and behind your head.
4. Pull across stretching the back of your arms (triceps) and the shoulder blade (scapula). Hold for 30 seconds and repeat on the other side.

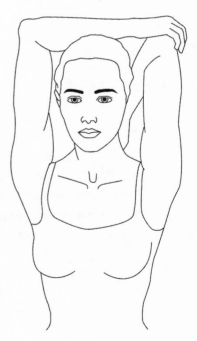

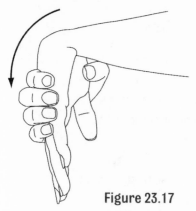

Figure 23.16
Tennis Elbow Forearm (Wrist Extensor) Stretch

1. Stand with your shoulders relaxed and chest up.
2. Turn your left palm down and with your right hand grasp the fingers and straighten the elbow until you feel the stretch. Hold for 30 seconds. Repeat with other hand.

Figure 23.17
Golfer's Elbow Forearm (Wrist Flexor) Stretch

1. Keep your right elbow straight with the palm up.
2. With your left hand, grasp your right hand and slowly bend your wrist down until you feel the stretch.
3. Hold for 30 seconds. Repeat for the other hand.

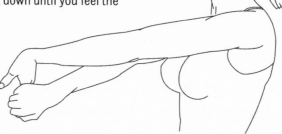

Figure 23.18
Hand Towel Roll Squeeze

This exercise has the same benefits as kneading dough. This strengthens the muscles of the hand and improves your grip, which makes it an important exercise for racquet sports conditioning and for the rehabilitation of hand and wrist injuries.

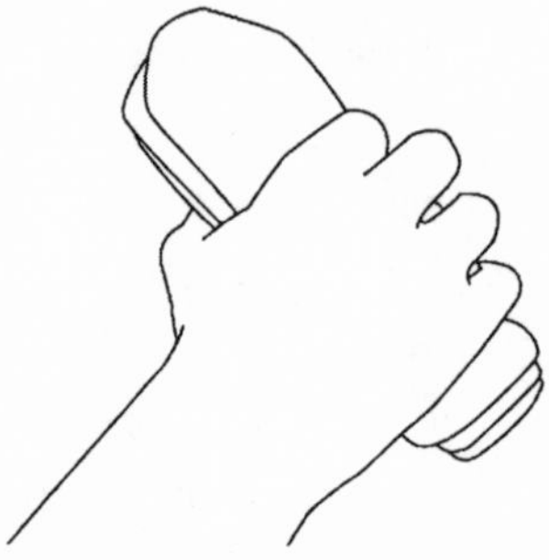

1. With your right forearm resting on a kitchen counter or a table, gently squeeze a towel. Repeat six times.
2. Rest for a few seconds and then do two more sets of six.
3. Switch hands and repeat.

PELVIC EXERCISES

Figure 23.19
Piriformis Stretch

The piriformis muscle is responsible for external (lateral) rotation of the hip. It is particularly important to athletes who have to change direction, such as tennis players and running backs in football. But though runners run straight ahead, keeping the piriformis muscle loose is important for overall flexibility.

1. Lying on your back, cross your legs just as you might if you were sitting in a chair.
2. Grasping the "under" leg with both hands, pull the knee toward your chest until you feel the stretch in your buttocks and hips.

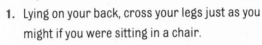

Figure 23.20
Pelvic Tilt

1. Lie on your back with your knees bent, your arms flat at your sides, and your feet flat on the floor.
2. Slowly raise your butt from the floor keeping your stomach and butt muscles tight and hold for the count of five. Repeat 12 times. *Do not perform this exercise if you have pain!* It can cause injury if you overdo it or if you do it incorrectly.

GENTLE STRENGTHENING FOR PELVIC, BUTT, AND ABDOMINAL MUSCLES

Do not do these if you have any pain in your back or abdomen. Do the first two the first day. Do the second two the next day and the last on the third day. After learning these exercises, you should be able to tense the correct muscles when standing or sitting, and you may not need to lie down to practice them anymore. You can also tense them up when doing stressful activities such as lifting a suitcase or whatever the particularly difficult movement is for you. Do these as many times as possible every day for the greatest benefit.

Prone Pelvic Floor Strengthening

1. Lie facedown in a relaxed position.
2. Tighten up the pelvic floor as if you are trying to stop yourself from urinating, then imagine there is something hot under your tummy and try and draw your abdomen up to your backbone. Do not tense up the chest or lift your hips off the surface. Keep breathing normally. Hold for 10 seconds and then relax.
3. Give yourself a short time to recover, then repeat the process until you have done it 10 times.
   You will find that when you breathe the muscles will tend to slacken, and when you tighten the muscles you'll stop breathing. Work steadily until you can both breathe and tighten your muscles at the same time.

Supine Pelvic Floor Strengthening

1. Lie on your back with your knees bent.
2. Gently tense the pelvic floor (as if you are trying to stop yourself from urinating). This usually tenses up the correct muscles in the abdomen.
3. Add a gentle drawing down of your abdominal muscles toward your spine.
4. Breathe normally as before and hold for 10 seconds each time.

Butt Strengthening

1. While lying on your back, tense up your muscles.
2. Hold the muscles tense and your pelvis stable while you let one bent leg gently out to one side a short way and back.
3. Repeat with other leg. Do five reps on each side.

Supine Straight Leg Raise

1. While lying on your back, lift one foot an inch off the floor only, and hold.
2. Do five repetitions for each leg.

Hip Flexor Strengthening

1. While lying on your back, tense up your muscles and hold.
2. Bend the left leg up toward the chest, reach out with the right arm, and gently push against the left.
3. Hold for 10 seconds. Alternate for five each leg.

HIP AND LOWER BODY EXERCISES

Figure 23.21
Stretch the Iliotibial Band

This exercise stretches the iliotibial band (ITB), which is very important for knee conditioning, especially in runners.

1. Cross your left leg over your right so that you feel a stretch over the outside of your hip. Hold eight seconds. Repeat 10 times.
2. Reverse legs and stretch. Hold eight seconds. Repeat 10 times.

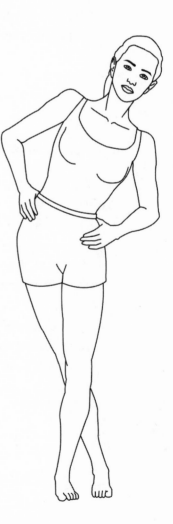

Figure 23.22
Hamstring Stretch

This is one of the most important stretches for the knee and lower back.

1. While sitting, bend your right leg as you straighten your left leg.
2. Reach for your left foot, keeping your spine straight. Hold eight seconds. Repeat 10 times.
3. Reverse legs and stretch. Hold eight seconds. Repeat 10 times.

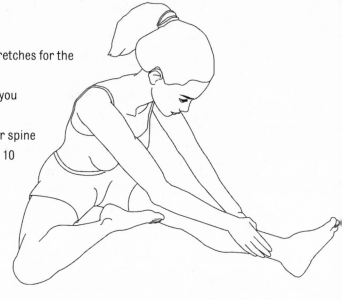

Figure 23.23
Hip Extension Strengthening

This exercise strengthens your lower back and buttocks. It can cause back pain if not done correctly or if overdone, so be careful.

1. Lying on your stomach, tighten the muscle on the front of your thigh, then lift your leg 8 to 10 inches off the floor keeping your knee locked.
2. Hold for five seconds and repeat 10 times or until your leg is really fatigued. *Do not perform if you have pain!*

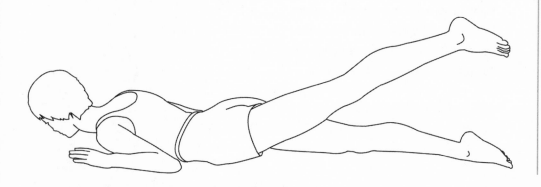

Figure 23.24
Hip Abductor Strengthening

This exercise is extremely important in knee conditioning for prevention of patellofemoral syndrome, patellar instability, and patellar tendonitis.

1. Lying on your side on the floor with a mat or towel under your body, tighten the muscle on the side of your thigh then lift your leg one to two feet away from the floor.
2. Repeat 10 to 100 times or until your leg is really fatigued. Turn over on your other side and repeat. *Do not perform if you have any pain!*

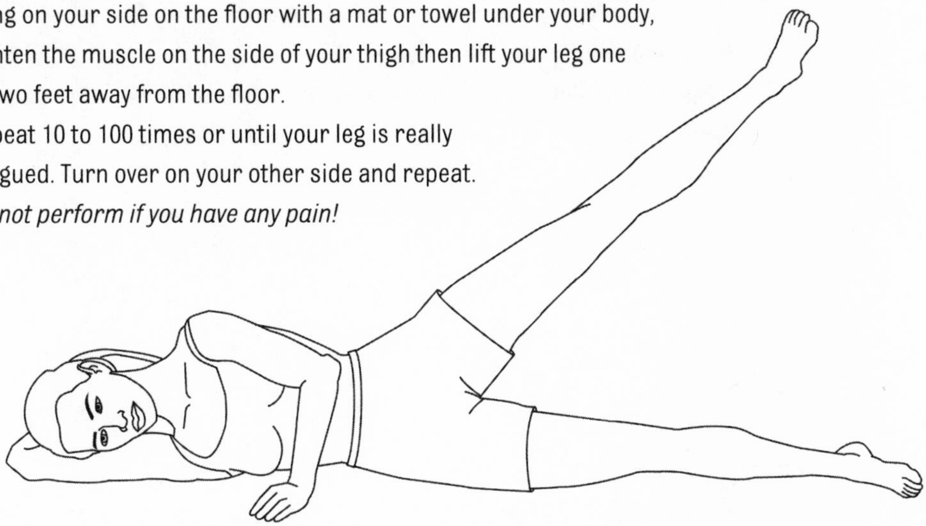

Figure 23.25
Hip Adductor (Inner Thigh) Strengthening

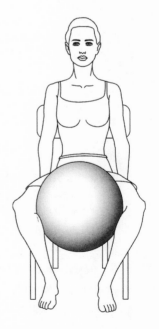

1. Sit in a chair leaning slightly forward, arms at your sides, and feet flat on the floor. Place a medium-size ball between your legs above your knees. Clamp your knees with just enough pressure to hold the ball in place.
2. Squeeze the ball with your inner thigh muscles for 5 to 10 seconds. Then release just enough to hold the ball in place. Start with 10 squeezes, and work up to 30.

Figure 23.26
Quadriceps Stretch

----

1. Seated on a chair, gently push one leg back with the other leg until you feel a stretch. Hold 10 seconds. Relax. Repeat with each leg.

2. Then, with one leg underneath the other, slowly lift the leg on top until it is straightened out. Repeat five times. Reverse legs and repeat. *Do not continue if you feel pain!*

Figure 23.27
Quadriceps Strengthening

This is one of the fundamental exercises for knee rehabilitation and prevention of patellar problems. It works the VMO (vastus medialis obliquus) of the quadriceps.

1. With your knee bent over a bolster, straighten the joint by tightening the muscle on top of thigh. Be sure to keep the bottom of your knee on the bolster.

2. Hold 10 seconds. Do three to five sets of 10 reps. *Stop if you have pain!*

Figure 23.28
Straight Leg Raises

1. Lie on your back, with your right knee bent and your right foot flat on the ground. Keep your left knee straight.
2. Contract your quad muscle by pushing the back of your left knee toward the floor and bending your ankle so your toes are pointed toward the ceiling.
3. Lift your whole leg off the floor approximately 10 inches keeping your knee straight and hold for 10 seconds before slowly lowering your leg. Start with three sets of 10 reps if there is no pain. When the exercise becomes easy, slowly add weights to your ankles to increase resistance and turn your foot outward so that the inner thigh muscles are doing the work of lifting the leg. This is a great exercise to strengthen the quads.

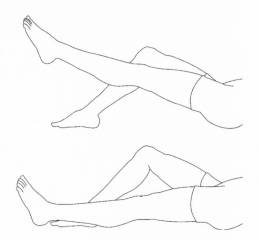

Figure 23.29
Wall Squat

This exercise strengthens your knees, thigh muscles, butt, and hamstrings. It's excellent conditioning for pivoting sports such as skiing, basketball, and tennis. *It can cause knee pain in the front of the knee if you are not performing it correctly or if you are out of condition, so stop if there is any pain.*

1. Lean your head and shoulders, lower back, and butt against a wall.
2. With your knees hip-width apart, slide slowly down the wall until you are in a position similar to sitting in a chair. Your knees should not bend any lower than a right angle to the floor. Hold this position for 30 seconds. Each day, increase the time until you can hold the position for several minutes.

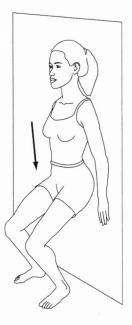

ACHILLES TENDON STRETCH AND STRENGTHENER

Figure 23.30
Wall Push-up

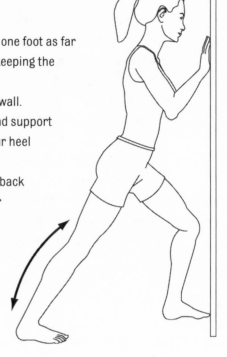

1. Facing a wall, place your palms flat. Place one foot as far away from the wall as you can while still keeping the heel flat on the ground.
2. Place the other leg a few inches from the wall.
3. Bending your elbows, lean into the wall and support yourself with your hands, but don't let your heel come off the ground.
4. Hold the stretch for 15 seconds and push back up. Bend the knee and hold the stretch for 15 seconds. Switch legs and repeat. This is an excellent stretch for the calf muscles and the Achilles tendon.

CALF STRENGTHENING

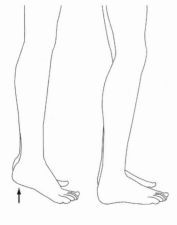

Figure 23.31
Calf Exercises

1. Stand on your toes for 10 seconds and then come down flat on the floor. Repeat until you feel real fatigue in your calf muscles.
2. When you come back up, you'll be strengthening the calf. If you really get strong, you can hold dumbbells or a barbell to increase your body weight while doing this exercise. As the calf muscles begin to grow stronger, you can perform this exercise while incorporating the calf stretch.

Figure 23.32
Calf Stretches

You can perform this exercise on a book or a step.

1. Stand on the balls of your feet on the step and let the heels come down slowly to the floor.
2. Hold the stretch for 5 to 10 seconds and then raise up again.

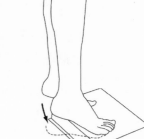

EXERCISES TO IMPROVE COORDINATION AND BALANCE

Figure 23.33
Cross Step

This exercise is great when you're preparing for activities like basketball or skating.

1. Start with knees bent and feet shoulder-width apart. Cross your right foot in front of your left.
2. With your left foot, step to the left.

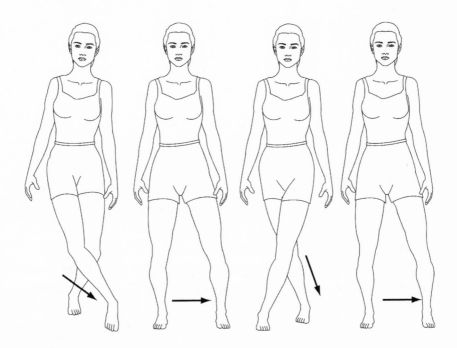

3. With your right foot, step behind your left foot.
4. With your left foot, step to the left.
5. After doing the cross-step sequence, switch directions. Repeat the entire exercise 10 times.

Figure 23.34
Side Step

Side steps prepare you for activities such as racquetball and tennis.
1. Put your right foot to the side and then draw your left foot toward it.
2. Use the motion to go across the room and then go back using the left foot first and drawing the right foot toward it.

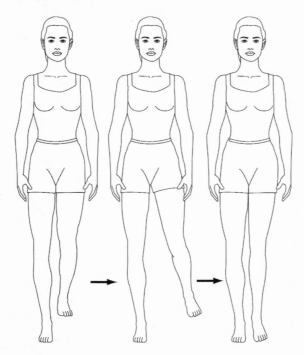

Cool Down

When you have finished your workout program, do a minimum of 5 to 10 minutes of slow walking, slow-paced exercises, and easy stretching.

Physical Therapy

Physical therapists use exercises and other special treatments to help people make their bodies healthier and stronger. A physical therapist can treat sports injuries in many ways, including massage, heat and ice treatments, ultrasound, or electric stimulation. He or she might also help you to use exercise equipment such as a treadmill, step or stair climber, or stationary bicycle.

Physical therapists work in hospitals, clinics, or individual practices. They design fitness training programs to help athletes improve performance in a sport or to recover from an injury and return to play. They can also help relieve sports-related pain and prevent complications from developing after surgical repair of an injury.

During the first visit, the physical therapist will evaluate your condition. He or she will figure out how flexible or strong your body is. In cooperation with your physician, the therapist will then create a treatment plan for you, including such therapies as massage, heat packs, ultrasound, whirlpool bath, and transcutaneous electrical nerve stimulation.

Most physical therapy sessions last 45 to 60 minutes. Your physician and the physical therapist will determine how long you will need to continue physical therapy. The therapist will usually give you exercises and treatments to perform at home as well. For more information about physical therapy or women's sports in general, contact:

AMERICAN PHYSICAL THERAPY ASSOCIATION (APTA)
1111 North Fairfax Street
Alexandria, VA 22314-1488
Telephone: (703) 684-APTA or
(703) 683-6748; (800) 999-2782
Fax: (703) 684-7343
apta.org
APTA is a national professional organization representing more than 63,000 members. Its goal is to foster advancements in physical therapy practice, research, and education.

AMERICAN ACADEMY OF ORTHOPAEDIC SURGEONS
orthoinfo.aaos.org
This organization is comprised of surgeons who specialize in the
diagnosis, treatment, rehabilitation, and prevention of injury and disease
of the body's musculoskeletal system. It provides a great deal of
information concerning sports injuries.

WOMEN'S SPORTS FOUNDATION
Eisenhower Park
East Meadow, NY 11554
Womenssportsfoundation.org
This is one of the most complete websites for female athletes, both
rookies and seasoned veterans. It has resources to help you play at the
top of your game, as well as descriptions of more than 100 sports and
fitness activities.

INDEX

Achilles' heel, 183–84
Achilles tendonitis, 327–29
  basketball and, 17–18
Acromioclavicular (AC) separations, 280–82
Aerobic exercises, 332
  for mature female athletes, 240–41
  pregnant women and, 233
Albright, Letha, 147–49
Alpine skiing, knee injuries and, 77–78
Altitude sickness, climbing and, 164–65
Amateur Softball Association of America, 48
Amenorrhea, 4–5
American Academy of Orthopaedic Surgeons,
  354
American Alpine club, 166
American Association of Cheerleading
  Coaches and Advisors, 213
American Bicycle Association, 145
American College of Sports Medicine, 249
American Cross Country Skiers, 87
American Gymnastics Association, 213
American Mountain Guide Association, 166
American Physical Therapy Association, 249,
  353
American Running Association, 185
American Safe Climbing Association, 166
American Swimming Coaches Association,
  The, 114
American Volleyball Coaches Association, 40
AmericanAlpineClub.org, 166
Ankle injuries
  climbing and, 162
  fractures, 326–27

gymnastics and, 206–7
peroneal tendon dislocations, 321–23
sprains, 324–25
stress fractures, 323–24
Ankle sprains
  basketball and, 16–17
  field hockey and, 70
  racquet sports and, 60
  skiing and, 81–82
  snowboarding and, 81–82
  soccer and, 23
  softball and, 44
  swimming and, 110
  volleyball and, 37
Anterior cruciate ligament (ACL) injuries,
  25–26
Attia, Magdt W., 222

Back injuries
  basketball and, 15
  biking and, 136–37
  golf and, 188–90
  gymnastics and, 207
  racquet sports and, 61
  skiing and, 85–86
  snowboarding and, 85–86
  swimming and, 107–8
  volleyball and, 39–40
  walking or running and, 179–80
Back pain
  mature female athletes and, 244
  pregnant athletes and, 228–30
Badminton. See Racquet sports

Ball throwing, men vs. women, 4
Baseball. *See* Softball
Baseball finger, 300–301
Basketball, 11–12
    Achilles tendonitis and, 17–18
    ankle sprains and, 16–17
    back and, 15
    fingers and, 15–16
    foot fractures and, 18
    hamstring muscles and, 16
    head protection and, 14
    knees and, 12–13
    neck and, 14–15
    organizations, 20
    shoulders and, 13–14
    stress fractures and, 18
    tips for preventing injuries, 19
    training and conditioning for, 18–19
    wrists and, 15
Biking, 127–28
    back injuries and, 136–37
    bottom pain and, 137–38
    choosing bike saddles for, 128–29
    dehydration and, 136
    elbow injuries and, 137
    face injuries and, 140
    foot injuries and, 138
    hand injuries and, 137
    head injuries and, 133–34
    hints for comfortable, 131–33
    hip pain and, 140
    knee injuries and, 139–40
    neck pain and, 136
    organizations, 145
    pregnant women and, 233
    proper fitting of bikes for, 129–30
    shoulder pain and, 136
    skin problems and, 134–36
    tips for, 143–45
    type of bikes for, 130–31
    types of injuries with, 134
Bodychecking, 98
Bone density, 4–5
Breast cancer, diving with or after, 120
Breast implants, scuba diving and, 119–20
Breasts, protecting, 5
Broken bones. *See* Fractures
Bruises, treating, 62
Bunion deformities, 47
Bursitis
    elbow, 285
    hip, 305–6
    kneecap, 319
    shinbone, 321

Caffeine, 260
Carbohydrate loading, 252–54
Carbohydrate metabolism, 251–52
Carpal tunnel syndrome, 296–97
CDC National Center for Chronic Disease
    Prevention and Health Promotion, 248
Charley horse (contusion), 24
Cheerleading, 205
    organizations, 213
    preventing injuries and, 211–12
    risk of injuries and, 209–11
Club Swim, 114
Collarbone fractures, 282–83
Collarbone pain, swimming and, 106–7
Collateral ligament tears, 313–14
Colles fractures, 291–93
Conditioning exercises, 2. *See also* Exercises
    aerobics, 332
    flexibility, 331
    for rehabilitation, 333
    for sports-injury prevention, 333
    for strengthening, 332–33
    warm up, 331
Conjunctivitis (red eye), 112
Contusion (charley horse), 24
Contusions, climbing and, 162–63
Creatine, 255–56
Cuts, treating, 62
Cycling. *See* Biking

Decompression sickness (DCS), 116–18
    Type I, 116–17
    Type II, 117–18
DeQuervain's tenosynovitis, 298
Diabetes, mature female athletes and, 246
Diets
    high-carbohydrate, 261–62
    high-protein, 262–63
    menu options for balanced, 265–67
    resources for, 267
Dislocations, shoulder, 276–77, 278–79
Divers Alert Network, 114, 126
Diving. *See* Scuba diving

Eating disorders, 5
Elbow injuries, 283–90
    biking and, 137
    bursitis, 285
    dislocations, 289–90
    fractures, 287–89
    golf and, 190–92
    golfer's elbow, 190–91, 283–85
    racquet sports and, 52–54
    snowboarding and, 79–80

softball and, 44–45
swimming and, 107
tendonitis, 286
tennis elbow, 283–85
Electrolytes, female athletes and, 258–59
Ephedrine, 260–61
Exercises. *See also* Conditioning exercises
  for Achilles tendon, 350
  for calves, 350–51
  for elbow and forearm flexibility, 340–42
  for hip and lower body, 345–49
  to improve coordination and balance,
    351–52
  for neck, back, and trunk, 334–37
  for pelvic muscles, 343–45
  for shoulder flexibility, 337
  for shoulder rotator cuff strength, 338–40
Eye injuries, racquet sports and, 61–62

Face injuries. *See also* Head injuries
  biking and, 140
  lacrosse and, 68
  soccer and, 29–30
Fats, female athletes and, 257
Female athlete triad, 5–6
Female athletes. *See also* Girl athletes; Mature
    female athletes
  bone-diet connection and, 256
  calorie requirements for, 264
  carbohydrate loading and, 252–54
  creatine and, 255–56
  electrolytes and, 258–59
  fats and, 257
  high-carbohydrate diet for, 261–62
  high-protein diet for, 262–63
  iron and, 257–58
  menu options for balanced diet for, 265–67
  nutrition for, 251–52
  pregame meal for, 263–64
  protein intake and, 254–55
  rest and, 264
Field hockey, 65, 69–70. *See also* Lacrosse
  improving game of, 70
50-Plus Fitness Association, 249
Finger injuries
  basketball and, 15–16
  softball injuries, 45–46
  volleyball and, 39
Flexibility exercises, 331
Fluids, female athletes and, 259–61
Foot injuries
  biking and, 138
  fractures, 330
  racquet sports and, 60

skiing and, 81–82
snowboarding and, 81–82
soccer and, 28–29
swimming and, 110
Foot pain, skating and, 97–98
Forearm injuries
  lacrosse and, 67–68
  snowboarding and, 79–80
Fractured pelvis, skiing and, 85
Fractures
  biking and, 140–42
  climbing and, 162
  finger, 302
Funny bone pain (Ulnar neuritis), 54,
    286–87

Germs, swimming and, 112–13
Girl athletes. *See also* Female athletes
  acute injuries and, 221–22
  overuse injuries and, 221
  special needs of, 218–21
  specific sport injuries and, 222–23
  sports and, 217–18
Goldstein, Irwin, 128
Golf
  aerobic training for, 195
  back injuries and, 188–90
  benefits of, 195–96
  conditioning for, 194
  elbow injuries and, 190–92
  flexibility training for, 194–95
  movements in, 187–88
  organizations, 197
  playing tips for, 196
  shoulder injuries and, 192
  strength training for, 194
Golf.com, 197
Golfer's elbow, 190–91, 283–85
Goose's foot, 321
Grip techniques, for rock climbing,
    152–53
Gymnastics, 205–6
  injuries and, 206–7
  organizations, 212–13
  tips for injury prevention, 207–9

Hallux valgus, 47
Hamate fractures, 294–95
Hamstring muscles, basketball and, 16
Hand injuries
  baseball finger, 300–301
  biking and, 137
  dislocated finger, 301–2
  dislocations, 301

finger fractures, 302
fractures, 301
golf and, 192–94
racquet sports and, 55–56
rock climbing and, 153–58
skier's thumb, 299–300
skiing and, 78–79
Head injuries. *See also* Face injuries
basketball and, 14
biking and, 133–34
climbing and, 159
lacrosse and, 68
skiing and, 86
snowboarding and, 86
soccer and, 30–31
Heart problems, mature female athletes and, 246
Heart rate, measuring, 332
Heel injuries
Achilles tendon, 17–18, 183–84, 327–29
heel pain, 329–30
softball and, 47
Heel spur syndrome, 182–83
Hip bursitis, 305–6
Hip fractures, skiing and, 84–85
Hip injuries, 304–7
Hip pain, 304–5
biking and, 140
Hockey. *See* Ice hockey
Hutchinson, Mark R., 209–10, 212
Hypothermia, climbing and, 163–64
Hysterectomy, diving after, 120

Ice hockey, 95
bodychecking and, 98
equipment and, 96
lower body injuries and, 98
organizations, 99
preconditioning for, 96
stopping and, 96–97
Ice skating
equipment and, 89–91
foot pain and, 97–98
improving balance and posture for, 92–94
organizations, 99
stopping and, 91–92
tips for, 94–95
Iliotibial band (ITB) friction syndrome, 178–79
International Masters Games Association, 237, 248
International Volksports Federation, 185
Iron, female athletes and, 257–58

Jogging, 167. *See also* Running; Walking
programs for, 171–74
Joint replacements, mature female athletes and, 245–46

Knee injuries
alpine skiing and, 77–78
anterior cruciate ligament (ACL) tears, 309–12
basketball and, 12–13
biking and, 139–40
bursitis, 319
climbing and, 162
kneecap instability, 316–18
lacrosse and, 67
ligament injuries, 308–9
men vs. women and, 2–3
meniscus tears, 314–16
patellofemoral syndrome, 316–18
plicas, 319–20
racquet sports and, 59–60
running and, 181–82
skiing and, 76–77
snowboarding and, 76
soccer and, 25–26
softball injuries, 46–47
swimming and, 108–9
tendonitis, 319
volleyball and, 35–36
Kristiansen, Ingrid, 169

Labral tears, 279–80
Lacrosse, 65–66. *See also* Field hockey
ball-related injuries and, 68
forearm and hand injuries, 67–68
knee injuries and, 67
organizations, 68–69
preventing injuries for, 68
tips for playing better, 66–67
Ladies Professional Golf Association, 197
Ladies Professional Racquetball Association, 63
Lamb, Sandra E., 49, 50
Lateral collateral ligament (LCL) tears, 313–14
Latus, Janine, 127
Leg injuries
racquet sports and, 59
skiing and, 82–84
snowboarding and, 82–84
soccer and, 27–28
volleyball and, 36–37
Levinson, Ben, 237

Ligament injuries, 308–9
  anterior cruciate ligament (ACL) tears,
    309–12
  lateral collateral ligament (LCL) tears,
    313–14
  medial collateral ligament (MCL) tears,
    313–14
  posterior cruciate ligament (PCL) tears,
    312–13
Lobo, Rebecca, 11–12, 20
Lobo, Ruthann, 11
Lower body injuries, ice hockey and, 98

Manganese, 256
Martin, Lawrence, 116
Mature female athletes, 237
  aerobic exercises for, 240–41
  balance exercises and, 241–43
  benefits of exercise for, 243
  body changes and, 238–40
  chronic conditions and, 243–46
  exercise tips for, 247–48
  resistance training and, 241
  resources for, 248
  sports opportunities for, 237
  stretching and, 241
Medial collateral ligament (MCL) tears,
    313–14
Meniscus tears, 314–16
Menstruation, diving before or during,
    118–19
Metabolism, men vs. women and, 3–4,
    251–52
Milano, Carol, 168–69, 178
Mountain biking. *See* Biking
Mountain climbing, 150–51. *See also* Rock
    climbing
Muscle strains
  climbing and, 161–62
  soccer and, 24–25
  walking or running and, 178

Naismith, James, 12
National Bicycle Tour Directors Association,
    145
National Collegiate Athletic Association
    (NCAA), 20
National Gay Volleyball Association, 40
National Masters Racquetball
    Association, 50
National Senior Games Association, 248
National Soccer Coaches Association of
    America, 33

National Strength and Conditioning
    Association, 203
Neck injuries, 271–72
  basketball and, 14–15
  racquet sports and, 60–61
  snowboarding and, 85–86
Neck pain, biking and, 136
Nerve injuries, volleyball and, 38–39
North American Racewalking Foundation,
    185

Oligomenorrhea, 5
Osgood-Schlatter disease, 220
Osteoarthritis, mature female athletes and,
    244
Osteoporosis, 4–5
  mature female athletes and, 244–45
Ovarian tumors, diving with, 120–21
Overuse injuries
  biking and, 142–43
  girls and, 221
  softball and, 43–44
Oxygen carrying ability, men vs. women, 4

Paddleball. *See* Racquet sports
Patellofemoral syndrome, 316–18
Peroneal tendon dislocations, 321–23
Physical therapy, 353
Piriformis syndrome, 306–7
Pitching injuries, 43–44
Plica syndrome, 109, 139
Posterior cruciate ligament (PCL) tears,
    312–13
Potassium, 258–59
Pregnancy, diving during, 119
Pregnant athletes
  aerobics and, 233
  back pain and, 228–30
  cycling and, 233
  exercises for, 231–32
  precautions for, 235–36
  running and, 232
  sports and, 225–28
  sports not recommended for, 234
  staying fit and, 230–31
  swimming and, 233
  tennis and, 233–34
  weight training and, 233
President's Council on Physical Fitness and
    Sports, The, 249
Professional Golf Association of America,
    197
Pulled muscles. *See* Muscle strains

Racquet sports
 back injuries and, 61
 common injuries, 50–52
 eye injuries and, 61–62
 hand injuries, 55–56
 knee injuries and, 59–60
 leg injuries and, 59
 organizations, 63
 shoulder injuries and, 56–59
 tennis elbow and, 52–54
 tips for improving game, 62
 tips for preventing injuries in, 62
 wrist injuries, 55–56
Racquetball, 49–50. *See also* Racquet sports
Red eye (conjunctivitis), 112
Resistance training, for mature female
 athletes, 241
Resting metabolic rate (RMR), men vs.
 women, 3–4
RICE therapy, 24, 303
Road Runners Club of America, 185
Rock climbing, 147–50
 basics of, 150–51
 common maladies of, 158–65
 grip techniques for, 152–53
 hand injuries and, 153–58
 injury prevention and, 165
 organizations, 166
Rotator cuff tears, 275–76
Running, 167–68. *See also* Walking
 back pain and, 179–80
 foot injuries and, 182–84
 iliotibial band friction syndrome and,
  178–79
 injuries from, 174–77
 knee injuries and, 181–82
 organizations, 185–86
 pregnant women and, 232
 programs for, 171–74
 sacroiliac joint pain and, 180–81
 selecting shoes for, 184–85
 tendonitis and, 177–78
 vs. walking, 169–70

Sacroiliac joint pain, running or walking and,
 180–81
Scaphoid fractures, 293–94
Schwart, Daylle Deanna, 199–200
Scuba diving, 115–16
 after hysterectomy, 120
 before or during menstruation, 118–19
 breast implants and, 119–20
 conditions for avoiding, 125–27

 conditions for delaying, 125
 decompression sickness and, 116–18
 hazards of, 121–25
 importance of instruction for, 121
 organizations, 126
 pregnant women and, 119
 with or after breast cancer, 120
 with ovarian tumors, 120–21
Scubacentral.com, 114
Senior Olympics, 237
Senior women. *See* Mature female athletes
Shin injuries, 320–21
 soccer and, 26–27
 walking or running and, 175
Shoulder injuries
 acromioclavicular (AC) separations,
  280–82
 basketball and, 13–14
 climbing and, 160–61
 dislocations, 276–77, 278–79
 golf and, 192
 labral tears, 279–80
 racquet sports and, 56–59
 rotator cuff tears, 275–76
 shoulder impingement/bursitis, 272–74
 skiing and, 80–81
 soccer and, 29
 subluxation, 277–78
 tendonitis, 276
 volleyball and, 37–38
Shoulder instability, 105–6
Shoulder pain, biking and, 136
Skating. *See* Ice skating
Ski Central, 87
Skier's thumb, 299–300
Skiing. *See also* Snowboarding
 alpine, 77–78
 ankle sprains and, 81–82
 back injuries and, 85–86
 conditioning for, 71–73
 developing sweet spot for, 74
 foot injuries and, 81–82
 fractured pelvis and, 85
 hand injuries and, 78–79
 head injuries and, 86
 hip fractures and, 84–85
 knee injuries and, 76–77
 leg injuries and, 82–84
 organizations, 86–87
 shoulder injuries and, 80–81
 Telemark, 76–77
 wrist injuries and, 79
Sliding into bases, 42

Snowboard.com, 87
Snowboarding, 74–75. *See also* Skiing
    ankle sprains and, 81–82
    back injuries and, 85–86
    elbow injuries and, 79–80
    foot injuries and, 81–82
    forearm injuries and, 79–80
    head injuries and, 86
    knee injuries and, 76
    leg injuries and, 82–84
    neck injuries and, 85–86
    organizations, 86–87
Sobek, Joe, 49
Soccer
    ankle sprains and, 23
    face injuries and, 29–30
    feet and, 28–29
    female athletes and, 21–22
    head and, 30–31
    injury rates for, 22–23
    knees and, 25–26
    leg fractures and, 27–28
    muscle cramps and, 24–25
    muscle strains and, 24
    organizations, 32–33
    preventing injuries and, 31–32
    shins and, 26–27
    shoulders and, 29
Softball
    ankle sprains and, 44
    finger injuries and, 45–46
    heel injuries and, 47
    knee injuries and, 46–47
    organizations, 48
    pitching injuries and, 43–44
    sliding injuries and, 42
    toe injuries and, 47–48
    wrist injuries and, 45
Spinal injuries. *See* Back injuries
Squash. *See* Racquet sports
Stress fractures, 5
    ankle, 323–24
    basketball and, 18
    walking or running and, 175–77
Stretching, for mature female athletes,
    241
Subluxation, shoulder, 277–78
Sunburn
    biking and, 138
    climbing and, 163
Swimmer's ear, 112
Swimmer's knee, 109
Swimmer's shoulder, 102, 104, 106

Swimming, 101–2
    ankle injuries and, 110
    back injuries and, 107–8
    collarbone pain and, 106–7
    elbow injuries and, 107
    foot injuries and, 110
    germs and, 112–13
    importance of good instructors for, 110–11
    knee injuries and, 108–9
    organizations, 113–14
    pregnant women and, 233
    red eye and, 112
    shoulder injuries in, 103–6
    stroke styles and strains, 102–3
    swimmer's ear and, 112

Tai chi, 241–42
Tarnopolsky, Mark, 252
Taylor, Bambi Lynne, 222
Telemark skiing, 76–77
Tendonitis
    elbow, 286
    knee, 319
    shoulder, 276
    walking or running and, 177–78
    wrist, 298
Tennis, 49. *See also* Racquet sports
    pregnant women and, 233–34
Tennis elbow, 52–54, 283–85
Tennis leg, 59
Terrible Triad of O'Donohue injury, 26
Thigh injuries, 307–8
Title IX, 1
Triangular fibrocartilage complex
    (TFCC), 55
Turf toe, 47
Type I decompression sickness, 116–17
Type II decompression sickness, 117–18

Ulnar neuritis, 54, 286–87
United States Amateur Soccer
    Association, 33
U.S. Field Hockey Association, 70
United States Figure Skating
    Association, 99
U.S.A. Gymnastics, 212
USA Hockey, Inc., 99
United States of America Snowboard
    Association, 87
U.S.A. Swimming, 113
U.S.A. Track & Field, 186
USA Volleyball, 40
USA Weightlifting, 204

United States Racquetball Association, 63
U.S. Ski and Snowboard Association, 86–87
United States Soccer Federation, 33
United States Tennis Association, 63
United States Water Fitness Association, 113
U.S. Youth Soccer, 32

Vamm, Richard, 119–20
Varsity.com, 213
Vitamin E, 261
Volleyball, 35
  ankle sprains and, 37
  back injuries and, 39–40
  finger injuries and, 39
  knees and, 35–36
  leg injuries and, 36–37
  nerve injuries and, 38–39
  organizations, 40
  shoulder injuries and, 37–38
Volleyball World Wide, 40

Walking, 167. *See also* Running
  back pain and, 179–80
  foot injuries and, 182–84
  iliotibial band friction syndrome and, 178–79
  injuries from, 174–77
  obtaining maximum benefits from, 171
  organizations, 185–86
  vs. running, 169–70
  sacroiliac joint pain and, 180–81
  tendonitis and, 177–78
Walking.about.com, 186
Warm-up exercises, 331

Weight training, 199–200
  benefits of, 200–201
  finding facilities for, 203
  precautions for, 201–2
  pregnant women and, 233
Weightlifting, competitive, 202–3
Wescott, Wayne, 200
Williams, Nancy, 170
Women athletes. *See* Female athletes;
  Girl athletes; Mature female
  athletes
Women's Golf Today, 197
Women's International Squash Players
  Association, 63
Women's National Basketball Association
  (WNBA), 20
Women's Pro Softball League, 42
Women's Sports Foundation, 354
Women's United Soccer Association
  (WUSA), 32
Wrist injuries
  basketball and, 15
  carpal tunnel syndrome, 296–97
  fractures, 291–95
  golf and, 192–94
  ligament tears, 295–96
  racquet sports and, 55–56
  skiing and, 79
  softball and, 45
  sprains, 290–91
  tendonitis, 298
Wryneck, 60–61

Yaffe, Kristine, 170
Yoga, 241–43